Yellowstone

Yellowstone

The History, Ecology and Future of America's First National Park

Hunt Janin *and*
Nicole Sheehan

McFarland & Company, Inc., Publishers
Jefferson, North Carolina

LIBRARY OF CONGRESS CATALOGUING-IN-PUBLICATION DATA

Names: Janin, Hunt, 1940– author. | Sheehan, Nicole, 1967– author.
Title: Yellowstone : the history, ecology and future of America's first national park / Hunt Janin and Nicole Sheehan.
Other titles: History, ecology and future of America's first national park
Description: Jefferson, North Carolina : McFarland & Company, Inc., Publishers, 2022 | Includes bibliographical references and index.
Identifiers: LCCN 2021054403 | ISBN 9781476681078 (paperback : acid free paper) ∞
ISBN 9781476644066 (ebook)
Subjects: LCSH: Natural history—Yellowstone National Park. | Yellowstone National Park—History. | BISAC: HISTORY / United States / State & Local / West (AK, CA, CO, HI, ID, MT, NV, UT, WY)
Classification: LCC F722 .J36 2021 | DDC 978.7/52—dc23/eng/20211116
LC record available at https://lccn.loc.gov/2021054403

BRITISH LIBRARY CATALOGUING DATA ARE AVAILABLE

ISBN (print) 978-1-4766-8107-8
ISBN (ebook) 978-1-4766-4406-6

Front cover: Bison in Yellowstone National Park (National Park Service)

Printed in the United States of America

McFarland & Company, Inc., Publishers
Box 611, Jefferson, North Carolina 28640
www.mcfarlandpub.com

In 1835–1839, the fur trapper Osborne Russell visited the Yellowstone area three times and was one of the very few early Yellowstone explorers to leave any written record of his thoughts and travels. Writing about Yellowstone's Lamar Valley in his 1835 *Journal of a Trapper*, he had this to say:

> *There is something in the wild scenery of this valley which I cannot describe: but the impressions made upon my mind while gazing from a high eminence on the surrounding landscape one evening as the sun was gently gliding behind the western mountain and casting gigantic shadows across the vale were such as time can never efface. For my own part I almost wished I could spend the remainder of my days in a place like this where happiness and contentment seemed to reign in wild romantic splendor.[1]*

Table of Contents

Preface

Yellowstone National Park and the huge ecosystem of which it is such an important part are subjects that have a wide domestic, international, and scientific appeal today.

"Ecosystem"—a term first used by the British ecologist Arthur Tansley in 1935—is the single most important concept in this book and will appear frequently in the following pages.[1] It can best be defined as *a biological community of interacting living organisms—including human beings—and their environments.* A simpler but equally-accurate explanation is that it simply means: "everything is interconnected."

This book is a detailed survey that blends Yellowstone's past into its present and into its likely future. We describe the first inhabitants; the bold explorers and visionary conservationists; the unsung early heroes of the park's ranger service; the flora, fauna, and spectacular geology of the region; and all the other elements that have culminated in the creation, preservation, and international popularity of the park. We also look at the future prospects for the park and for the national forests and other public lands surrounding it.

A "systemic shift" is a major change that affects all the parts of a given system. Climate change is precisely such a systemic shift, and it is occurring right now throughout the Greater Yellowstone Ecosystem. In a later chapter, we will discuss the impacts of climate change on this ecosystem.

To clarify one important point in advance, although the two terms "global warming" and "climate change" are sometimes used interchangeably, global warming is in fact only one aspect of climate change.[2] "Global warming" refers to the rise in global temperatures which is due mainly to the increasing concentrations in the atmosphere of heat-trapping, human-caused, emissions of greenhouse gases such as carbon dioxide (CO_2). These emissions stem from a wide range of human activities such as vehicle use, power plant operations, and the destruction of forests (deforestation). Prehistoric fossil records reveal that the earth's climate is now warming 40 times faster than during any other period in our planet's history.[3]

"Climate change," on the other hand, refers to the shifts perceived when tracking climate over a long period of time—including snow and rain precipitation, temperatures, and wind patterns. Since climate change is now considered to be a broader and more accurate scientific term than global warming, it will be used in this book.

Our thanks are due to many helpful experts in the Yellowstone region and elsewhere. Listed in random order, these men and women include Kari Gunderson, John Gross, Paul Schullery, Ursula Carlson, Bob Strawbridge, Chuck Preston, Doug Smith, Rachel Phillips, Bruce Gourley, Jenny Golding, Chelse Grohman, Richard Parks, Lee Whittlesey, Alicia Murphy, Ann Rodman, Andy Hansen, Tony Perri, Bill Davis, Mark McBeth, Bob Crabtree, Jesse Logan, and Corinne Janin-Nuis.

Everything written in this text is the responsibility of the authors alone. Conditions in the Yellowstone area are never static, however, so visitors must always be sure to check with Yellowstone National Park itself or with other reputable sources in order to get the latest information.

Setting the Stage

What are the main functions of the Yellowstone ecosystem, and how does it fit into the international framework?

Any ecosystem is a complex biological community of interacting organisms and their physical environment that is often subject to human intervention. A wide range of interrelated cycles and processes form the essential connections within any ecosystem, which is always changing and evolving.[1] For example, photosynthesis, predation, scavenging, eventual decomposition, climate, and precipitation all make possible the essential flows of energy and raw materials; in the process, all living things release, absorb, transform, and circulate energy and raw materials.[2]

Although these cycles and processes are going on everywhere in Yellowstone and at all times, they are perhaps most easily seen and studied in the animals and vegetation of the Northern Range, much of which is located in the northeastern sector of Yellowstone National Park. It is in many ways a microcosm of all of Yellowstone's issues, both warmly-welcomed and highly-controversial.

This book has interrelated parts. It offers at the same time:

1. A concise history of the multifaceted Greater Yellowstone Ecosystem, which will be described later. It encompasses a total of about 22 million acres in northwestern Wyoming and parts of eastern Idaho and Montana, a large part of which consists of public lands and 14 mountain ranges[3] in moderate-to-strict protection status.

2. An analysis of the environmental challenges this ecosystem is now facing.

3. The long-term prospects for the future of Yellowstone Park itself.

Park managers and citizens have already experienced some disturbances that have significantly altered the ecosystem's functioning. These include increased mountain pine beetle attacks, more severe wildfires, and reduced annual snowpack. Moreover, international and American experts report a decadal global temperature increase of 1–1.2 degrees F, and a continuing upward trend in temperatures.[4]

The Greater Yellowstone Ecosystem itself consists of such a confusing assemblage of component parts that it will be easiest just to list most of them here. They may be mentioned again in later pages, but taken collectively they include:

All of Yellowstone and Grand Teton National Parks

- The John D. Rockefeller National Parkway
- Ten wilderness areas (Gros Ventre, Fitzpatrick, Popo Agie, Jedediah Smith, Winegar Hole, Washakie, Teton, North Absaroka, Absaroka/Beartooth, and Lee Metcalf)
- Six National Forests (Beaverhead-Deerlodge, Gallatin, Custer, Shoshone, Bridger-Teton, and Caribou-Targhee)
- Three wildlife refuges (the National Elk Refuge and Red Rock and Camas Lake National Wildlife Refuges)
- Parts of the Wind River Indian Reservation, Bureau of Land Management Lands, state lands, and significant areas of private land, many of which are protected by land trust conservation easements.

Perhaps this huge ecosystem can best be understood both in environmental terms and in cultural terms—the latter evoking *the human beings who lived there in the past or who live there now.* Both these aspects surface repeatedly in this book.[5]

From an environmental point of view, this mountainous ecosystem basically includes the Yellowstone Plateau itself and all the elevations in the 14 surrounding ranges that rise above the 7,000-foot level. Its lowest elevation is only about 1,600 feet; the highest is above 10,800 feet. The Greater Yellowstone Ecosystem also embraces the headwaters of three major continental-scale river systems, namely, the Missouri-Mississippi, the Snake-Columbia, and the Green-Colorado.

Changing levels in elevation—and the accompanying variations in snowfall and rainfall, temperature, landforms, and river and stream networks—all exert very strong pressures over the distributions of plant and animal species in the whole region. Appendix 5 discusses some of the waters of Yellowstone.

From a cultural point of view, this ecosystem not only made possible vibrant Native American cultures in the past, but also most of the many modern economic and leisure-time activities. These include timber harvests; oil and gas exploration and development; reservoir operations; flood control; farming and ranching; hunting and fishing; livestock grazing; and hiking, boating, skiing, wildlife viewing, artistic expression (painting and photography), and many other kinds of recreation.

In the literature on these subjects, the Greater Yellowstone Ecosystem itself is often referred to simply as the "GYE" but, in the interest of clarity, it is spelled out in this book.

Located in three American states (chiefly in western Wyoming, but also with small parts tucked into southwestern Montana and eastern Idaho), the Greater Yellowstone Ecosystem now plays a starring role for tourists and scientists alike. The reason is that it is a world-class outdoor mosaic consisting of Yellowstone Park and of many other nearby Federal and otherwise-protected lands. They encompass about 22 million acres, but it must be kept in mind that all descriptions of the size, boundaries, and contents of any given ecosystem are only approximations and may vary considerably from one writer to another.

Most remarkably, the enormous *biodiversity* of this ecosystem, i.e., its natural environmental diversity, is still essentially unchanged after all these years. This is due chiefly to its relative remoteness in and near the Rocky Mountains; to the lack of intensive exploitation by human beings; to its legally-protected status; and to the very different habitats that characterize this region. Such habitats range from very high alpine areas to the very extensive low sagebrush steppes and flats (which are already among the most altered ecosystems in the intermountain West), and from boiling-hot hydrothermal areas to cold rivers, streams, and lakes.

It is worth quoting here the views of Jerry Altermatt, a Wyoming Game and Fish habitat biologist who works out of Cody, Wyoming. This is what he has to say about sagebrush:

> Lots of people think of sagebrush drylands as expendable. Yet, sage grouse depend on these areas, which also provide indispensable food and cover for mule deer, pronghorn, wild birds, and rodents. Fire keeps competing plants from crowding out sagebrush, but it's getting harder to allow natural fires to burn when we have to protect all the homes that border public lands. That's the big reason sagebrush is one of the most threatened habitats in Wyoming.[6]

In historical, scientific, political, economic, social, and even in legal terms, the Greater Yellowstone Ecosystem now presents us with a very complicated package.

Physically, it embraces national parks, national forests, wildlife refuges, and other assorted other land holdings. On the legal front,

Yellowstone National Park itself lies within the jurisdiction of the United States District Court for the District of Wyoming, making it the only federal court that includes portions of *more than one state*, i.e., Idaho, Montana, and Wyoming.

It has even been argued that, in legal terms, it might be impossible to impanel a jury in compliance with the Vicinage Clause of the Constitution's Sixth Amendment for a crime committed solely in the unpopulated Idaho portion of the park, and that it might also be very difficult to do so for a crime committed in the lightly-populated Montana portion. (The Vicinage Clause regulates the "vicinity" from which a jury pool may be selected.)

In any case, we should turn now to the much less-complicated matter of the difference between U.S. National Parks and U.S. National Forests. This difference is a simple one: the National Parks are basically designed to *preserve* existing conditions in the parks, while the National Forests are basically designed to encourage *multiple uses and sustained yields* of the lands they administer.

These sustainable uses can include timber production, recreation, livestock grazing, wildlife production, and hunting and fishing during regulated seasons. Within the Greater Yellowstone Ecosystem there are also three national wildlife refuges; extensive holdings of the Bureau of Land Management; and assorted state, tribal, and private properties, too. Some of these places will be described later.

Not surprisingly, the extensive literature discussing this ecosystem is quite complicated as well, both chronologically and in scope. As a result, this book provides a clear overview of this ecosystem. To orient the reader to the scope of this gigantic ecosystem, envision an area that stretches from the southern tip of Wyoming's Wind River Mountains to Butte, Montana, and from north of Billings, Montana, to Bear Lake, just above the Utah border.[7]

The concept of the Greater Yellowstone Ecosystem was first established in 1872, chiefly to help protect the geothermal areas that still contain about half of the world's active geysers. Geysers are hot springs with constrictions in their natural "plumbing systems" (i.e., their internal structures) that prevent the hot water from circulating freely to the surface where its heat can escape. In some cases, tremendous amounts of steam force the water up and out of a vent on the surface. When such an eruption begins, water is expelled faster than it can enter the "plumbing system"; heat and pressure gradually decrease; and the eruption finally comes to an end when the water reservoir empties or when the whole system cools down.

Fortunately, Yellowstone National Park has so far lost only a small number of geysers due to tourism-related damage or other activities, but there is always the potential for greater damage if geothermal developments take place outside the park.[8]

The Greater Yellowstone Ecosystem is noteworthy because of its world-class beauty, natural history, wildlife populations, and the intractable environmental challenges it is certain to face in the coming years. Today, it is home to the largest concentration of animals in the lower 48 states. It is especially famous for the predator-prey complex of large mammals. These include eight ungulate (hoofed mammal) species—i.e., bighorn sheep; American bison (the scientific name for this species is Bison bison: see endnote[9]); elk (30,000–40,000 of them, the most abundant large mammal in the Greater Yellowstone Ecosystem); moose; mountain goats; mule deer, pronghorn, and white-tailed deer.

There are also eight large carnivores, namely, black bears, grizzlies (which now number more than 700 and are bigger, stronger, and far more dangerous than black bears), mountain lions (also known as cougars), coyotes, Canada lynxes, wolverines, wolves, and human beings. These creatures are extremely important because they are critical to the smooth functioning of ecosystems. They exert direct control over smaller predators, over prey, and can strongly influence, indirectly, the plant world as well.[10] For more on this matter, see the comments on "trophic cascades" later in this book.

The grey wolf, for its part, can range in color from pure white to solid black, but the most common shade is a tawny brown in which the wolf's guard hairs are banded with black, white, gold, and brown. This banded coloration is known as "agouti," and is found in a number of wild species. The subspecies of wolves native to the Yellowstone area prior to extirpation was the Northern Rocky Mountain Wolf, but the species that was brought into Yellowstone was Canada's Mackenzie Valley wolf. As a practical matter, both subspecies were very similar and their ranges overlapped across the whole region. In this book, "wolf" will mean the Mackenzie Valley wolf.

Yellowstone National Park has many different types of ecosystems, but the lodgepole pine is the most abundant tree in its forests. In Yellowstone, this ecosystem is unique because so many different international and domestic stakeholders (i.e., individuals or institutions that have financial or other interests in the issue) are deeply involved in studying or administering it.

The park has long won international praise. When setting up the International Biosphere Reserve in 1976, for example, the United Nations said of the region: "Yellowstone National Park is recognized as part of the international network of biosphere reserves.... It provides a standard against which the effect of man's impact on the environment can be measured."[11]

Moreover, and more significantly, in 1978 it also became a UNESCO World Heritage Site. A World Heritage Site is a key landmark or an area that has been chosen by the United Nations Educational, Scientific, and Cultural Organization as having cultural, historical, scientific, or other forms of significance, and for this reason *it is legally protected by international treaties.* As the United Nations explained, "Through the collective recognition of the community of nations.... Yellowstone National Park has been designated as a World Heritage Site and joins a select list of protected areas around the world whose natural and cultural resources form the common heritage of all mankind."[12]

Other key stakeholders include the U.S. Government; American state governments; tribal governments; business interests; private individuals; scientists; and a wide variety of nonprofit organizations, many of which have strong international ties.

Yellowstone National Park itself probably has the widest range of dramatic features but the Grand Teton National Park, located along the southern border of Yellowstone, is equally impressive and should not be missed if you are a visitor to northern Wyoming. The Grand Teton park is particularly stunning because it has no foothills, so the Teton Mountains soar up abruptly from the flat valley floor of Jackson Hole to a maximum of 13,772 feet at the summit of Grand Teton. Perhaps a bit of local background information will be useful here.

The term "hole" was historically used to mean a high-altitude flat area or a valley floor surrounded by tall mountains. Jackson Hole is thus a broad valley, nearly 15 miles wide and 55 miles long, nestled in the mountains. The now-booming town of Jackson was named in memory of David Edward "Davy" Jackson (1788–1837), who in the late 1820s trapped beaver in the area together with his partners.

The last of the original mountain men who trapped and hunted in the Jackson Hole area was Richard "Beaver Dick" Leigh (1831–1899).[13] He was variously a trapper, a hunting guide, a boatman (i.e., ferryman), a Mexican war veteran, and an all-around mountain man. He began his long career trapping for the Hudson Bay Company, but much later became an independent "free trapper" and a guide for the hunting parties that began to trickle into the Rocky Mountains in the 1860s and 1870s. Beaver Dick also helped in the survey of Yellowstone. Sadly, his Shoshone wife and their six children perished together from smallpox and were buried near Henry's Fork River, a tributary of the Snake River, in Idaho.

The great American photographer Ansel Adams (1902–1984) loved the Tetons and took many remarkable shots of their three craggy peaks, with the Snake River twisting in the foreground. He would move up and down the Jackson Hole valley to find different perspectives on his subjects, and would catch the sun hitting the Tetons from different angles at different times of the day.[14]

In the late 1800s, efforts commenced to preserve the area as a national park. After a long controversy between local landowners and the U.S. Government over its establishment, Grand Teton National Park was finally dedicated in 1929. The original boundary of the park encompassed only the major peaks of the Tetons, plus the lake region at the foot of the mountains.

The first expansion occurred—accompanied by many local protests from Wyoming ranching and mining advocates—with the establishment of the Jackson Hole National Monument in 1943. The present boundary, which encompasses approximately 310,000 acres, was created in 1950, thanks in large part to the very generous philanthropic efforts of John D. Rockefeller, Jr.[15]

The Greater Yellowstone Ecosystem remains one of the biggest nearly-pristine northern temperate ecosystems left on earth. When it was founded in 1872, the boundaries of Yellowstone National Park itself were laid out to include only the geothermal basins in the region. No other ecological criteria were incorporated in this initial decision.

In 1872, naturalists did not understand how much "room to roam" a grizzly bear really needs. In 12-year-long study beginning in 1959, however, the brothers Frank and John Craighead radio-tracked grizzlies and found that these bears regularly roamed far and wide in their movements in and around Yellowstone. By the 1970s, it had become evident that the grizzly bear's normal range was in fact much bigger than the 1872 boundaries of the park itself. New boundaries were therefore needed. At first, it was thought that four million acres would be sufficient, but a 1994 speech by the pro-environment Greater Yellowstone Coalition, which had led the fight against the New World gold-silver-copper mine, with a proposed location of about four miles from the northeast entrance to Yellowstone Park, enlarged the estimate to a new total of 20 million acres. (The park itself now totals 2,222,000 acres.)

This is now the most commonly-accepted "best size" of this ecosystem. It includes all of the 20 contiguous counties in Wyoming, Montana, and Idaho that surround Yellowstone National Park. Yellowstone National Park is widely considered to be its core and its centerpiece. The park now totals 3,437.5 square miles of lakes, canyons, rivers, and mountain ranges. Most of it lies above 7,500 feet in elevation, and is located on a high volcanic plateau in northwestern Wyoming, with smaller segments in southern Montana and eastern Idaho.

These higher lands are covered with snow much of the year, and support vast forests of lodgepole pine (often used in the past by the Native Americans to support their lodges or tepees), interspersed with wet alpine meadows. Lower elevations provide vitally-important winter forage for elk, bison, bighorn sheep and, indirectly, for a host of smaller creatures as well. There are about 10,000 thermal features in the park, including about 500 geysers.

What is perhaps most important for all visitors to understand (there are more than four million of them every year) is that, in the park itself, approaching on foot within 100 yards of bears or wolves, or within 25 yards of other wildlife, is strictly prohibited. To see them closely and safely, use binoculars or telephoto lenses. It is illegal to willfully draw near or remain near wildlife, including birds, within any distance that disturbs an animal or causes them to move.

It must be kept in mind, too, that wild animals, especially females with their young, are very unpredictable and are potentially very dangerous. In fact, every year a number of people are injured in Yellowstone by wildlife—and some have been killed—simply because they have approached the animals too closely. For this reason, carrying bear spray—*and knowing how to use it quickly and safely*—is also strongly recommended by local experts.[16]

1

The First Peoples

The first peoples who lived in or passed through the Yellowstone area were most notably the Sheep Eater Indians and the Nez Percé, including legendary Chief Joseph. In overview, almost all of the indigenous peoples of the United States (except for those of Hawaii and the territories of the United States) are now variously known as American Indians, Native Americans, Indigenous Americans, or by other terms. For the purposes of simplicity and clarity, in this book the indigenous peoples of the Yellowstone region will be referred to as Native Americans.

The ancestors of these peoples are believed to have crossed into North America via the then ice-free region known as the Bering Straits, travelling along dry land, and possibly by canoes or reed vessels that hugged the shoreline, which was rich with shellfish, fish, and birds.

The National Park Service (NPS) explains that, ultimately, the Greater Yellowstone Ecosystem became a place where the Native American cultures of the Great Plains, the Great Basin, and the Yellowstone plateau all overlapped.[1] A number of tribes are believed to have held the Yellowstone region to be a sacred place—one especially suited for vision-quests, i.e., rigorous spiritually-oriented exercises; prayer-making; and ceremonial exchanges of gifts.[2]

For thousands of years, it was actively used by many Native American. These included, in overview and at different times, by the following 26 tribes[3]:

- Assiniboine and Sioux
- Blackfeet
- Cheyenne River Sioux
- Coeur d'Alene
- Colville Reservation
- Comanche
- Crow
- Crow Creek Sioux
- Eastern Shoshone, including the Sheep Eaters
- Flandreau Santee Sioux
- Gros Ventre and Assiniboine
- Kiowa
- Lower Brule Sioux
- Nez Percé
- Northern Arapaho

- Northern Cheyenne
- Oglala Sioux
- Rosebud Sioux
- Salish and Kootenai
- Shoshone-Bannock
- Sisseton Whapeton
- Spirit Lake
- Standing Rock Sioux
- Turtle Mountain Band of the Chippewa
- Umatilla Reservation
- Yankton Sioux

The indigenous peoples who inhabited the Yellowstone area for thousands of years had to adapt to ever-changing climatic conditions. The long, slow process of ecological succession (i.e., biological progression) is outlined below very briefly.[4] There are two different types of ecological succession, which involves the natural progression of biological life from a given condition to another. This succession occurs on many different timescales, ranging from three months to hundreds or even thousands of years.

Primary succession marks the beginning of natural progression that includes the "pioneering" of plant life that occurs on an entirely new habitat which has never been colonized before, such as a newly-quarried rock face or moving sand dunes. Secondary succession is the progression of life that follows the disruption of the primary succession due to disturbances that have reduced the number of the initial inhabitants, such as a large forest fire.

Primary succession took place in Yellowstone about 13,000 to 14,000 years ago, after glacial ice covered the area over what is now Yellowstone Lake and slowly scraped away all the soil and vegetation of the region. This dramatic act set the stage for primary succession. Streams, lakes, and soils appeared. Plant and animal life began to recolonize the area: tundra and steppe vegetation formed first, but were replaced by subalpine and montane parkland as the climate gradually warmed. Recolonization continued, and what is now the park became host to bison, wolves, elk, cutthroat trout, and such open vegetation species as Douglas fir woodlands.

As the climate gradually warmed up and dried out, the animals, vegetation, and human lifestyles all had to change. For example, the huge Ice Age animals that had previously flourished under very cold and very wet conditions now became extinct. Retreating glaciers left behind them sediment-filled valleys where grasses and sagebrush could thrive. The now-uncovered, i.e., ice-free, volcanic plateau gradually became well-stocked with forests of aspens, fir trees, and lodgepole pines.

The local Native Americans, for their part, quickly adapted to such new conditions by developing a more diverse diet that included medium and small animals, including deer and bighorn sheep. They began to use the more powerful, longer range, and relatively rapid-firing bow and arrow, rather than the primitive single-shot atlatl (spear-thrower). They also perfected sheep traps in the hills and bison corrals on the plains.[5]

That the Native Americans (and their predecessors, the Paleoindians) have lived in the Yellowstone region for about 11,000 years was proved by the local discovery in 1929 of a "Clovis point" (i.e., a fluted projectile point for an arrow or a spear), dating from some 11,000 years ago and made from a cliff of Yellowstone obsidian.

Because obsidian can be given an exceptionally sharp cutting edge through a process known as pressure-flaking, it was by far the best material to use when making arrowheads, skinning knives, and spear tips. A geological formation now known as the Obsidian Cliff, located in Wyoming near the Grand Loop Road between Mammoth Hot Springs (a large complex of hot springs set on a hill of travertine in Yellowstone Park, created over thousands of years as hot water from the spring cooled and deposited calcium carbonate—up to two tons each day in a solution) was the primary source of obsidian for Native Americans living as far away as western Canada and the Ohio River Valley.

Technology aside, today fragmentary tribal oral histories can sometimes cast a bit of light on remote earlier times but offer no details on how the earlier Native Americans actually lived. Kiowa legends, for example, place the Kiowa ancestors in the Yellowstone area from around 1400 through the 1700s. The Shoshone, for their part, believe that their own ancestors came to Yellowstone to gather obsidian, which they used to field-dress bison. The forest now named in their honor—the 2.5 million-acre Shoshone National Forest in Wyoming—was first created in 1891 as part of the Yellowstone Timber Reserve. As such, it was the first national forest in the United States.

Some tribes also used the Fishing Bridge in the park, not only for fishing but also as a convenient meeting point. The Crow are said to have occupied the lands generally to the east of the park. The Blackfeet liked the area to the north. The Shoshone, Bannock, and tribes of the plateau-lands to the west had to cross the park every year to hunt bison on the eastern plains. Other Shoshonean groups hunted in the non-forested areas west and south of Yellowstone.

Pottery containers now known as "Intermountain Ware" have been discovered in the region, and indicate that the Shoshone were living and working there about 700 years ago. Another echo from the distant past is an ancient Native American trail, referred to today as the "Bannock Trail," that cut east-west across what is now northern Wyoming. Its exact location still remains unknown due to contradictory contemporary accounts and to errors in an early (1869) map.

The Lakota Sioux first began exploring the Yellowstone area in the

1700s. Around the same time, some tribes first began to acquire horses, which had been brought into the New World by the Spaniards and which were available to North American tribes beginning in the mid- to late 1600s. Mastering the horse fundamentally changed the lifestyles of many tribes. They could now travel much further and faster to hunt; could easily move their camps in response to seasonal changes; and were able to fight their enemies much more effectively.

The best-known component of the Shoshone tribe was the Tukudika, or "Sheep Eaters." They are remembered today chiefly because they continued to use dogs to carry their food, hides, and other provisions— long after most other Native Americans had shifted to the horse. The Tukudika followed, on foot, the migrations of the bighorn sheep that formed a significant part of their diet. There were probably two reasons for this.

The first was that these sheep preferred the rocky, steep slopes of the upper Yellowstone River watershed. The Yellowstone River, a tributary of the Missouri River, is about 670 miles long. It drains a wide area of the Rockies and the high plains of southern Montana and northern Wyoming. (The Missouri River itself does not begin in the Greater Yellowstone area, but its three tributaries do.)

This river, which is now the longest free-flowing river in the lower 48 states, flows north through Yellowstone National Park, feeds into Yellowstone Lake, then tumbles over the upper and lower falls of Yellowstone, which are located at the entrance to the Grand Canyon of Yellowstone. Its very steep slopes were not good hunting country for Native Americans on horseback, so they never ventured there. The river eventually empties into the Missouri River in North Dakota.

The second reason was that early reports, those written before the park was established, indicate that a great many sheep were in fact living near the upper reaches of the river. As a result, Native American hunters, even afoot, probably had little trouble bagging as many sheep as they needed. A male sheep can weigh more than 300 pounds and a female up to 130 pounds, so there was easily enough meat to sustain the hunters and their families.

The Native Americans also made useful implements from the sheep carcasses—for example, by steaming their heavy curving horns in hot springs to make them pliable enough to bend into powerful bows. They then bartered the bows and the sheepskins to neighboring tribes.

The last and most tragic drama of any free-roaming Native American band in Yellowstone began in the summer and fall of 1877, when the Nez Percé Indians fled from the U.S. Army and passed through what is now Yellowstone National Park. Their story is a short but very sad one that deserves to be briefly recounted.

Chief Joseph (1840?–1904) of the Nez Percé led his people, who lived in the Wallowa Valley of northwest Oregon, in a vain attempt to resist the takeover of their tribal lands by white settlers in the Oregon Territory. When some members of his tribe killed a group of white settlers, he tried to flee to Canada with his followers, traveling over 1,500 miles through Oregon, Washington, Idaho, and Montana. Along the way, he fought several skirmishes with the pursuing U.S. Army, spending a total of 13 days in Yellowstone before finally being forced to surrender in October 1877 near the Bears Paw Mountains in Montana—less than 40 miles from the Canadian border.

The speech that he made when surrendering has gone down in American history as the most moving speech ever made by an Native American. Speaking in his native language, Chief Joseph said on 5 October 1877 at Bears Paw in northern Montana:

> I am tired of fighting. Our Chiefs are killed. Looking Glass [a famous warrior] is dead. Toohulhulsote [a wise old man] is dead. The old men are all dead. It is the young men who say yes or no. He who led the young men is dead.
>
> It is cold and we have no blankets. The little children are freezing to death. My people, some of them, have run away to the hills and have no blankets, no food. No one knows where they are—perhaps freezing to death. I want to have time to look for my children and see how many I can find. Maybe I shall find them among the dead.
>
> Hear me, my chiefs. I am tired. My heart is sick and sad. From where the sun now stands I will fight no more forever.[6]

In recent years in the park, the Native Americans have not been forgotten. In 2014, for example, the park's archeology staff completed a Lewis and Snake River Headquarters Survey, which included an intensive inventory of about 23 square miles of the Lewis and Snake river valleys. These valleys served as major transportation corridors for many nomadic peoples. Newly-identified sites there include prehistoric quarries; campsites; lithic (i.e., stone) scatters dating to between 10,000 and 1,500 years ago; and Native American quarries, campsites, and refuse dumps.

The prehistoric sites are changing scholars' understanding of how early human beings procured suitable stones and turned them into useable tools. Most sites show a heavy reliance on Obsidian Cliff materials and on chert, a cryptocrystalline sedimentary rock. Along the Lewis and Snake rivers, a wider and more diverse range of materials was in use. Obsidian was primarily locally-sourced (from the nearby Warm Spring, Teton Pass, and Park Point quarries), but orthoquartzite, a classic sedimentary rock, was the most common material that was used to make tools.[7]

2

Exploring and Protecting the Greater Yellowstone Region, 1784 to 1871

The term "Greater Yellowstone" was first used in print only in 1919 but in this chapter the reader will meet the "Northwestern Mystery" and 17 individual explorers or expeditions that worked in or near the Yellowstone area.[1]

It was the great historian of the American West, Bernard DeVoto (1897–1955), who coined the term "the Northwestern Mystery." By these evocative words he meant the trans–Missouri West, which he defined as "an area … that contained *the key features of continental geography which were the last to be discovered and understood*" by non–Native Americans.[2] The gradual and unrelenting history of exploration of the Rocky Mountain West by many different peoples eventually resolved the Northwestern Mystery. In the process, the complicated scope, extent, and details of the Yellowstone ecosystem itself were gradually laid bare, too.

This chapter and the next sketch out, briefly, two consecutive blocks of time covering the general topics of Yellowstone's exploration and preservation. To begin with, some of the most interesting personalities involved in this long process were the following:

(1) DAVID THOMPSON. This celebrated early explorer and geographer of the British fur trade throughout much of the western Canada and the Pacific Northwest may have been the first to use the English words "Yellow Stone." This was his translation of the Native American phrase "Mi tse a-da-zi" ("Yellow Stone River") in the notes he wrote in 1797–1798 when he was visiting the villages of the Mandan Indians along the Upper Missouri River.[3]

Many aspects of Thompson's career are remarkable. He came to Canada from London in 1784 as a 14-year-old Hudson's Bay Company apprentice. Established in 1670 by an English royal charter, this company gradually expanded into such a powerful exploring, trading, and political institution that it eventually influenced, both directly and indirectly, much of the native and non–Native American life in what is now northern and western Canada.

Working out of the frontier settlement of Churchill, on the western shore of Hudson Bay, and using snowshoes as well as dog teams, Thompson explored and trapped as far west as Lake Athabasca in present-day Alberta. A bright and hard-working lad, he undertook a serious study of wilderness map-making under the tutelage of the Hudson's Bay Company's chief surveyor. As a result, Thompson himself would soon be able to draft the first accurate maps of the western regions of Canada that had never been explored by non–Native Americans.

In 1797, for example, he explored and mapped new routes to the Company's far-flung chain of posts lying east of the Rockies. The next year, traveling by snowshoes and dog teams to trade with the Native Americans of North Dakota and Manitoba, he learned why travel there was almost impossible in the winter. He noted in his diary, for example, how he had managed to survive a potentially-fatal winter storm. This was, he wrote on the spot in his journal:

> A most terrible Storm with thick snow and excessively high Drift … it is as much as we can [do] to Keep from being buried under the Snow, it is without doubt the worse day I ever saw in my Life. We have no Meat [i.e., no food], fortunately yesterday I picked up a Marrow Bone of a Buffaloe which had been pretty well Knawed by a wolf—this was my day's allowance of food.[4]

Toward the end of his life (he died in 1857), when he was blind and ailing, he finally had his lifelong experiences committed to paper. The narrative of his explorations, entitled *Travels in Western North America,* was annotated in 1971. It contains this justifiably-proud statement by him:

> Thus I have fully completed the survey of this part of North America from sea to sea, and by almost innumerable astronomical Observations have determined the positions of the Mountains, Lakes and Rivers, and other remarkable places of the northern part of the continent.[5]

(2) Lewis and Clark. Their famous expedition, also known as the Corps of Discovery Expedition, undertaken from May 1804 to September 1806, is important today because it was the first American expedition to explore large parts of the western mountains of what is now the United States.[6] As such, it would be a key step toward understanding Yellowstone itself.

At that time, this expedition did not excite any local, let alone any national or international, attention. Today, in the broader sweep of American history, it is hailed as a major epic of exploration; as a key advance in scientific and ethnographic knowledge; as a seminal event that set in motion the settlement and domination of the Rocky Mountain West by non–Native American newcomers; and as a tragic death-knell for many of the Native American tribes that Lewis and Clark had encountered during their travels.

Commissioned by President Thomas Jefferson, this now-famous expedition set off from Pittsburgh, Pennsylvania, and made its way westward to the Pacific Coast, eventually returning to St. Louis to report its many findings to Jefferson. It was jointly led by U.S. Army Captain Meriwether Lewis and his close friend, Second Lieutenant William Clark. Today, the journals of Lewis and Clark still deserve our careful attention for the historical information, drawings, and the local color they contain.[7]

The Lewis and Clark expedition traveled along the northern edge of the Greater Yellowstone Ecosystem, coming within 50 miles of what is now Yellowstone Park, and saw many species of large mammals in great abundance. Lewis made the following observations in his journal (spelling and punctuation have been modernized):

> I decided to camp on the bank of the Yellowstone River, which made its appearance two miles south of me. The whole face of the country was covered with herds of buffalo, elk, and antelopes; deer are also abundant but keep themselves more concealed in the woodland. The buffalo, elk, and antelope are so gentle that we pass near them without appearing to excite any alarm among them, and when we attract their attention they frequently approach us more closely to discover what we are. In some instances they follow us at a considerable distance for this purpose.[8]

En route, the two leaders also heard distant volcanic explosions but thought that these sounds must have been thunder. Although they made the very ground shake, Lewis and Clark did not pause to investigate the source of these strange sounds. Their assignment from Jefferson was to get to the Pacific Ocean and back again without any dawdling along the way. So, like the good soldiers they were, these pathfinders simply followed their President's orders. Therefore, they did not explore the Yellowstone River itself beyond what is now Livingston, Montana.

After Clark returned to St. Louis, he added the following statement to his notes (the spelling and other errors in this and other quotes are as in the original):

> At the head of this river [the Yellowstone] the natives give an account
> that there is frequently herd a noise, like Thunder, which makes the earth

Tremble, they State that they seldom go there because their children Cannot sleep—and Conceive it possessed of spirts, who were averse that men Should be near them.[9]

In 1805, when the expedition reached the junction of the Missouri and Yellowstone Rivers, Lewis climbed up a bluff above the Missouri and saw, for the first time, the jagged peaks of the Rockies looming above him. He later wrote:

When I reflected on the difficulties which this snowy barrier would most probably throw in my way to the Pacific, and the sufferings and hardships of myself and party in them, it in some measure counterbalanced the joy I had felt in the first moment in which I gazed upon them.[10]

Remarkably, despite the very rugged mountainous terrain through which much of the Yellowstone River flowed, Lewis did not understand its true nature. Indeed, he wrote (incorrectly) in 1806 that "the Yellow Stone river is navigable at all seasons of the year," and he further assumed that this alleged navigability characterized the entire course of the river from source to mouth. It was, he mistakenly claimed, "a large and navigable river with but few obstructions quite to the rocky Mountains."[11]

The Hidatsa Indians knew the region very well. It is very likely that they had in fact already explained to Lewis that only one part of the Yellowstone River was navigable even by canoes or dugouts.[12] The reason is that, in Yellowstone Park itself, the river tumbles, first, over the 109-foot-high Upper Yellowstone Falls; then over the much smaller and lesser-known Crystal Falls, located between the upper and lower falls; and, finally, over the 308-foot-high Lower Yellowstone Falls at the head of the 20-mile-long and more than 1,000-foot deep Grand Canyon of the Yellowstone. All this makes an uninterrupted river passage quite impossible.

On other sections of the river even steam navigation would turn out to be quite feasible. For example, *Yellowstone*, a 120-foot-long side-wheel steamer, was, in 1831, the first steamboat to proceed above Council Bluffs, Iowa, on the Missouri River. Today, naval historians often refer to a ship only by her given name, such as *Yellowstone*, without adding the prefix "the." In 1832, *Yellowstone* was also the first steam-powered trading vessel boat to reach the mouth of the Yellowstone River itself. The dramatic reactions of the Mandan Indians in the 1830s to this new and totally strange vessel are mentioned in Appendix 1, giving George Catlin's views on the Prairie Native Americans.

Yellowstone had been built for the American Fur Company to support the fur trade between St. Louis, Missouri, and its trading camps along the Missouri River, up to the mouth of the Yellowstone River. In

1829, this company had built a large central post, known as Fort Union, located in what is now Montana. It was set on the north bank of the Missouri River about five miles above the mouth of the Yellowstone River.

In 1832, the artist George Catlin used Fort Union as a base from which he carefully studied and sensitively portrayed the Mandan Indians. He later wrote of his Yellowstone experiences:

> I have wandered over a good part of the [historical Kansas and Jefferson] Territories and have seen much of the varied scenery of the Far West, but that of Yellowstone retains its hold upon my imagination with a vividness as of yesterday. The impression made upon me by the stupendous and remarkable manifestations of nature's forces will remain with me as long as memory lasts.[13]

From Fort Union and its string of lesser posts, the company then began to woo the Native Americans away from their former trading contacts and had some success, even with the potentially-hostile Blackfeet. In addition, large, well-equipped brigades of American and other trappers directly employed by the American Fur Company were soon sent out into the mountains, not only to trap-out the beaver but also to try to ruin the Rocky Mountain Fur Company and any other rivals.[14]

The Yellowstone River was sometimes fatal for steamboats. In 1833, *Yellowstone* grounded on a sandbar but managed to get off safely after some of her heavy cargo had been offloaded. In 1870, another steamer, also named *Yellowstone*, was swept downstream onto the rocks below when she failed to winch her way up a foaming rapid. Once on the rocks, she quickly filled with water and sank in a matter of minutes.[15]

(3) JOHN COLTER. This explorer is the source of one of the most dramatic adventure accounts in the entire history of the Rocky Mountain West.[16] Traveling alone in the wilderness for months on end, the mountain man John Colter (c. 1770–1775–May 7, 1812, or November 22, 1813), who had served with Lewis and Clark, was very probably, during the winter of 1807–1808, the first non–Native American to get a good look at the Yellowstone region. His story is quite remarkable.

During his travels, Colter skirted the northwest shore of Yellowstone Lake, which at 7,731 feet is the largest high-elevation lake in North America, and crossed the Yellowstone River near today's Tower Fall, where he noted the presence of what he called "Hot Spring Brimstone." His experiences are truly the stuff of legend, both because both they are so interesting and because they so lightly documented. When trying to separate historical fact from adventuresome fiction, modern historians are left with something like the following account:

After serving as an excellent and much-valued hunter and guide for the Lewis and Clark expedition from 1803 to 1806, Colter left its homeward-bound journey on 15 August 1806 at the Mandan villages of what is now North Dakota. He had just encountered two trappers—Joseph Dixon and Forest Hancock—who were now retracing the expedition's out-bound route, hoping to find some virgin beaver-trapping territory. Very eager to join them, Colter asked Lewis and Clark for an honorable discharge, and he received their immediate permission to join the trappers.

The next documented sighting of Colter was not until the spring of 1807, when he was seen paddling down the Missouri, all alone, in a dugout canoe he had made from a hollowed-out cottonwood log. There is no information about what happened to Dixon and Hancock, but when Colter reached the mouth of the Platte River near today's Omaha, Nebraska, he ran into the first well-organized group of trappers to follow the route of Lewis and Clark up toward the Rocky Mountains.

Led by the St. Louis entrepreneur Manuel Lisa, a native of Spanish Louisiana, this large group also included three former members of the Louis and Clark expedition, who warmly welcomed Colter and encouraged him to join them, which he did. Legend has it that at some later point he decided to leave them and to set out, alone, on a remarkable single-handed 500-mile-long journey to trade with the Native Americans.

During this process, in what is now the Cody area and Yellowstone National Park, he saw the geysers and hot springs in a part of northern Wyoming that would jokingly become known to his unbelieving fellow outdoorsmen as "Colter's Hell." The American historian William Goetzmann has described Colter's journey as "the first great exploring trek after Louis and Clark, and one of the least remembered in history."[17]

In addition to being a highly-skilled outdoorsman, Colter was also a gifted storyteller. When the English naturalist John Bradbury was traveling up the Missouri in 1811, he met Colter who told him the following tale: In the autumn of 1809 he had been captured by the Blackfeet Indians. Then, barefoot and stripped naked, he had been forced to run for his life, while the Native Americans, after giving him a short head-start, began to chase him.

During this race, he had survived only by his courage, his stamina, and his quick thinking. First, he ran as hard as he could. Then, seeing that the fastest Native American was about to overtake him, he came to a sudden and totally unexpected stop. He then instantly turned, faced the pursuing opponent, and spread his arms wide open. At that instant, Colter was bleeding profusely from his nose because of his fierce exertions. This very gory appearance—coupled with the suddenness of Colter's stop—literally put the Native American off his stride.

The Native American tried hard to stop running, but he stumbled as he threw at Colter the spear he was carrying in his hand. The spear point stuck in the ground, and the wooden shaft broke in two. Colter instantly seized the half which had the spear point, stabbed and killed the man with it, and then ran on. He had then hidden in the water under a raft of drift timber until the other Native Americans finally got tired of hunting for him and went away. Bradbury ended his account, now known to historians as "Colter's Run," by concluding laconically that these were "circumstances under which almost any man but an American hunter would have despaired."

By about 1810, Colter decided that he had pressed his luck far enough. He announced to some of his fellow trappers: "If God will only forgive me this time and let me off I will leave this country day after tomorrow—and be damned if I ever come to it again!"[18] He was true to his word, retiring to St. Louis and spending some of his remaining years farming on the Missouri River frontier. During the War of 1812, he enlisted and fought in Nathan Boone's Ranger unit. The cause and the year of his death are not known, but it may have been due to jaundice in 1812 or 1813. Since then, Colter's remarkable story has been the subject of several motion pictures and novels. A historical marker to his memory is now located at Stuart's Draft, Virginia, his birthplace.

(4) ANDREW HENRY. The expeditions of this American trapper and miner after 1809 opened up parts of the Rocky Mountains in Wyoming, Montana, and Idaho that had never been explored before by non–Native Americans.[19] A partner of the great trader Manuel Lisa, in 1810 Henry led the first American trapping expedition to cross the Rockies and, that same year, he also set up the first American trading post west of the Continental Divide. It was located at what is now Henry's Fort on Clark's Fork, a tributary of the Snake River.

In 1822, Henry joined another famous trader, William H. Ashley, and formed the Rocky Mountain Fur Company. Having run ads in the help-wanted section of the *Missouri Gazette and Public Advertiser* in 1823, these men found many adventuresome trappers quite eager to open up the Rocky Mountains to the beaver-trapping business by joining one of the two expeditions sent out for this purpose and by helping to build a trading post at the mouth of the Yellowstone River. The ads ran along the following lines:

FOR THE ROCKY MOUNTAINS. The undersigned wishing to engage ONE HUNDRED MEN, to ascend the Missouri to the
ROCKY MOUNTAINS, There to be employed as Hunters. As a compensation to each man fit for such business,
$200 Per Annum, will be given for his services, as aforesaid.[20]

The first expedition was led by Henry himself in the late summer of 1823. It crossed today's Nebraska and the Dakotas and pressed on into the central Rockies. The second expedition was led by another well-known explorer, Jedidiah Smith. In the spring of 1824, Smith's group would discover South Pass, Wyoming, which would later become the chief trade and migrant route through the Rockies.

(5) STEPHEN H. LONG. An able officer of the U.S. Army's prestigious Corps of Topographical Engineers, Long saw himself as the natural successor to Lewis and Clark but, unfortunately, his own achievements would fall far short of his ambitious dreams.[21] In 1818, the War Department chose Long to lead an expedition into the Rockies. His party included soldiers, scientists, and—remarkably—two excellent artists, namely Titian Peale and Samuel Seymour.

The expedition traveled by steamboat up the Mississippi and Missouri Rivers to Council Bluffs, where they spent the winter. They later met with both success and failure. On the positive side, three of Long's men made the first documented ascent of 14,110 foot–high Pikes Peak south of present-day Denver. Perhaps even more importantly, the artistic work by Peale and Seymour was so good that it gave millions of stay-at-home American men and women their first dramatic and accurate pictures of the frontier West in that time.

On the negative side, after leaving Pike's Peak, Long set out to find the Red River, which formed the boundary between American territory and Spanish territory. The bad news was that he mistook the Canadian River in today's Oklahoma for the Red River, and never reached the Red River.

Another problem was a map that Long made of the region lying between the Missouri frontier and the Rocky Mountains. This map was relatively accurate and could be useful for travelers but on it Long had repeated the dramatic but very inaccurate description by an earlier explorer (Zebulon Pike) that the Great Plains were literally nothing more than a "Great American Desert."

The result of his error was that, for many years to come, this ominous phrase would continue to discourage farmers who were weighing the pros and cons of moving to the Great Plains.

In a related move, in 1820, the Spanish commander in Santa Fe, Facundo Melgares, sent out a reconnaissance mission as far as the Yellowstone Valley in Wyoming to check on a report of illegal American encroachment, such as Long's expedition, into the "Spanish Dominion," namely, the territory claimed by Spain in this region. This effort by Melgares came to naught because the United States had already prevailed in the western boundary dispute through signing the 1818–1819 Adams-Onís (or Transcontinental) Treaty.

The treaty officially established the western boundary line of the Louisiana Territory and also settled some issues regarding Florida itself. When the very long, zigzagging western boundary line finally reached the Pacific Ocean, it officially separated Oregon from the Spanish holdings in California. The end result was that it gave the United States its own long-sought "dominion" from coast to coast.[22]

6) PRINCE MAXIMILIAN AND KARL BODMER. Maximilian was the hereditary German ruler of the small Prussian principality of Wied-Neuwied, which was located on the east bank of the Rhine. Bodmer was a 24-year-old Swiss artist who accompanied him to record their travels.[23] The purpose of their epic 1833–1834 journey up to the headwaters of the Missouri River was to make an accurate, scientific, written and visual record of a part of North America that was then very little known.

Traveling more than 2,500 miles, Maximilian took copious notes which he later distilled into a magisterial multi-volume work titled *Travels in the Interior of North America, 1832–1834*. This would be the crowning achievement of his long, distinguished career. Even better than this text, on the other hand, were Bodmer's many vivid, colorful, and sensitive engravings of the Native Americans. During their Missouri River passage, Bodmer and Maximilian encountered at least 20 Native American tribes and recorded their varied ways of life. The two men also studied many of the landscapes, plants, and animals of the upper Missouri River. Bodmer's vivid engravings and drawings illustrated the book; today they are still hailed as outstanding. The catalog of a modern exhibition has described them in these glowing terms:

> In illuminating the haunting natural beauty which abided in the interior of North America at the time, Bodmer's work, like a sentient candle in the dark, continues to surprise and delight us. It causes us to look with new eyes at a pristine America—the raw freshness of its flora and fauna, its verdant riverbottoms, its limpid intercontinental waterways, its landscapes which extended as far as the eye could see on either side of the broad Missouri River.[24]

A modern historian of the West, William H. Goetzmann, summarized the route of this expedition by noting that from April 1833 to April 1834 Bodmer and Maximilian travelled up the Missouri River, first aboard the steamboats *Yellow Stone* and *Assiniboine*, and then by via a keelboat (a sturdy, long, narrow, cigar-shaped riverboat that could be either rowed or poled), all the way up to Fort McKenzie, the last American outpost in the Upper Missouri region.

This fort was almost 3,000 miles upstream from St. Louis and was located in the very heart of lands dominated by the Blackfeet Indians. It would become the farthest point in their journey because of the extreme hostility of the Blackfeet toward both neighboring tribes and visiting travelers. Their fear of this hostility forced Bodmer and Maximilian to retreat downriver and to spend the winter at Fort Clark on the Missouri. After five miserable months of hardship there, they were finally able to set off for St. Louis and from there managed to return safely to New York. They were back in France in August 1834.

(7) OSBORNE RUSSELL. This trapper (1814–1892), a trapper in the 1820s and 1830s, was one of the very few early Yellowstone explorers to leave any written record of his travels. The reader may refer to the quotation on the opening page of this book, but it is worth learning a little bit more about him.[25]

Russell was neither a heroic explorer nor a world-famous trapper, but—even better for our purposes—he was a sensitive, excellent observer. He managed to keep a unique journal, which was not published until 1921, that documents his experiences in the mountains between 1834 and 1843. Its full, sonorous title is: *Journal of a Trapper: or, Nine Years in the Rocky Mountains, 1834–1843; being a general description of the country, climate, rivers, lakes, mountains, etc., and a view of the life led by a hunter in those regions.*

After working for several major fur-trading companies, Russell decided to find a better job. The companies' low prices for prime beaver pelts (his pay for 18 months of hard, dangerous labor was only $250); the growing scarcity of beaver; and the declining demand for their fur due to the shift in men's fashion from beaver-pelt hats to silk hats—all combined to make him a "free trapper."

Such a trapper was a very independent-spirited and resourceful man who, unchained by any formal commitment to a fur company, could go wherever he pleased, trap wherever he liked, and sell his furs to the highest bidder. The writer and historian Washington Irving (1783–1859), who was the best-known American man of letters of his time, wrote of these free trappers: "We find them ... hardy, lithe, vigorous, and active; extravagant in word, and thought, and deed; heedless of hardship; daring of danger; prodigal of the present, and thoughtless of the future."[26]

Russell himself wrote compassionately, accurately, and very well. He was present when the beaver and bison populations were being decimated, and for this reason recorded in his journal that "it is [now] time for the white man to leave the mountains." Long before then, he had faced many near-death situations. In his trapper's journal, for example, he recounts how he had wounded a grizzly bear while out hunting buffalo with a companion. As the two men approached the bushes where the bear had hidden,

> ... we heard a sullen growl, which was instantly followed by a spring of the Bear toward us, his enormous jaws extended and eyes flashing fire. Was there anything so hideous?
>
> We could not retain sufficient presence of mind to shoot at him but took to our heels, separating as we ran, the Bear taking after me. I was obliged to turn about and face him.
>
> I pulled the trigger and I knew not what else to do, and hardly knew that I did this, but it accidently happened that my Rifle was pointed towards the Bear when I pull[ed], and the ball piercing his heart, he uttered a deathly howl and fell dead: but I trembled as if I had an ague fit for half an hour after.[27]

In 1834, Russell described the region of the Lamar River (a 40-mile-long tributary of the Yellowstone River) as "A Garden of Eden Inhabited by a Small Party of Snake Indians" in the following words:

> On the 28th [of July 1834] we crossed the mountain in a westerly direction through the thick pines and fallen timber, about twelve miles, and encamped in a small prairie about a mile in circumference. Through this valley ran a small stream in a northerly direction, which all agreed to be a branch of the Yellowstone.
>
> [29 July 1834]. We descended the stream about fifteen miles through the dense forest and at length came to a beautiful valley about eight miles long and three or four wide, surrounded by dark and lofty mountains. The stream, after running through the center in a northwesterly direction, rushed down a tremendous canyon of basaltic rock apparently just wide enough to admit its waters.
>
> The streams of the valley were low and skirted in many places with beautiful cottonwood groves. Here we found a few Snake Indians comprising six men, seven women and eight or ten children, who were the only inhabitants of this lonely and secluded spot.[28]

As a free trapper, Russell had plenty of time to hunt game, to make friends with the local Native Americans, and—perhaps most surprisingly because so many trappers were illiterate—to read the Bible. It was while doing the latter that he experienced a religious conversion that led him to abandon the raucous life of a mountain man and to join a wagon train of emigrants heading for the Willamette Valley of Oregon. In 1843, he lost his right eye and sustained other injuries while blasting rocks for a millrace at Oregon City. Always resourceful, while convalescing he studied law, later became a judge, and was deeply involved in local Oregon Territory politics.

After joining the 1848 Gold Rush to California, Russell was still in poor health due to his earlier injuries and was thus forced to become a merchant rather than a prospector. He was financially ruined by a dishonest partner and had to spend the rest of his life trying to pay off his creditors, finally dying in Placerville, California, in 1892. He never married.

(8) DANIEL T. POTTS. In the early 1800s, trappers were beginning to roam through the Rockies for the first time, looking for beaver. Trapper brigades had already reached the Yellowstone plateau by 1826, and in 1827 an anonymous account of a trapper's adventures in what is now Yellowstone Park was published in *The Philadelphia Gazette and Advertiser.*

Much later, the author was discovered to have been a fur trapper named Daniel T. Potts, who had sent a letter to his brother on July 8, 1827. This letter is now thought to be the first written description of the thermal features of the Upper Yellowstone by someone who had actually seen them. Potts wrote the letter at what is now Bear Lake in northern Utah, which he called "Sweet Lake" to distinguish it from the Great Salt Lake. The following is verbatim, with bracketed editorial additions.

Respected Brother,

Shortly after writing to you last year I took my departure for the Blackfoot Country.[29] We took a northerly direction about 50 miles where we cross Snake River or the South fork of Columbia—which heads on the top of the great chain of Rocky Mountains that separate the water of the Atlantic from that of the Pacific. Near this place Yellowstone South fork of Missouri and the Henrys fork head at an angular point. The head of the Yellowstone has a large fresh water lake on the very top of the mountain—which is about 140 miles in diameter and as clear as crystal.

On the south borders of this lake is a number of hot and boiling springs—some of water and others of most beautiful fine clay, resembling a mush pot [a simple metal cooking pot], and throwing particles to the immense height of twenty to thirty feet [these are the geysers, mud springs, and "paint pots" of the thermal region west of Yellowstone Lake.]

The clay is white and of a pink. The water appears fathomless; it appears to be entirely hollow underneath [i.e., seemed to be very deep].

There is also a number of places where the pure sulphur is sent forth in abundance [from the springs]. One of our men visited one of those whilst taking his recreation. There at an instant the earth began a tremendous trembling. With difficulty he made his escape when an explosion took place resembling that of thunder. During our stay in that quarter, I heard it every day.

From this place by a circuitous route to the northwest, we returned. Two others and I pushed on in advance for the purpose of accumulating a few more beaver. In the act of passing through a narrow confine in the mountain, we were met plumb in face by a large party of Blackfeet Indians. Not knowing our number, they fled into the mountain in confusion—and we to a small grove of willows. Here we made every preparation for battle. After finding our enemy as much alarmed as ourselves, we mounted our horses which were heavily loaded we took the back retreat.

The Indians raised a tremendous yell and showered down from the mountaintop. They had almost cut off our retreat when [we] put whip to our horses. They pursued us in close quarters until we reached the plains where we left them behind.

Tomorrow I depart for the west. We are all in good health and hope that this letter finds you in the same situation. I wish you to remember my best respects to all enquiring friends, particularly your wife.

Remain yours most affectionally.
[Signed] Daniel T. Potts[30]

(9) JOE MEEK. In about 1829, this 19-year-old fur trapper was en route with a trapping party along the Yellowstone River when a hostile band of Blackfoot Indians attacked and scattered his party, forcing Meek to escape by himself into what is now Yellowstone National Park. In the later years of his life, he recounted his adventures to an Oregon historian, Frances Fuller Victor, who published them in 1870 in a book entitled *The River of the West*.

Meek had strong memories of his many years in the mountains and was able to highlight his account with colorful anecdotes of his life as a mountain man. Here are some of them (summarized from or quoted from *The River of the West*).

The volcanic region Meek describes is now known as the Norris Geyser basin. It is subject, he reported, to "thermal disturbances," lasting from a few days to a few weeks. During these events, water levels fluctuate, temperatures and pH vary, colors change, and different eruptive patterns occur throughout the basin.

To avoid being immediately captured by the Native Americans when they attacked, Meek was forced to flee into the high mountains overlooking the Yellowstone River.

Traveling to the southeast, he first crossed the river and then, while still among the mountains, decided to abandon his mule and his camping equipment. He kept only his single-shot rifle with some gunpowder and bullets for it, and one blanket. After five days trekking alone on foot through the wilderness, he climbed a low mountain near his camp and saw the following:

> … Behold! the whole country beyond was smoking with the vapor from boiling springs, and burning with gasses, issuing from small craters, each of which was emitting a sharp whistling sound.…
>
> The extent of the volcanic region was immense, reaching far out of sight. The general face of the country was smooth and rolling, being a level plain, dotted with cone-shaped mounds. On the summit these mounds were small

craters from four to eight feet in diameter. Interspersed among these, on the level plain, were larger craters, some of them four to six miles across. Out of these craters issued blue flames and molten brimstone....

On descending to the plain [which was lower than these craters], the earth was found to have a hollow sound, and seemed threatening to break through. But Joe found the warmth of the place most delightful, after the freezing cold of the mountains, and remarked to himself again, "If it war [i.e., if it were] hell, it war a more agreeable climate than he had been in for some time."[31]

When he finally managed to rejoin the other trappers, Meek found that they simply refused to believe his vivid accounts of the Yellowstone region. They thought that he was drunk, or mad, or both. On the other hand, they probably had less trouble believing his report that "The whole country, lying upon the Yellowstone and its tributaries, and about the headwaters of the Missouri, at the time of which we are writing, abounded not only in beaver, but in buffalo, bear, elk, antelope, and many kinds of small game."[32]

(10) JIM BRIDGER. This American frontiersman was one of the most famous explorers and mountain men. His hands-on knowledge of the frontier was so extensive that the modern historian Bernard DeVoto would praise him as "an atlas of the West." A mountain traveler who knew Bridger personally in 1837–1838 later wrote that Bridger had

> ... a complete and absolute understanding of the Indian character in all its different phases, and a firm, though no means over cautious, distrust with regard to these savages....
>
> ... his bravery was unquestionable, his horsemanship equally so, and ... he had been known to kill twenty buffaloes by the same number of shots....
>
> ... To complete the picture, he was perfectly ignorant of all knowledge contained in books, not even knowing the letters of the alphabet, and was unutterably scandalized if even the most childish of the superstitions of the Indians were treated with anything like contempt or disrespect; for in all these he was a firm and devout believer.[33]

Bridger visited the Yellowstone region and its geysers in 1830. His only problem in this adventure lay in the fact that he was now too well known—not only as a world-class wilderness guide but also as a world-class spinner of tall tales.

He found, as Meek had before him and others would find later on, that no one believed his outlandish accounts of waterfalls spouting upwards and of petrified "birds and trees" in the "Yaller Stone" country. (See Appendix 2, The "Putrified" [i.e., Petrified] Forest of Black Harris.) Bridger's most exaggerated stories usually contained some elements of truth, which would later be confirmed by scientific expeditions.

Bridger became famous for all his exploits; indeed, a monument to him was set up at the Kansas City Cemetery where he was buried. The epitaph on it gives a good summary of his danger-ridden, strenuous life. Annotated and edited, it reads:

1804—James Bridger—1881

Discovered Salt Lake, 1824; [discovered] the South Pass [a broad, easily-crossed passageway through the Rocky Mountains which shortened the Oregon Trail by 61 miles and would later become the chosen route for the Union Pacific Railroad and for Interstate 80], 1827; visited Yellowstone Lake and Geysers, 1830; Founded Fort Bridger [a small trading post in southwestern Wyoming], 1843; Opened Overland Route by Bridger's Pass to Salt Lake. Was Guide for Exploring Expeditions* [for] Albert Sidney Johnson's Army in 1857, and [for] G.M. Dodge in U.P. [Union Pacific Railroad] Surveys and Indian Campaigns in 1865–66.

(11) WARREN ANGUS FERRIS. This clerk of the American Fur Company once overheard some fur trappers talking among themselves about the remarkable features to be seen along the Firehole River in northwestern Wyoming. Surrounded by geothermal features that pour water into it, and named by fur trappers for the steam that makes it look like it is on fire, this river is located in northwestern Wyoming and is one of the two major tributaries of the Madison River.

To add to its charms, the Firehole River also flows over three of Yellowstone's major waterfalls, namely, Kepler Cascade, south of Old Faithful; Firehole Falls; and the Cascades of the Firehole in Firehole Canyon. Ferris very much wanted to see all these wonders with his own eyes, and, solely for this reason, he visited the geyser basins in 1834.

Today he is credited with having written the first factual description of them: he kept a careful journal during his trip and later published it in the *Western Literary Messenger* of Buffalo, New York. He may also have been the first genuine Yellowstone "tourist," in the sense that in making this visit he was motivated by intellectual curiosity alone, not by any hope of financial or other gain.

(12) ELIJAH NICHOLAS (NICK) WILSON. Nick (1842–1915) was not an explorer but his unique in-depth knowledge of Shoshone Indian life, coupled with his own remarkable adventures, would put most "real"

For example, in 1855–1857 Bridger was the guide for the Irish nobleman and hunter Sir St. George Gore, who by his own count, during a three-year-long hunting expedition supported by 40 employees, 112 horses, three milk cows and "enough champagne to float a small boat," traveled 6,000 miles and killed 2,000 buffalo; 1,600 deer and elk; and 105 bears.

explorers to shame.[34] He was an uneducated but very bright pioneer boy who crossed the Great Plains in 1850 by ox-team with his Mormon parents and lived with them in a frontier settlement south of the Great Salt Lake.

Life there in the 1850s was exceptionally hard. Without very much to eat, he and his family lived chiefly on vegetables they grew and on "lumpy-dick," an unappetizing porridge made by mixing a little water and flour to form pea-sized lumps, which were then cooked in hot milk. The work on their subsistence-level farm was unending, exhausting, and stressful. The nearby presence of hostile Native Americans kept the settlers heavily-armed and on a constant state of alert. As a result of these tribulations, when he was only 11 years old, Nick ran away from the farm (in the company of a friendly Native American), seeking adventure and a more promising way of life.

The best news was that the mother of Chief Washakie, a prominent Shoshone leader, who had recently lost her youngest son in an avalanche, kindly adopted Nick as her own boy. He spent the next two years living with the Native Americans, learning their language, their culture, and the outdoor skills he needed to become a useful member of the tribe. He took part in buffalo hunts, fought off grizzly bears, watched Native American wars, and even survived being shot in the head with an Native American arrow and then being left to die.

As if all this was not enough, in his adult years Nick also became a trapper; was one of the original Pony Express riders; worked as an overland stagecoach driver; served as a U.S. Army scout and interpreter; was called on to track down hostile Native Americans; had to shoot his way out of a confrontation with three Sioux thieves; finally settled down in Jackson Hole, Wyoming, in 1889; and a few years later founded a little town near it, named "Wilson" in his honor. An important point to be made here, both for historical accuracy and for local color, is that at the age of 14, in 1856, Nick went with his Native American "mother" to visit an extensive Native American encampment then being held in the Big Hole Basin of the Snake River. In his own words:

One morning we saw seven head [of buffalo] on the bench [a long narrow strip of land bounded by steeper slopes above and below about a mile away]. Ten Indians started after them. One having a wide spear with a long handle would ride up to a buffalo and cut the hamstrings of both legs and [another Native American] would come along and kill it.

About fifteen squaws went up to skin the buffaloes to get the meat. Mother and I went with them. The squaws would rip the animals down the back from the head to the tail and then rip them down the belly and take off the top half of the hide and cut all the meat on that side from the bones. They would then tie ropes to the feet of the buffaloes and turn them over with their ponies, and do the other side the same way.

After they got the meat home, they would slice it up into thin pieces and hang it up to dry. When it was about half dry they would take a piece at a time and pound it between two rocks until it was very soft, and then hang it up again until it was dry. The dried meat was put into a sack and the older it got the better it was.

This was the way they did all of their buffalo meat. The meat was generally kept for use in the winter and during the general gatherings of the tribe. I know that we had about five hundred pounds of it when we got to the place where the tribe was to assemble [in Deer Lodge Valley, Montana].

It was a great sight to see so many Indians together.... As nearly as I could find out, there were about six thousand Indians in this great camp, but there might have been more. When I asked the chief [Chief Washakie] how many there were, he said that there were so many that he could not count them.[35]

(13) CAPTAIN WILLIAM F. RAYNOLDS. In 1859 this U.S. Army surveyor, set out on a two-year survey of the northern Rocky Mountains. Raynolds and his party spent the winter in Wyoming and then, in May 1860, tried to cross the Continental Divide over Two Ocean Plateau from the Wind River drainage in northwest Wyoming.

Deep spring snows made this venture quite impossible but if the group had been able to cross that divide, it would then have been the first organized survey to enter the Yellowstone region. Later, the Civil War tied up the U.S. Government but as soon as the war ended in 1865, several official Yellowstone expeditions were planned. None of these actually ever got underway.

(14) THE COOK-FOLSOM-PETERSON EXPEDITION. The first formal and well-organized—but still unofficial—expedition into the Yellowstone region was the privately-funded journey organized and led by David E. Folsom, Charles W. Cook, and William Peterson in 1869.[36] These three very competent outdoorsmen lived in Diamond City, Montana, a gold-prospecting settlement in the Big Belt Mountains east of Helena, Montana. They pointedly ignored a concerned friend's alarmed warnings that their travels from and then back to Helena would be nearly-suicidal because of the "Indian troubles" he was certain that they would face along the way.

In fact, their 36-day trip was both extensive and quite safe. From Bozeman, they traveled down the divide between the Gallatin and Yellowstone rivers and then crossed the mountains to Yellowstone and made their way into what is now the park. The wonders they saw there included Tower Fall, the Grand Canyon of the Yellowstone, Mud

Volcano, Yellowstone Lake, West Thumb, Shoshone Lake, and, finally, the geysers of the Firehole River. The expedition updated an earlier 1865 explorer's map; wrote an article for *Western Monthly* magazine (see below); and rekindled the interest of scientists in studying these wonders on a rigorous scientific basis.

The only problem they had, upon their return to Helena, was that magazine editors there initially refused to publish the articles they had written, which described the environmental wonders they had seen. Cook wrote of a lovely spot now known as Artist Point:

> I sat there in amazement, while my companions came up, and after that, it seemed to me it was 5 minutes before anyone spoke. Language is inadequate to convey a just conception of the grandeur and sublimity of this master-piece of nature's handiwork.[37]

Their editors were convinced that they were merely repeating the tall tales of Jim Bridger and other mountain men who had long been trading yarns around their campfires.

Eventually, their exploits were published in Chicago by the *Western Monthly Magazine.* Their journals, coupled with their firsthand accounts to friends, led to the next—and the first *official*—expedition (described below), which took place the next year, in 1870.

(15) THE WASHBURN-LANGFORD-DOANE EXPEDITION. Surveyor-General Henry D. Washburn; politician and businessman Nathaniel P. Langford (who would in 1872 be appointed the first super-intendent of the new Yellowstone National Park); attorney Cornelius Hedges; and U.S. Army First Lieutenant Gustavus C. Doane, who led a small military escort from Fort Ellis (near present-day Bozeman, Montana), all set out together in 1870 on an official expedition to explore the Yellowstone region.

Doane had no camera or artist on hand to record his impressions. He was forced to rely on his own journal to record, for posterity, his own sense of wonder at the Jackson Hole region. He wrote, movingly:

> The moonlight view was one of unspeakable grandeur. There are twenty-two summits in the line [of mountains], all of them mighty mountains, with the gleaming spire of Mount Hayden rising in a pinnacle above all.
> There are no foothills to the Tetons. They rise suddenly in rugged maj-esty from the rock strewn plain. Masses of heavy forest appear on the glacial debris and in the parks behind the curve of the lower slopes, but the general field of vision is glittering glacial rock. The soft light floods the great expanse of the valley, the winding silvery river and the resplendent deeply carved mountain walls.[38]

This expedition visited many local sights, including the geyser basins. During their travels, the expedition members drew up detailed maps, made scientific observations, explored numerous lakes, climbed several mountains, and studied the wildlife. Moreover, they also visited both the Upper and Lower Geyser Basins where, memorably, after noting the regular eruptions of one particular geyser, they decided to christen it "Old Faithful" because it could be relied on to erupt about once every hour.

Other results from this expedition included excellent publicity for the Yellowstone region as a whole. Nathaniel Langford, for example, went East during the winter and spring of 1871; lectured on all the Yellowstone marvels he had seen; and, then, in May 1871, published an article in *Scribner's* magazine that he entitled "Wonders of the Yellowstone."

A year before, in 1870, he had written candidly about his own strong personal reactions at such sites as the Grand Canyon of the Yellowstone: "As I took in the scene, I realized my own littleness, my dread exposure to destruction, my inability to cope with or even comprehend the mighty architecture of nature...."[39]

On that earlier expedition, Doane, then perched on the 10,243-foot summit of Mount Washburn far above the Yellowstone River, had noticed that "something was missing," i.e., a stretch of the high mountains, from a section of the Rocky Mountains when he looked to the south.[40] For miles and miles, he remembered, the high peaks there loomed up only at a great distance—forming, as it were, parentheses around one huge forested *basin*. He correctly guessed that this great basin "has been formerly one vast crater of a now extinct volcano." Doane was certainly right in one sense: Yellowstone is a indeed a volcano. He was wrong in another sense: this volcano is not extinct but is still very much alive today.

In any case, Doane was not only a perceptive observer but also wrote very well. He circulated throughout the U.S. Department of War his official report on the expedition. This account was so interesting and so persuasive that it spurred Congress to authorize another official expedition in 1871.

The oldest member of the Washburn expedition was Truman C. Everts. As winter approached, he became separated from the party and as a result he became hopelessly lost in the Yellowstone wilderness for 37 days. He survived chiefly by eating the root of a thistle now known as the Everts thistle or the elk thistle. This kept him alive as he managed first to walk and then to crawl his way around Yellowstone Lake, and down the Yellowstone River.

At last, in mid–October, he was found among the rocks near

Crescent Hill in the north end of what is now the park by two men who were out looking for him. At first they thought he was a wounded bear slowly crawling among the rocks. Remarkably, he was none the worse for his ordeal. He was quickly offered a job as the first superintendent of Yellowstone Park and very much wanted to take it, but he could not afford to do so because there was no salary for the position. Undaunted, Everts later moved away from Montana and lived until 1901, dying in Maryland at the age of 85. In the meantime, his unique experience helped to further arouse the nation's growing interest in Yellowstone.

(16) THE FERDINAND V. HAYDEN GEOLOGICAL SURVEY OF 1871. This expedition was headed by the very able chief of the U.S. Geological and Geographical Survey of the Territories, Ferdinand V. Hayden.[41] In an account published in 1904 by the Historical Society of Montana, Nathaniel P. Langford, who was himself an explorer, the first superintendent of the park, and a member of the Washburn-Cook-Doane Expedition that had visited the park in 1870, had this to say about these early expeditions:

> We [can now] trace the creation of the park from the Folsom-Cook expedition of 1869 to the Washburn expedition of 1870, and thence to the Hayden expedition (U.S. Geological Survey) of 1871. Not to one of these expeditions more than to another do we owe the legislation which set apart this "public park or pleasuring-ground for the benefit and enjoyment of the people."

Although Hayden had already briefly been to Yellowstone on a preliminary survey of the region in 1870, the history of the scientific exploration of Yellowstone formally begins only with his 1871 expedition.[42]

He was not the first person to have the idea of creating a park in the Yellowstone region but he became its first well-known and its most enthusiastic supporter. Indeed, it was Hayden himself who convinced Congress to make Yellowstone a national park in 1872. The Yellowstone National Park Protection Act would be signed into law by President Ulysses S. Grant on March 1, 1872, and the world's first national park was thus born. Its unique attractions include more than 10,000 hydrothermal features. The National Park Service tells us that five types of these features are readily visible in Yellowstone:

> **Hot springs:** pools of hydrothermally-heated water.
> **Geysers:** hot springs with constrictions in their "plumbing," which causes them to erupt periodically in order to release the pressures that build up inside them.
> **Mudpots:** hot springs acid enough to dissolve the rocks surrounding them, but typically lack water in their systems.

>**Travertine terraces:** hot springs that rise up through limestone, dissolve the calcium carbonate, and deposit the calcite that makes the travertine terraces.
>
>**Fumaroles** (also known as steam vents): hot features that lack water in their systems and that release only hot steam.

Yellowstone now has the largest concentration of active geysers in the world—i.e., more than half of the world's total. It has numerous "cooler" wonders, too, for example, large herds of animals, and the Grand Canyon of the Yellowstone River.

The local Native Americans of the northern plains had nicknamed Hayden as the "Man Who Picks Up Stones Running" because of the speed in which he ranged over the Western landscape during his geological surveys. To fund the ambitious exploration projects he had in mind, he was equally quick to cultivate what the British would call "the great and the good"—in this case, the rich men of the very powerful railroad interests. He also made friends with many of the working-class Westerners he met during his work in the field.

This was the first Federally-funded geological survey to explore and further describe some of the most dramatic natural features of what would soon become Yellowstone Park. His expedition was heavily staffed with experts: it included two botanists, a meteorologist, a zoologist, an ornithologist, a mineralogist, a topographer, an agricultural statistician/entomologist, an artist, and a photographer. There were also numerous guides, cowboys, cooks, and other support personnel.

The expedition was an unqualified success. It confirmed, by means of photographs, watercolors, and paintings, that the earlier glowing reports of Yellowstone, which had often been dismissed by stay-at-home skeptics, were in fact quite true.

The excellent photographs taken by William Henry Jackson (his 1873 photo of Mammoth Hot Springs was one of the first to reveal the thermal wonders of the Yellowstone region); the dramatic watercolors painted by Henry W. Elliot; and the fine paintings by Thomas Moran all combined to excite the interests of the scientific community.[43] They appeared in Hayden's 500-page report to Congress, which made a very favorable impression there and aroused even more national interest in Yellowstone.

It is worth remembering here that Jackson and the other early photographers had to cope not only with all the hardships and hassles of being part of complicated expeditions, but also had to man-handle all their heavy, bulky, and generally unwieldy photographic gear. In addition to their large and bulky wet-plate cameras, for example, they also need a range of chemicals; fragile glass negatives; tripods; and light-proof tents in which to prepare their emulsions. In the mountains, their 300-odd pounds of equipment had to be strapped to teams of mules.

The act of taking a picture was anything but quick or easy. When photographing 132-foot Tower Falls in the Yellowstone canyon from the bottom of the canyon, Jackson had to climb down the steep sides of the gorge with his camera. He then had to scramble up again, prepare a photographic plate and rush down again. As soon as he took the picture, he had to wrap the plate in a wet towel to keep it from drying, and then had to climb back up the gorge to develop it. This process took so long that in a whole day's work he could shoot only five exposures.[44]

Another lasting achievement of the Hayden Expedition was that, under the supervision of Hayden himself, the first precise large-scale map of Yellowstone Lake was drawn up and was published in 1871 in the U.S. Geographical Survey of Montana and Adjacent Territory.[45]

As a result of all these activities, the first intrepid "pioneer tourists" now began to visit Yellowstone—as purely private visitors, not as members of any organized expedition.[46] One of the earliest recorded groups was the 1871 visit of six gentlemen, including the writer Calvin Clawson, who recorded details of his trip in a book entitled *A Ride to the Infernal Regions—Yellowstone's First Tourists*. Their route was via Virginia City, Montana; then past Henry's Lake in Idaho; and, finally, following the Madison River into what is now the park. They had to travel on horseback because there were no wagon roads then.

Before long, their rough trail was improved to the extent that wagons and stagecoaches could now use it. The first recorded commercial stagecoach trip into the park area was established by the Marshall & Goff line from Virginia City. Even after the Northern Pacific Railroad reached Livingston, Montana, in 1882 and then soon added a spur to Cinnabar (close to the north entrance to the park), stagecoaches continued to carry passengers thorough the park until 1917, when all large-scale park transportation was converted to motor vehicles.

The upshot of all the adventures discussed in this chapter was that, by the early 1880s, Yellowstone was beginning to be much better known and much better understood. This process would pick up speed in the years ahead. By 1904, for example, the Northern Pacific railroad would carry as many as 14,000 passengers to Yellowstone a year.

(17) THE EARL OF DUNRAVEN. The Earl of Dunraven and Mountearl, Windham Thomas Wyndham-Quin, was the owner of 30,000 lush acres of land in Ireland and Wales. He arrived in Colorado in the

summer of 1874 to check on some tracts of rangeland that he had bought there as an investment. Then, as he later wrote,

> Having two or three months of spare time, I determined to pay a visit to the far-famed region of the Upper Yellowstone, and to judge for myself whether the thermal springs and geysers were deserving of the superiority claimed for them.... The pursuit of large game is [also] to me a great delight.[47]

Dunraven was a rich adventurer, not a death-or-glory explorer, but he was very fit, wrote well, and had a nice, self-deprecating sense of humor. All this is evident in his fine 1876 book on travel reminiscences, which he entitled *The Great Divide.* Traveling in the grand style favored by 19th-century British aristocrats, he was accompanied by his local guide, the rancher Fred Boteler; the noted frontiersman "Texas Jack" Omohundro; his own English artist; his personal physician; his Scottish gunbearer; his all-purpose servant; and his collie, Tweed.

Together with Boteler, Dunraven climbed Mount Washburn near the northern border of Yellowstone, despite the fact it was already very late in the afternoon and that rain was threatening. When they reached the summit, he was so struck by the magnificent visa he saw before him that he described it as follows in his book:

> Stretching out its arms between the streams [which variously feed the Missouri, the Colorado, the Green, the Snake, and other powerful Western rivers], it seems to say to one, "Run in this direction," and to another, "Flow in that." From it has been traced out the geography of the country. The main divisions, the great centres of trade, together with the natural features that sway the fates of men and nations, radiate thence.[48]

Dunraven did not take himself too seriously. As he lamented in the book,

> I never have had an adventure worth a cent; nobody ever scalps me; I don't get "jumped" by highwaymen. It never occurs to a bear to hug me, and my very appearance inspires feelings of dismay or disgust in the breast of the puma or mountain lion. It is true that I have often been horribly frightened, but generally without any adequate cause.[49]

3

Later Efforts to Safeguard
the Yellowstone Region,
1872–1887

Seven additional events or explorers need to be mentioned to round out the history of the important undertakings relating to Yellowstone in the late 19th century. When he was studying the history of the park, the explorer Nathaniel Langford made the key point that it was chiefly thanks to *the cumulative impact of all of these earlier undertakings* that the public came to benefit permanently from the legislation that created Yellowstone Park in 1872. The "protection and exploration" entries below continue the numbering begun in the previous chapter.

(18) THE YELLOWSTONE PROTECTION ACT. The 1872 Act of Dedication that established the park carefully explained the purpose of this document. The 1872 law defined this legislation as:

An Act to set apart a certain tract of land lying near the headwaters of the Yellowstone River as a public park. Be it enacted by the Senate and House of Representatives of the United States of America in Congress assembled, That the tract of land in the Territories of Montana and Wyoming ... is hereby reserved and withdrawn from settlement, occupancy, or sale under the laws of the United States, and dedicated and set apart as a public park or pleasuring ground for the benefit and enjoyment of the people; and all persons who shall locate, or settle upon, or occupy the same or any part thereof, except as hereinafter provided, shall be considers trespassers and removed there from....

This Act was signed on March 1, 1872, by President Ulysses S. Grant; Vice-President Schuyler Colfax; and James G. Blaine, Speaker of the House.

There was a great deal of local opposition to the park in its earliest years. Opponents were worried that the strict Federal prohibitions against resource development and population settlement would stifle the local economy and therefore impoverish them. They also wanted to reduce the size of the park and, at the same time, they argued that hunting, mining, and logging in it should all be strongly encouraged for economic reasons.

Fortunately for later generations, the good news was that the numerous bills introduced into Congress by local legislators to remove the Federal land-use restrictions all came to naught.

(19) GEORGE BIRD GRINNELL. An American anthropologist, historian, naturalist, writer, and publisher, Grinnell was born in Brooklyn, New York, in 1849 and graduated from Yale University with a B.A. in 1870 and a Ph.D. in 1880.[1] By the time of his death in 1938, he was recognized for his strong influence on public opinion and for his successful efforts to preserve both Yellowstone National Park and the American bison.

In 1875, Grinnell served as a naturalist and mineralogist on an expedition to Montana and to the newly-established Yellowstone National Park. He prepared an attachment to the expedition's report, in which he carefully documented the slaughter—by poaching—of buffalo, mule deer, elk, and antelope for their hides. For example, he estimated that, during the winter of 1874–1875 alone, at least 3,000 buffalo had been killed in the regions he visited, together with comparable numbers of mule deer, elk, and antelope. Such wanton destruction led Grinnell to write the first of his many magazine articles on the importance of conservation.

A new set of problems arose in 1883 when the Northern Pacific Railroad was finally completed. This made it possible for many more tourists from the East to travel to Yellowstone in much greater speed and comfort. As a result, visitation increased five-fold in the first year alone of railroad service.

The increased popularity of Yellowstone was a mixed blessing. Much of the Yellowstone region was still directly under the influence of the Yellowstone Park Improvement Company, which had been awarded a monopoly for all the activities it would undertake within the park. For example, this firm, which had very close ties to the Northern Pacific company, was permitted to cut as much timber as it needed to power its trains and, probably, to build train-related buildings as well. In addition, the Northern Pacific was allowed to kill game for food; to farm the land; and even to rechannel some of the hot springs. Finally, the contract also permitted the Yellowstone Park Improvement Company to select, for its own use, some very big (one square mile) parcels of land at seven different locations within the park.

This state of affairs persuaded Grinnell that the prime attractions of Yellowstone were now in grave danger of being surrounded and exploited by commercial interests. In his capacity as a publisher, he therefore began a crusade to stop what he called "The Park Grab." In Washington, D.C., he took on the railroad lobby directly, calling for an investigation into the park contracts, proposing an expansion of the size of Yellowstone, and trying to write into law the park's then-unenforced regulations prohibiting hunting.

The bill to expand Yellowstone failed but Congress did appropriate $40,000 for the park's maintenance, and also approved an amendment authorizing U.S. Army troops to be used to enforce the new regulations against hunting and vandalism. Over the next few years, Grinnell fought to stop various attacks on the integrity of the park by a series of inept superintendents. He made maximum use of a poaching incident in 1894 to win more public support for his cause. His life-long efforts were rewarded when, in 1894, President Grover Cleveland signed a law that would finally protect the park, its geysers, and its wildlife.

(20) WILLIAM ADOLPH BAILLIE-GROHMAN. This explorer was a man for all outdoor seasons. He was variously a prolific Anglo-Austrian author of books on the dialects, culture, and animals of the Tyrol mountains in Austria, where he had grown up; an excellent shot; a big game hunter; an expert mountaineer; and, finally, a pioneer in the Kootenay region of British Columbia. Baillie-Grohman was a very wealthy and a physically-fit explorer. He devoted some of his considerable fortune and much of his boundless energy to traveling throughout the American Far West in the 1870s and 1880s to hunt big game there. This was the era in which the Rocky Mountains were first becoming accessible to rich sportsmen who lived on the East Coast of the United States or abroad.

His 1882 book on *Camps in the Rockies: Being a Narrative of Life on the Frontier, and Sport in the Rocky Mountains, with an Account of the Cattle Ranches of the West* gives the reader a firsthand account of his outdoor experiences in Wyoming and Idaho. He was what was then known as a "topshelfer," namely, a rich, well-equipped, and well-connected outdoorsman. At the same time, he was also a good friend and supporter of the local trappers and Native Americans.

His book, which contains accurate and sympathetic passages describing the Native Americans and the local customs, is a valuable account of the American and Canadian West just before and after the coming of the railroad. Baillie-Grohman was as excellent traveler, ranging widely over the Pacific Slope, the Central Rockies, and exploring the Selkirks (a mountain range spanning the northern portion of the Idaho

Panhandle, eastern Washington, and southeastern British Columbia). Consider, for example, his description of the Jackson Hole region:

> At our feet lay the perfectly level expanse, about eight or ten miles broad and five-and-twenty in length. Traversing the basin lengthwise, we saw the curves of the Snake River—its waters a beautiful beryl green—winding its way through groves of stately old cottonwood trees....
>
> Beyond the river the eye espied several little lakes, nestling in forest-girt seclusion under the buckling cliffs of the boldest-shaped mountain I am acquainted with, i.e., the Grand Teton Peak, rising in one great sweep.... It was the most sublime scenery I have ever seen.[2]

(21) THE SNAKE RIVER EXPEDITION. Concern over safeguarding Yellowstone grew apace. In a letter of 1876, for example, Martin Maginnis, a Montana Territorial official, complained to the Secretary of the Interior that "spoliations in the park are great" and that there was then no way to stop them. "Several of the geysers are now nearly ruined," he complained, and he urged the Federal government to "take some action to preserve these wonderful and beautiful curiosities before it is too late."

Probably in response, in 1876 an expedition was sent to the Snake River. That fall, Lieutenant Doane had returned to Fort Ellis after dealing, over the summer, with the aftermath of the Battle of the Little Big Horn. (Also known as Custer's Last Stand, this battle was the most decisive Native American victory and the most decisive defeat suffered by the U.S. Army during the long Plains Indian conflicts.) Very ambitious and very eager to make a lasting name for himself by becoming the first non–Native American to explore the unknown regions south of Yellowstone, Doane went over the head of his immediate commander and got permission from higher-ranking officers to lead the 1876 Snake River expedition. Unfortunately, this undertaking was ill-advised, poorly-planned, and badly-led; not surprisingly, it turned out to be a complete failure.

Doane took his soldiers over the Yellowstone plateau—but after winter had begun—and then planned to float down the Snake River in a wooden boat that had been taken apart and loaded onto pack mules. His expedition soon ran into bitter cold and deep snows. The boat could not handle the whitewater rapids of the Snake River, and when this craft was heavily damaged by the river, vital supplies in it were lost downstream. Eventually, it was totally wrecked and had to be abandoned.

Doane and his men then nearly starved to death before they managed to reach a trapper's cabin on the Snake River. They finally got to Fort Hall, Idaho, in January 1877. When word of their plight reached Fort Ellis, Doane and his troops were ordered to end their expedition and to return to Fort Ellis at once. This they did—over Doane's strong objections. His ill-fated expedition was, understandably, the last time he ever ventured out onto the Yellowstone plateau.

(22) PRESIDENT ARTHUR'S EXPEDITION. The next exploratory-protection effort, which had much better results, was President Chester A. Arthur's expedition of 1883. Heavily burdened by the pressures of his office, the President had been encouraged by his advisers to take a good rest. One of these men—Senator George Vest of Missouri—recommended a trip to Yellowstone, the new national park. A two-week trip, without any journalists but with an official photographer was therefore arranged for President Arthur in August 1883. He was accompanied by about a dozen friends, a 75-man cavalry escort, and 175 pack animals.

The year before, in 1882, Vest had learned that railroad executives and other businessmen were planning to corrupt the concessions planned for Yellowstone and wanted to set up unregulated monopolies there for themselves. He therefore introduced and helped to pass legislation that required the Secretary of the Interior, in order to prevent corruption and other abuses, to submit all concession and construction contracts to the Senate first for its approval.

Vest strongly encouraged the Arthur expedition and by so doing helped to bring Yellowstone into wider national attention. He continued his voluntary oversight role during the rest of his career in the Senate and was warmly hailed by conservationists as "the self-appointed protector of Yellowstone National Park."

During President Arthur's trip, the President met with the famous Shoshone leader, Chief Washakie, at Fort Washakie, which is located in the foothills of Wyoming's Wind River Range, just east of the Continental Divide. Native American Agent James Irwin, who served as the interpreter, commended Washakie for the latter's efforts to educate his people and said to him: "President Grant is one of your admirers." Irwin then asked the chief: "What reply from you should I send to the Great Father in Washington?"

It is said that Washakie remained silent, with his arms folded and his face immobile, but tears welled up in his eyes. When Irwin asked him again, and the chief finally replied along these lines: "When a kindness is done to a white man, he feels it in his head, and his tongue speaks. But when a kindness is shown to an Indian, he feels it in his heart, and his heart has no tongue. I have spoken."

(23) THE HAGUE GEOLOGIC SURVEYS. These surveys of 1883–1889 had very desirable results. Arnold Hague, appointed in 1883 as

geologist in charge of the survey of the Yellowstone National Park and its vicinity, began his field work that year, leading a large party of well-qualified assistants.

In the summer of 1883, the completion of the Northern Pacific Railroad line had brought a great deal of public attention to the Yellowstone region. Hague himself played an active and prominent role in this process by advising government officials in Washington on how new laws and regulations could best be administered to protect the unique natural features of the park, and on how its multifaceted roles as a "pleasure resort," a safe haven for wildlife, and a forest preserve could all be safely maintained.

He strongly advocated the preservation of major features in their natural conditions, stressing that no hotels or other buildings should be placed where they would destroy the natural beauty. Hague was especially opposed to an attempt to extend the railroad into the park itself. He and his assistants surveyed, during seven seasons in the field, an area of more than 3,000 square miles. Moreover, they also explored and mapped the geology of the region north of the park that is now known as Montana's "Livingston quadrangle."

(24) Frederick Schwatka's Winter Expedition. Despite much greater understanding of the Yellowstone region thanks to prior expeditions, surveys, and government protection, crossing the park was still quite difficult. In December 1886, for example, the experienced Arctic explorer Frederick Schwatka planned to organize an ambitious winter tour through the park. This expedition, sponsored by the *New York World* newspaper and by *Century Magazine*, set off from Mammoth Hot Springs in January 1887.

On skis and snowshoes, while pulling heavy sleds laden with all their camping gear, Schwatka, Frank Jay Haynes, and 11 other participants (all of whom were guides or professional outdoorsmen) quickly made their way from Mammoth Hot Springs to the Norris Geyser Basin in only two days. The high elevation told so heavily on Schwatka himself (he was used to Arctic cold, but not to Yellowstone's heights) that he was forced to drop out of the expedition. Nevertheless, Haynes and three other men decided to press on in order to visit the geyser basins and Yellowstone Falls. This decision nearly cost them their lives. At one point, when they were stranded on Mount Washburn for 72 hours in a freezing, blinding snowstorm, with little or no food or shelter, they almost died. Finally, when the weather did improve, they were able to make their way safely back to Mammoth Hot Springs.

Their 29-day outing had covered nearly 200 miles, in temperatures

The Haynes expedition in the winter of 1887 (photographer unknown, NPS).

down to minus-52 degrees F below zero. Remarkably, Haynes returned home successfully with 42 photographs of Yellowstone taken in the very depths of the winter—the first photos ever taken during that time of year. Schwatka himself later came to a very sad end. Badly overweight and addicted to opium, he died in Portland, Oregon, in 1892 at the age of only 43.

4

Early Days of the Park Rangers in Yellowstone, 1872–1918

Timothy R. Manns was a National Park Service naturalist and historian in the 1980s. His 10-page unpublished manuscript, entitled "History of the Park Ranger in Yellowstone National Park" and completed on April 18, 1980, is (lightly edited and annotated here) a key source of the information used in this chapter. All the quoted matter come from this manuscript, so no endnotes are needed. Because of the importance of park rangers today, it is worth learning how they came to be.

Timothy Manns begins by making the important point that, when Congress designated Yellowstone in 1872 for preservation as the first national park in the United States, Congress was silent in response to the questions of just how this preservation was to be accomplished, and how this huge new park was to be run. Indeed, Congress left it entirely up to the Secretary of the Interior to draw up any necessary rules to protect the park's future and to prevent the "wanton destruction of the fish and game" there. No money at all was appropriated by Congress to accomplish these commendable ends. As a result, the Yellowstone explorer Nathaniel P. Langford, who became the park's first superintendent and who was the *only member* of the park's staff, had to serve without any pay for the duration of his tenure.

The park had become an increasingly a popular place to visit but, fundamentally, it had no real protection and was thus subject to desecration by tourists. For example, Edwin Stanley, a visitor in 1877, described the geyserite formations near Old Faithful as being "though so delicate in appearance, so solid that a hatchet is often necessary to obtain a choice piece for your cabinet." At that time (in the early years of the park), hunting was still legal but it was totally unregulated. Alas, nothing could be done to stop the slaughter of game, given the facts that the park's staff was then much too small and that no legal machinery was in place to enforce the few rules that might exist on paper.

Yellowstone's second superintendent was Philetus Norris, who in 1877 appointed J.C. McCartney as the first "protection man" for the park. The latter's duties were to "guard well … against wanton slaughter of the game, spoliation of geyser cones and other curiosities, and especially against forest fires." Unfortunately, McCartney and later assistants proved quite unequal to the tasks assigned to them. Their duties were unclear; their training was nonexistent; and their pay was bad. Moreover, they were too thin on the ground, and there was no legal support mechanism to back them up in case of need.

In his 1881 letter of resignation after only one year of service as the park's first and only "gamekeeper," the famous wilderness guide Harry Yount (1839–1924) recommended a much wiser policy: to have the park protected by "officers stationed at different points of the park with authority to enforce the observance of the laws of the park." This would become the pattern later successfully followed in Yellowstone under both U.S. Army and National Park Service administrations. Horace Albright, the second director of the National Park Service, warmly praised Yount as "the father of the ranger service, as well as the first national park ranger." Moreover, in 1994 the National Park Service established the Harry Yount Award, which is given each year to an employee whose "overall impact, record of accomplishments, and excellence in traditional ranger duties have created an appreciation for the park ranger profession."

Legislation enacted in 1883 approved more assistant superintendents (up to a total of 10), and made hunting and trapping in the park illegal. Alas, most of the new assistant superintendents were quite unable to protect the park, being political appointees who lacked the knowledge, skills, and often even the *interest* to do a competent job.

There was some good news, though. The 1883 bill also allowed the Secretary of the Interior to ask the Secretary of War for help in protecting Yellowstone. Thus, in 1886, when Congress refused to appropriate any money for the park, troops from the U.S. Cavalry were sent to Yellowstone, and stayed there until 1918. Ironically, it was thus the Cavalry that first learned how to protect and how to manage the world's first national park. U.S. Army regulations allowed one civilian scout to be hired for each troop of cavalry. This was an extremely important development because these scouts became the principal models for the future park rangers of Yellowstone. Jack Baronett, a widely-traveled adventurer who had also been an assistant superintendent, was hired as the first army scout in Yellowstone in 1886.

The historian Aubrey Haines, who is quoted in the Manns

manuscript, described the merits of stationing troops and scouts around the park during the winter to prevent poaching:

> While the [soldiers] on patrol usually did their best, they could seldom equal the [poachers] in woodsmanship or native craftiness....
>
> The solution, insofar as there was one, lay in the use of civilian scouts (who were as good as the poachers in woodcraft and in their ability to travel and survive under any winter conditions) to instruct the soldiers, visit them in winter, and lead them on difficult patrols. The scouts passed along the lore of their way of life, the use of skis, how to dress and what to carry on patrols, where to travel and what to look for, and, occasionally, how to get out of a tight scrape [by use of their firearms in case of an emergency].

In summers, the scouts continued to carry out and to supervise backcountry patrols, while the soldiers checked wagons entering the park, protected the geyser basins, and answered the many questions that visitors had. Indeed, soldiers were giving "cone talks" at Old Faithful Geyser as early as 1887. The U.S. Army's protection of Yellowstone was strict and successful, but it was never seen as a permanent solution to the problem of administering the national parks. Thus it was that, in 1905, the equivalent of scouts—now relabeled as "park rangers"—were deployed fulltime in Yellowstone, where the Army had been present only during the summer.

In the park Superintendent's Annual Report for 1907, retired General S.B.M. Young suggested creation of a "civilian guard" for Yellowstone. Since President Theodore Roosevelt supported this idea, it had very good political traction. Young then outlined his criteria for scouts in Yellowstone, setting very high—indeed, very *aspirational*—standards. He wrote:

> I am convinced that with a properly-organized civil guard the administration of this park could be brought to a higher and better standard, in two or three years, than could ever be attained by the successive changes of troop detailed by roster from the Army....
>
> It is quite obvious that any man assigned to duty in any capacity in the park should possess special qualifications for the proper discharge of that duty, and he should be by natural inclination interested in the park and its purposes.
>
> In addition, every man should be an experienced woodsman, a speedy traveler on skis, and expert trailer, a good packer who with his horse and pack animal could carry supplies to subsist himself for a month alone in the mountains and forests, and besides he should be able with his rifle and pistol to enable him to find and overcome the wily trapper and the ugly large game head and teeth hunter. [Poachers killed elk not only for their meat but also for their teeth, which could be sold to the members of a fraternal order.]
>
> He should be well-informed on the history of the park and thoroughly

cognizant with all the curiosities and points of interest therein; he should also be qualified to pass a reasonable examination in zoology and ornithology.

A visiting tourist should always be favored by an intelligent and courteous answer on any subject pertaining to the park from any guard interrogated. Inattention or discourtesy should subject the guard to proper discipline or dismissal from the park when in the judgment of the superintendent the discipline of the park service would thereby be promoted.

Young wanted practical men, who would demonstrate diligence, interest, intelligence and courtesy in the protection of the park and their service to the public.

In one of his first acts as Assistant to the Secretary of the Interior, Stephen Mather put into effect the "Regulations Governing Rangers in National Parks," largely written by Mark Daniels, who served as General Superintendent of National Parks before Mather's appointment. But the Army still remained in Yellowstone and, lacking money to hire park rangers, kept its scouts, who were the only civilians the Army was authorized to employ. The result was that with the Army still guarding Yellowstone, the park's first employees with the title of "park ranger" had to be hired with funds from the Department of the Interior. In 1915, to control the use of automobiles first admitted to the park that year, four rangers were hired to operate entrance stations. Later, in the autumn of 1915, two more rangers were hired and assigned to kill coyotes, cougars, and wolves.

The Army's withdrawal from the park was scheduled for October 1916, and 23 men from the scouts and the Army's Yellowstone Park detachment had been carefully selected to be transferred to the Department of the Interior as park rangers. First local and then Congressional opposition to closing the Army's Yellowstone post forced the Army to stay in the park until 1917. The formal creation of a permanent Yellowstone ranger force thus did not occur until November 1, 1918—the day after the official closing of Fort Yellowstone.

On that day, there were only 21 permanent rangers. This mere handful of men replaced the approximately 400 soldiers who had been protecting the park. The day of the Yellowstone park rangers had arrived. Approximately 733 people now work in Yellowstone for the National Park Service during the peak summer season. About 330 of them are permanent, year-round employees. Park rangers work in education, resource management, law enforcement, emergency medical services, and backcountry operations.

5

The Greater Yellowstone Ecosystem

At 22 million acres, this ecosystem is one of the largest temperate-zone ecosystems on Earth. It is so big and so complicated that this short chapter can provide only a few glimpses into its unusual history and wildlife.

This chapter discusses the ecosystem's biological consumers and producers and the Federally-managed lands that comprise the ecosystem. Because they are relevant to understanding the area just outside of Yellowstone Park, also recounted are the history of Jackson Hole and dude ranching itself, the formation of Grand Teton National Park, and the surrounding national forests and their flora and fauna. The most important thing to remember is that *this is one of the last expansive intact ecosystems in the world.* It now has much the same plant and animal species that it had long before humans ever arrived in North America.[1]

Located in the northern Rocky Mountains, i.e., in northwestern Wyoming, southwestern Montana, and eastern Idaho, the Greater Yellowstone Ecosystem is one of the world's best natural laboratories, both in terms of its ecology and of its Holocene geology (dating from about 14,000 to 9,000 years ago). It is home to many diverse plant and animal species—and to an ever-growing number of humans as well—and is a major year-round recreational asset for local, regional and international visitors alike.

In simple terms, the natural history of Greater Yellowstone Ecosystem can best be understood in terms of biological *producers* and *consumers.*[2] Some of the Yellowstone areas most prolific *producers* are wheatgrass, pond lilies, lodgepole pines, quaking aspen, green algae, and willows. These organisms are known as "autotrophs," which means they can make their own food. Moreover, they can also produce food for the more complex organisms that are higher on the food chain. Wolves and bears are at the very top of the Yellowstone food chain and prey on other animals such as elk and bison.

Wherever there are producers, there are also *consumers,* too. This great ecosystem is thus home to many primary consumers, namely, the organisms that derive their own energy from the autotrophs. These primary consumers include pronghorns, beavers, elk, cutthroat trout, mayflies, and deer mice. They play a vital role in the food chain: they not only keep the producer populations under control, but they are also sources of energy for the secondary and tertiary consumers described below.

Secondary consumers include osprey, bald eagles, bighorn sheep, grizzly bears, coyotes, red-tailed hawks, and bison. They get their energy from primary consumers and producers, and are themselves sources of energy for tertiary consumers. These tertiary consumers are organisms that feed primarily on secondary and primary producers. The wolf is probably this ecosystem's most-publicized tertiary consumer.

The 22 million acre Greater Yellowstone Ecosytem is centered on Yellowstone National Park (NPS).

The complicated human history of some the Federally-managed parts of the Greater Yellowstone Ecosystem can usefully be highlighted. It should be noted that (1) all the National Parks are managed by the Department of the Interior; (2) all the National Forests are managed by the Department of Agriculture; and (3) all the components of the National Wildlife System are managed by the U.S. Fish and Wildlife Service, which itself is part of the Department of the Interior. The Federally-managed areas of this ecosystem include:

- Yellowstone National Park, Grand Teton National Park, and John D. Rockefeller, Jr. National Parkway. All of these are managed by the United States National Park Service.

- National Elk Refuge, Red Rock Lakes, and Camas Lake National Wildlife Refuges. All of these are managed by the United States Fish and Wildlife Service.
- Gallatin, Custer, Beaverhead-Deerlodge, Caribou-Targhee, Bridger-Teton, and Shoshone National Forests. All of these are managed by the United States National Forest Service.
- In addition, 11 distinct National Wilderness Areas have been established within these National Forests since 1966, providing a much higher level of habitat protection. These are also managed by the Forest Service.

The Greater Yellowstone Ecosystem encompasses some privately-held lands and some state lands surrounding the lands managed by the U.S. Government. Moreover, the Trust for Public Land, a nonprofit institution founded in 1972, has protected 67,000 acres in this ecosystem, which are now the sites of about 40 environmental projects

In historical terms, the Homestead Act of 1862 strongly encouraged the settlement of the West but homesteaders did not begin to come to the Jackson Hole region until 1884. A group of Mormon families settled in South Park in 1889. More Mormons followed and homesteaded on what was known as "Mormon Row," located east of Blacktail Butte, and in the Wilson area. Moreover, some trappers and guides settled down along the meandering streams and rivers of the area in order to give ranching a try.[3]

Although lush summer grass and abundant water apparently made Jackson Hole a perfect site for raising livestock, the settlers faced an uphill battle there. The soil was thin, sandy, and rocky. Winters were long, cold, and snowy. Summers were dry: settlers had to work very hard then to raise crops for themselves and to put up hay for their livestock. Moreover, an agricultural depression swept the region in about 1920.

The good news was that some rich Easterners fell in love with Jackson Hole and wanted to have a "real cowboy experience" there. Local ranchers quickly realized that "dude ranching" ("dude" was a joking Western term for a city-dwelling man or woman[4]) was much easier, much more profitable, and probably much more fun than cattle ranching. The golden age of dude ranching was thus born in the 1920s.[5]

It also gave rise, among the real cowboys, to the harmless pastime known as "stuffing dudes," i.e., telling the dudes, tongue firmly in cheek, the tallest of tall tales about past times in the Rocky Mountain West. It is important to keep in mind, though, that these yarns always contained at least a nucleus of truth.

For example, when relaxing around a campfire with his dudes at the end of a long day's ride, a cowboy might begin stuffing his dudes with a story along these lines. It starts very slowly but picks up pace over seven pages of text, which will not be quoted here in the interest of brevity. It begins thus:

> And there was the time when John Colter [whose exploits are discussed earlier in this book] was jumped by two Indians on the Stinking Water [i.e., the Shoshone River].
>
> Old Colter was a-squattin' down alongside a beaver pond, doctorin' up one of them lures with that come-hither-beaver stuff the old trappers carried in a bottle slung 'round their necks [this "stuff" was castoreum, an oily and odorous secretion from the glands of a beaver], when out of the tail of his eye he seen a bush startin' to shake but he knowed the wind wasn't blowin' that hard. So just as calm as a stuffed mule he started linin' up the best way to make a run for his gun, a-leanin' agin a tree a good rope's throw away....[6]

Human interest and humor aside, the downside of dude ranching was that a sudden influx of visitors from all walks of life now expected cheap cabins, gas stations, dancehalls, billboards, and racetracks—and all this at the very feet of the Tetons. Some local ranchers and businessmen, on the other hand, wanted to protect the valley as, to use their own words "a museum on the hoof," and to preserve the remaining open spaces there from any commercial development. They therefore held what may have been the earliest Jackson Hole "environmental meeting" at Maud Noble's cabin, in 1923.

In an enormous stroke of luck for environmental causes, in 1926 John D. Rockefeller, Jr., toured the area with Yellowstone Park Superintendent Horace Albright (who appears again later in this book). Rockefeller was charmed by the stunning mountain scenery and, over the next two decades, he secretly began buying 35,000 acres of land for what was known only as the "Snake River Land Company"—with the intent of donating it to become part of Grand Teton National Park.

He did this as anonymously as possible so that sellers would not inflate their prices. Nevertheless, he was not able to buy *all* the ranches at that time, so the park continues to buy the remaining inholdings to this day. (An inholding is privately-owned land located inside the boundary of a national park, national forest, or similar publicly-owned protected area. When the park system was formed, many such pieces of property had been in private ownership for generations and were not for sale when the park was formed.)

Some ranchers negotiated lifetime leases in Yellowstone so that they and their families could stay in the valley for as long as possible. Many local residents strongly opposed Rockefeller's plan—on the grounds that it would mean a loss of local tax revenue and would take political control out of their own hands. These contentious issues would finally be resolved by a Congressional hearing.

Nevertheless, it still took decades to establish Grand Teton National Park officially. Congress created the original park in 1929 to protect the Teton Range and several lakes at the foot of the mountains. In 1943, Franklin Delano Roosevelt declared the remaining Federal land in the valley as Jackson Hole National Monument. In 1949, John D. Rockefeller, Jr., donated the land he had purchased to the Federal government to be included in the national park. Finally, in 1950, Congress combined the original park, the national monument, and the Rockefeller lands to establish today's Grand Teton National Park. Moreover, in 1972 Congress also established the John D. Rockefeller, Jr., Memorial Parkway to honor his generosity and commitment to the National Park System. The Parkway connects Yellowstone and Grand Teton National Park.

Today, Grand Teton National Park hosts a very wide range of dramatic landscapes, ranging from shrub-grasslands to riverside, mountain, and subalpine forests, lush wet meadows, lakes, waterways, rocky slopes, and alpine tundra. Although it is less than half the size of Yellowstone National Park, Grand Teton has nearly the same broad assortment of plants and animals as its bigger northern neighbor.[7] Moreover, it is less crowded and has more dramatic mountains.

◆ THE CUSTER-GALLATIN NATIONAL FOREST. In 1891, Congress passed the Forest Reserve Act which allowed President Benjamin Harrison to set aside, i.e., to "reserve," parts of the public domain in order to protect natural resources.[8] In March of that year, the President established the nation's first Forest Reserve, i.e., the "Yellowstone Park Timberland Reserve." This was created to set up a protective buffer around the park itself.

The historic Main Boulder Ranger Station, located 30 miles south of Big Timber, Montana, is perhaps the oldest facility in the U.S. Forest Service System today. It served as both the district Ranger headquarters and as the home of Harry S. Kaufman, who signed on as a guard ranger in 1903. At that time, modern concepts of conservation and livestock and forest management had not yet taken root in the Rocky Mountains. The immediate result was that Kaufman had to provide two horses, riding and pack outfits, camp equipment, and his services for 24 hours a day—all in return for $60 per month. In the absence of any institution to provide law and order, he also had to be ready to use his own Colt single action revolver to deal with any trespassing livestock owners, cattle rustlers, and wildlife poachers. (This iconic revolver held six cartridges, usually .45 caliber, but it had to be cocked by hand—i.e., by thumb—for each shot, and was very slow to reload.[9])

In 1905, Kaufman built a permanent one-room Ranger Station at the mouth of the Main Boulder River Cabin, some 34 miles north of Yellowstone Park. From this modest headquarters-and-home, he administered U.S. Forest Service activities in about 300,000 acres of the National Forest lands. He also married and later raised a family at this Ranger Station, to which additional rooms were eventually added. It has been preserved and restored, beginning in 1991, and is now open to the public.

◆ THE BEAVERHEAD-DEERLODGE NATIONAL FOREST. This is now the largest of the National Forests in Montana, covering 3.5 million acres.[10] The early exploration of southwestern Montana by Euro-Americans began in 1805 with the arrival of the Lewis and Clark expedition. A Lewis and Clark campsite has now been identified in the Forest but what is more important is that Lewis and Clark singlehandedly opened up Montana to the fur traders, who were eager to expand their operations into the virgin lands lying beyond eastern Canada and the Great Lakes region.

Between 1810 and the late 1840s, every major fur trading company in the West passed through territory that is now part of, or adjacent to, Beaverhead-Deerlodge National Forest. Based on the entries in fur trade journals, it is very likely that traders and local Native Americans worked together and shared a common culture that was an amalgam of Euro-American frontier culture and Native American tribal culture. This fleeting common culture did not leave any durable archeological sites that can be studied today.

The first profitable quantities of gold in Montana were found in 1860 in what is now Deer Lodge County. Gold was also discovered in a tributary of the Big Hole River. Other gold strikes followed but the free gold (i.e., gold dust and small gold nuggets lying in creek beds) was soon exhausted, forcing miners to turn to lode mining by the mid–1870s. Today this forest has one of the most extensive and best-preserved collections of historic mining resources in the region.

The Civilian Conservation Corps (CCC) is an excellent example of the monumental social programs put in place in the United States to ease the widespread unemployment caused by the Great Depression of the 1930s. In the Beaverhead-Deerlodge National Forest, for example, CCC work is evident in the multi-building Ranger Stations and the isolated Guard Stations used by Forest Officers to patrol remote areas of the Forest. The Birch Creek CCC camp in the east Pioneer Mountains is one of the best remaining examples of a CCC camp in the U.S. Forest Service today.

◆ THE CARIBOU-TARGHEE NATIONAL FOREST. When explorers and fur traders arrived in this area early in the 19th century, they were not alone: mounted bands of Shoshone and Bannock Indians often crossed the mountains of the Targhee in order to hunt bison on the northwestern Great Plains.[11] The explorers and fur traders also encountered groups of horseless Shoshone who were scattered throughout the mountains and who gathered plants and hunted the bighorn sheep on foot.

Gold was discovered near Caribou Mountain in 1870. The resulting gold rush lasted for nearly 20 years and produced $50 million worth of placer gold before finally petering out. In another milestone of that region, President Theodore Roosevelt established a Forest Reserve in 1903 that was known as the Pocatello Forest Reserve. Since then, phosphate mining, sawtimber harvesting, and livestock grazing have been the major economic activities in what is now the Caribou National Forest. Targhee National Forest, for its part, was established by President Theodore Roosevelt in 1908. Named after a Bannock Indian warrior, it is now used chiefly for timber harvesting and livestock grazing.

◆ THE BRIDGER-TETON NATIONAL FOREST. This forest includes the Wyoming Range, located south of Jackson. It contains 3.4 million acres and constitutes a good chunk of the Greater Yellowstone Ecosystem.[12] It contains some of the most pristine areas within this ecosystem, while its clean air and remoteness contribute to an unusually brilliant night sky. The Teton Division of the forest encompasses three sides of Jackson Hole and borders on both Yellowstone and Grand Teton national parks.

In cultural terms alone, this forest is arguably the most interesting National Forest of this part of the United States: it is adjacent to the Great Plains in the east, to the Great Basin in the west and the southwest, and to the Columbia Plateau in the northwest. As a result of this unique geographical location, it is very likely that the Native Americans who initially lived in this region had close trade and other contacts with the many other tribes that migrated to or simply passed through the mountains of western Wyoming.

The recorded era of this forest began in 1807 with the arrival of the first Euro-American fur trappers. This period ended in 1840 but it was followed by the blazing of the Lander cut-off of the Oregon Trail, and then by the "Tie Hack" era of 1867 to 1952, when lumber from the forest was urgently needed to make railroad ties for the rapidly-expanding rail network. A number of isolated tie hack cabins can still be found in this forest.

In March 1891, President Benjamin Harrison set aside the Yellowstone Park Timber Land Reserve, located along the eastern and southern boundary of the park. In its original form, this Reserve totaled about 1.23 million acres. Portions of this Reserve now lie within the Teton Wilderness of the Bridger-Teton National Forest. In February 1897, President Cleveland created the Teton Forest Reserve from more than 829,000 acres of public domain land.

After various name changes over the years, in 1973 the Bridger and Teton National Forests were combined to form a single unit, now consisting of some 3,439,000 acres of public land in northwestern Wyoming.

◆ THE SHOSHONE NATIONAL FOREST. The Shoshone was America's first national forest.[13] It was set aside by President Benjamin Harrison in 1891 as part of the Yellowstone Timberland Reserve. Today its 2,400,000 acres are a key part of the Greater Yellowstone Ecosystem. More than half of the Shoshone's acreage lies in five designated wilderness areas. Remarkably, this forest still has virtually all of the original animal and plant species present when the earliest non–Native American explorers, such as John Colter and Jim Bridger, first visited the region.

The North Absaroka wilderness of Shoshone National Forest was the site of "Camp Monaco," where Prince Albert of Monaco, accompanied by the outdoorsman and showman William F. "Buffalo Bill" Cody, successfully hunted big game in September 1913.[14] This remote location is still accessible by trails open only to hikers and horseback riders. It is also frequented by grizzly bears, so any visitors are strongly urged to take anti-bear precautions. (See also Appendix 3 on Grizzly Bear Hazing Guidelines for Livestock Owners, Homeowners and the General Public.)

Prince Albert, backed up by Cody and a guide, bagged a trophy elk and a black bear. To mark this event, the prince's artist painted the camp's name and the date on the trunk of a spruce tree that had been blazed for this purpose. This tree was killed in the great forest fires that raged through Yellowstone Park 1988, but an unburned portion of it was salvaged in 1994 and is now on exhibit at the Buffalo Bill Historical Center in Cody, Wyoming.

The western boundary of the Shoshone Forest south of the park runs along the crest of the Continental Divide. The U.S. Forest Service says that people now visit the Shoshone for many reasons: it offers hundreds of alpine lakes, three mountain ranges, back country trails, scenic byways, and an abundance of wildlife.[15] It also has one of the few remaining grizzly bear populations in the lower 48 states.

The ghost town of Kirwin, an early-day mining town, is a window into the past, recalling a colorful era of Wyoming's history. The remains of "hack tie" flumes and cabins in the southern end of the forest bring to mind the years when millions of railroad ties were "hacked out" of the forests.

◈ THE NATIONAL ELK REFUGE. This refuge and the other wildlife refuges discussed below are all administered by the U.S. Fish and Wildlife Service.

As human settlements (and fences) in the Jackson Hole, Wyoming, region increased at the turn of the 20th century, the migratory routes of wild animals had to change.[16] The native elk, for example, now had to compete with cattle for a dwindling supply of natural grasses. The hungry elk often raided ranchers' haystacks, eating the hay put up at such great labor for the ranchers' livestock. A series of very cold winters resulted in the starvation of thousands of elk. The winter of 1909, for example, caused the death of almost half of the elk herd wintering near Jackson Hole. As a result, the community in Jackson Hole became quite concerned that its elk herd would no longer be able to survive without significant human help.

Stephen Leek, a successful local rancher who had come to the Teton Valley[17] in 1888, attracted national attention to the plight of the starving elk in the Jackson Hole area through his writings, photographs, and lectures. The Wyoming Legislature responded to the crisis by appropriating $5,000 for Leek and others to use in order to buy hay for the elk. The eventual outcome was that the National Elk Refuge was established by Acts of Congress and other mechanisms to provide, preserve, restore, and manage lands for wintering elk, birds, and other big game animals. It was an unqualified success, and the Refuge celebrated its centennial in 2012.

◈ THE RED ROCK LAKES NATIONAL WILDLIFE REFUGE. Located in the middle of an important wildlife corridor linking the Greater Yellowstone and Bitterroot regions, this refuge protects more than 82,000 acres of the Centennial Valley in southwest Montana.[18] It encompasses the largest wetland complex in the Greater Yellowstone Ecosystem and continues to provide critical nesting habitat for a tri-state flock of trumpeter swans. The Centennial Valley was well-known to the nomadic tribes as a safe travel route between the headwaters of the Big

Hole River and the Yellowstone country. Settlement by Euro-Americans did not occur until 1876, but the long winters, great distances to market, and small land parcels all combined to make life very difficult for them. Indeed, many local ranchers were forced out of business by the great depression of the 1930s.

In 1935, President Franklin D. Roosevelt established this refuge. Since then, the U.S. Fish and Wildlife Service has acquired more lands from willing landowners or by receiving donations. The Service now owns about 51,000 acres and manages conservation easements on more than 23,000 acres. Visitors to the spectacular scenery of such a refuge must be prepared for a very remote wilderness setting. There are few roads and no services there (i.e., no fuel or groceries).

◆ THE CAMAS NATIONAL WILDLIFE REFUGE. Before the arrival of European settlers, this area was never inhabited on a permanent basis by the Native Americans.[19] Members of several tribes sometimes camped here for short periods to hunt and to gather foods, notably the nutritious roots of the Camas plant, a staple in the diets of many tribes. Camas grew very well in the watery meadows of the mountains. The Canadian artist and explorer Paul Kane (1810–1871) said it was a bulbous root that looked like an onion but, when cooked, tasted more like a potato and was very good to eat. A modern cookbook describes a roasted camas bulb as tasting something like a baked pear or a cooked fig.

In the late 1880s, much of the present refuge became part of a big Idaho ranch known as Idaho Livestock Lands, Inc. At about the same time, a short section of a wagon and stagecoach road passed through the region, stopping overnight at Sandhole Lake in the southeast corner of what is now the refuge. Before the establishment of the refuge itself in 1937, part of the marshland was used to raise muskrats for the fur industry. Once the refuge was founded, the wetlands habitat was managed to benefit both nesting and migrating waterfowl. In the 1930s and early 1940s, crews from the U.S. Government's Works Progress Administration (WPA) built the refuge headquarters, water control structures and bridges.

This refuge is situated in a remote area that is basically a high-elevation hardstem bulrush marsh, not a true lake. In recent years, trumpeter swans have reestablished themselves there as an important nesting species, and Camas Lake is a fine place to see these rare birds. Moreover, this refuge is also an important nesting and staging area for sandhill cranes. In fact, with over 200 pairs nesting there, this lake hosts the largest nesting population of sandhill cranes in the world. On broader terms, the specific track record and long-term status of individual species have historically been more important to the Greater Yellowstone Ecosystem than highly generalized ecological principles.[20]

There are two kinds of long-term status at play here. The first kind is the known, or at least the probable, trend of given species, based on historical or perhaps on tribal information. The second kind is the objective result of formal scientific studies in modern times. On this latter point, some care is needed. Even though, say, 70 years of data may sound impressive, it still may not be long enough to give researchers a reliable picture of how much a given species can vary when it lives in a wild ecosystem. Some cases to this point can be mentioned here.

Historical accounts of grizzly bear abundance, for example, date from before the mid–1800s. Wildlife experts have been making informal guesses about the numbers of grizzly bears for many years. Their estimates suggest that these bears were very common and roamed freely throughout the Yellowstone region when the first mountain men arrived. In addition, before the 1930s, the bear population was not isolated—but it certainly is now, chiefly because the wilderness itself has been so fragmented. These experts do not know for sure whether in the past grizzly bears were more, or less, common than they are today. What is clear is that, in the Greater Yellowstone Ecosystem, a grizzly bear can weigh over 600 pounds and can keep up its weight and strength only by being what ecologists term "an opportunistic omnivore."

This means that Yellowstone grizzly bears eat a wide variety of foods, ranging from herbaceous plants, tubers, berries, and nuts to animals, insects, and fungi. Their diets can shift on a daily, weekly, seasonal, and annual basis—a fact that has thus far enabled them to adapt to ever-changing food supplies.[21] That said, grizzlies range over hundreds of square miles and, especially when human food is present, there is always the danger that they will come into conflict with human beings.

Writing in 2006, the grizzly bear experts Doug and Andrea Peacock had this to say in a moving account:

> The grizzly is a thing of beauty and grace, a magnificent beast in his own right who is capable of stirring deep reverence and humility in humans. The awe-inspiring bear is, however, married to danger.
>
> For thirteen thousand years, grizzly bears occupied the top of the food pyramid in North America, their dominance barely contested until the nineteenth century. This is the one animal who challenged human impulses to extend our domain over all lands and creatures, informing us that we still live close to but not quite at the top of that pyramid.
>
> In that, they take us back to the dawn of humanoid consciousness: they are a reminder of the ancient fear of falling prey to a wild bear. This primal

awareness has helped direct the evolution of human intelligence throughout all time.[22]

In recent years, the estimates of grizzly bear numbers in the Greater Yellowstone Ecosystem have ranged from about 229 in 1974 to about 718 in 2017. Even though the grizzly population now appears to be rising, climate change, continued habitat loss and the ever-increasing activities by more and more human beings could easily reverse this trend. A related if underlying problem here is, *How many grizzly bears should there really be in this ecosystem*? There is at present no agreed-upon answer to this question—which, of course, applies to all other species in the ecosystem, too. In 2020, a panel of Federal judges ruled that the grizzly bears in the Greater Yellowstone Ecosystem must remain under Endangered Species Act protections.[23]

In terms of fish, the Yellowstone cutthroat trout (the most widespread native trout in the park) was the dominant fish species there before the European-American settlement. Today they are still an important source of food for an estimated 16 species of birds, and for mammals such as bears, river otters, and mink. Genetically pure Yellowstone cutthroat trout have declined throughout their range in the Intermountain West, including in the Yellowstone Lake ecosystem, for four reasons: competition with and predation by non-native fish species; a loss of genetic integrity through hybridization; habitat degradation; and fishing by humans. In Yellowstone Lake, lake trout are a major predator of cutthroat trout. Because of the lack of natural barriers in the lower reaches of most river drainages, non-native fish have been moving upstream and are threatening to displace the native cutthroat trout.

The Northern Range is a unique wildlife-hub set in the wide grasslands bordering the Yellowstone River and extending into Montana itself. In order to protect the remaining cutthroat trout in the Lamar River of the Northern Range, electricity has been used since 2013 to kill the lake trout there. This has been a success, and the U.S. Fish and Wildlife Service now does not list Yellowstone cutthroat trout as a threatened species under the terms of the Endangered Species Act of 1973.[24]

The North American pronghorn (incorrectly often referred to as a pronghorn *antelope*: true antelopes are found only in Africa and Southeast Asia) is making a modest comeback today.[25] These animals, second only to bison in sheer numbers in the early 1800s, were nearly destroyed by the hunting encouraged by the conversion of rangeland to cropland; by the professional hunters who sold the tasty meat; and by the ranchers who believed that pronghorns were competing with their livestock for forage.

Grizzly sow in Yellowstone National Park, June 2016 (Jim Peaco, NPS).

Thanks to transplant programs, good management, and carefully-regulated hunting, pronghorns again roam the sagebrush prairies of the western United States in herds that cumulatively total nearly half a million animals. In 2018, there were an estimated 505 pronghorns in Yellowstone National Park itself—the highest count since the 1992 estimate of 536 animals. They can best be seen in summer in the Lamar Valley, and near the North Entrance to the park at the small town of Gardiner, Montana (named after Johnson Gardiner, a fur trapper who worked in the area from 1830 to 1831). In winter, they are often found between the North Entrance and Reese Creek.

Thanks to their oversize windpipes and hearts, which allow huge amounts of oxygen and blood to be carried to and from their unusually large lungs, adult pronghorns can sustain sprints of 45 to 50 miles an hour for short periods. Such great speed, coupled with excellent eyesight, make it very hard for any natural predators to kill the adults. Their fawns often fall prey to coyotes, bobcats, wolves, bears, and golden eagles. The pronghorn does have one weakness which was very quickly recognized and capitalized on by human hunters. It has such a high degree of curiosity about things it has never seen before that it will sometimes come too close to them. In the 19th century, for example, a small flag, flapping in the wind and set up by a hidden hunter, could often lure them into rifle-range.

In the northern Rockies, both grizzly bears and black bears depend very heavily on whitebark pine nuts, whose high fat content helps the bears fatten up in preparation for their long winter hibernation.[26] Bears raid squirrel middens—i.e., caches—of stored white pinebark nuts in the fall. This adds to their layers of fat and also improves the chances that grizzly bear mothers will have successful pregnancies. When the whitebark pines in the high mountains around Yellowstone have good years, the bears do, too. If the nut crop fails or if it fares poorly, this forces the bears to look for their food in other places—for example, in the plentiful, human-supplied food sources (livestock, birdfeeders, orchards, and garbage) so easily found in the valley bottoms. This can lead to conflicts that result in them being shot.

All across the Greater Yellowstone region, whitebark pine—an important component of the ecosystem—is facing serious decline. There are four problems here: *First,* the more effective suppression of forest fires has meant that there are now far fewer fires, and thus fewer opportunities for whitebark pines to regenerate. This in turn means that there are fewer young whitebark pines and greater numbers of older mature whitebark pines. *Second,* mountain pine beetles attack mature whitebark pines and kill the healthy trees that have inner bark thick enough to support the larvae of hungry beetles. *Third,* white pine blister rust (an exotic species native to Eurasia that was inadvertently introduced into western North America in 1910 near Vancouver, British Columbia) can take up to a decade to kill a tree, but it leaves "ghost forests" of dead trees in its wake. White pine blister rust is already present in the Greater Yellowstone Ecosystem. *Fourth,* the full impact of global climate change is now unknown but is likely to be significant. For example, warmer temperatures and milder winters have allowed the mountain pine beetle to accelerate its life cycle from two years into one year, thus allowing more rapid infestations.

A related point to be made here is that estimates of the decline of quaking aspen in the Northern Range vary from 50 percent to 95 percent. The exact reasons for this falling-off are not known today, but speculation has touched on the some or all of the following possibilities:

- The impacts of the Native Americans on some mammal species and on fire-return intervals before the creation of the park in 1872. The Native Americans had used fire to clear away dead wood, to encourage the growth of new grass in order to attract game, and to open up their fields of view when they were out hunting.
- Lesser fire-frequency after 1886, when the U.S. Army took charge of the park.

- Regional climate warming.
- Human harvests of beaver and hoofed mammals in the first 15 years of the park's history, and of wolves and other predators before 1930.
- Denser human settlements along traditional hoofed animal migration routes north of the park since 1872.
- Impacts of elk and other hoofed mammals on all other parts of the ecosystem since 1900.
- The human pressures, namely, culling (killing), on elk numbers and on their distribution in the park.[27]

In conclusion, one may usefully consider what Charles R. Preston, who was both the Chief Curator of the five museums of the Buffalo Bill Historical Center and the Founding Curator-in-Charge of the Draper Museum of Natural History, has said about the Greater Yellowstone Ecosystem. In his view, the ecosystem is now important for persuasive reasons, but still more needs to be done:

Beyond its symbolic meaning to people throughout the world, the Greater Yellowstone Ecosystem supports globally significant biological, geological, and cultural resources, and provides substantial opportunities for economic, scientific, recreational, aesthetic, and spiritual fulfillment for residents and visitors alike. This remarkable place holds great value for people with diverse backgrounds and interests.

Yet our numbers and activities are presently increasing threats to its integrity and identity. It is not too late to forge a comprehensive strategy that will preserve the integrity and uniqueness for future generations, but we must move quickly, decisively, and collaboratively to do so....

[In order to forge such a strategy, five elements, first recommended in 1988 but still valid today, are as follows:]

1. The collection and dissemination of good data before undertaking major management actions.

2. The creations of forums or mechanisms for civic dialog where information can be discussed and used in a constructive manner.

3. The decision to give stakeholders a voice on resource management issues and an opportunity to play a greater role in management decisions.

4. Identification of a set of shared management goals.

5. Continual evaluation and modification to reflect changing conditions.[28]

6

The Influence of Volcanism and Other Geological Events on the Greater Yellowstone Ecosystem

It is fundamentally important to understand the geology of the Greater Yellowstone Ecosystem because geology is the building-block of any ecosystem. This chapter discusses the history and present state of play of volcanism and other geological events in the Greater Yellowstone Ecosystem.[1] The ceaseless interchanges between volcanic, hydrothermal, and glacial processes, on the one hand, and the distributions of plant, animal, and human life, on the other, are intricate indeed.

Most of Earth's pre-history is known as the Precambrian era, which extended from the formation of the earth 4.6 billion years ago to roughly 541 million years ago. Rocks dating from this time are found in northern Yellowstone and in the nearby Teton, Beartooth, Wind River, and Gros Ventre mountain ranges. During subsequent geologic eras (i.e., 541 to 66 million years ago), much of the western United States was sometimes covered by seas, sand dunes, tidal flats and plains. During the Cenozoic era—the past 66 million years of our planet's history— the Yellowstone region was subjected to volcanism, mountain-building, faulting, and glaciation. Later (about 30 million years ago), huge parts of today's American West began stretching apart along an east-west axis. This stretching process increased about 17 million years ago and created the present basin-and-range topography that now characterizes Nevada and many other parts of the West, including the Yellowstone area. This topography is often marked by north-south mountain ranges that are divided by long north-south valleys.

Two explanations are useful: A caldera is a large cauldron-like hollow that forms shortly after the emptying of a magma chamber of molten rock during a volcanic eruption. Plate tectonics is a scientific concept that describes the large-scale motion of seven large plates and the movements of a larger number of smaller plates of Earth's lithosphere. The lithosphere (literally, the "stone ball") is the rigid envelope of the earth that includes the Earth's crust and part of the upper mantle. It is divided into a number of tectonic plates. When the edges of these plates meet, they may slide past one another, they may pull away from each other, or they may collide with each other.

About 16.5 million years ago, there was an intense period of volcanism near the borders of what are now Nevada, Oregon, and Idaho. Later volcanic eruptions also occurred in southern Idaho and Yellowstone, leaving a 500-mile trail of more than 100 calderas that were created as the North American tectonic plate slid in a southwestern direction over a shallow body of very hot magma. Some 2.1 million years ago, the movement of this plate carried the Yellowstone area ever closer to this magma body. The Yellowstone–Snake River Plain has been in slow motion for 16 million years; the youngest manifestation of its travels is the caldera system in Yellowstone.

Volcanism remains a major force in the Yellowstone area, where magma is quite close to the surface. This shallow body of molten rock is caused by heat convection in the mantle of the Earth. During this process, plumes of magma rise through the mantle and then melt in the crust, creating magma reservoirs of very hot rock that are partly-melted and partly-solid. The mantle plumes carry heat from deep within the mantle up into to the crust, thus creating what is known as "hot spot" volcanism. These hot spots create a wake of volcanic activity as the tectonic plates slide over them. For example, as the North American plate has moved westward over the last 16.5 million years, the hot spot that is now under the 15 million acres of Federal lands in the Greater Yellowstone Area has left a trail of volcanic deposits across Idaho's Snake River Plain.

Heat from the mantle plume has not only melted rocks in the crust but has also created two magma chambers of partially-molten and partially-solid rock near Yellowstone's surface. Heat from the lower magma chamber forced the crust above it to expand and rise, and stresses on the overlying crust led to earthquakes along the newly-formed faults. These faults eventually reached the magma chamber and magma began to ooze out through the cracks. The escaping magma lowered the pressure within the chamber, which allowed volcanic gasses first to escape and then to explode in a massive volcanic eruption.

This eruption of 2.1 million years ago coated 5,790 square miles with ash, extending all the way east to Missouri. It blasted huge amounts of volcanic gas and ash up into the atmosphere, which, in the process of rising, sent pyroclastic flows of super-hot fast-flowing debris coursing over the landscape. The net result was that the underground magma chamber was emptied; the land around it collapsed; and the first of Yellowstone's three calderas was thereby born. The total amount of volcanic material ejected during the above eruption was about 6,000 times greater than that ejected during the 1980 eruption of Mt. St. Helens in the State of Washington.

A second but smaller volcanic eruption occurred some 1.3 million years ago within the western edge of the first caldera. The third and most recent massive eruption was 640,000 years ago and created today's 30-by-45-mile-wide Yellowstone Caldera, which is located in the south-central portion of the park.

Since then, 80 smaller eruptions have occurred. About 174,000 years ago, one of them created what is now the West Thumb of Yellowstone Lake. During and after these explosive events, huge lava and basalt flows partially filled the caldera floor and its surrounding terrain. The youngest of these lava flows is the 70,000-year-old Pitchstone flow in the southwest corner of Yellowstone National Park.

There are still some very slow land movements going on in the Yellowstone region. Since the last of three caldera-forming eruptions, for example, upward pressures from the shallow magma body have formed two "resurgent domes" inside the Yellowstone Caldera. Both of these domes inflate and subside in response to changes in the volume of magma or hydrothermal fluids beneath them. In addition, the entire caldera floor rises and falls very slowly, too, but not to the same extent as the two resurgent domes. Over the past 100 years, the caldera floor has tilted very slightly toward the south. The result has been that Yellowstone Lake's southern shore has subsided: trees there that were once on dry land now stand in the water. By the same token, at the northern end of the lake, the water has risen up onto a sandy beach at Fishing Bridge.

Recent movements have been somewhat more dramatic. By 1985, vertical-motion surveys showed that, since the earliest measurements, the entire caldera had risen three feet. Later GPS measurements, however, revealed that the caldera had subsided—but that then it began to rise again, moving up 10.6 inches between 2004 and 2010. This increase slowed in 2008 and the caldera began to sink again during the first half of 2010.

Such up-and-down events will certainly continue and are believed to be caused by the movements of deep hydrothermal fluids or molten rock into the shallow crustal magma system at a depth of about 6 miles beneath the surface. It should be noted that a caldera may experience periods of both uplift and subsidence for thousands of years without erupting. Indeed, the lateral discharge of these fluids away from the caldera, accompanied by small earthquakes, subsidences, and uplifts, can relieve internal pressures and may act as a natural pressure-release valve. If so, it may keep Yellowstone safe from major volcanic eruptions in the foreseeable future.

In broader terms, most of the park lies above 7,500 feet in elevation and is underlain by volcanic bedrock. The Yellowstone Plateau as a whole is in fact the result of the ground moving upward as a result of hot spot volcanism. Today, this process is most dramatically seen in the park's extraordinary display of more than 10,000 hydrothermal features, such as geysers, hot springs, mudpots, and steam vents. Remarkably, the great uplift also influences the local weather by forcing the westerly storm systems to rise ever higher, i.e., over the plateau itself, where they drop their heavy loads of snow.

The 30-by-45-mile-wide Yellowstone Caldera itself has very nutrient-poor soils. As a result, this region can only support extensive stands of lodgepole pine, which tolerate drought very well and which have shallow roots that can take maximum advantage of the few nutrients available in the soil. Other parts of the park area have volcanic rocks that are very rich in calcium, magnesium, and iron. Because these minerals degrade well into soils that are able to store more water and provide useful nutrients, they can support more vegetation, which in turn adds organic matter and thus enriches the soil.

Scientists believe that geology can also directly influence the movements and distribution of wildlife. Some soils, for example, encourage the growth of whitebark pine nuts (an important food source for grizzly bears in the fall), while other soils produce the extensive grasslands of the Hayden and Lamar valleys which support herds of grazing animals, such as elk and bison. Finally, in the warm geothermal areas, the grasses and other food sources are never deeply buried under the snow, making it possible for animals there to graze on them during the long, bitterly-cold winter months.

It is reasonable to ask: will Yellowstone's volcano ever erupt again? The short answers are: over the coming thousands+ of years, *probably yes,* but over the next few hundred years, *very unlikely.* In 2001 the Yellowstone Volcano Observatory was set up to monitor volcanic and seismic activity in the region. Scientists there monitor the immense Yellowstone volcano with a real-time and near real-time network of 26 seismic stations, 16 GPS receivers, and 11 stream-gauging stations. In addition, they collect information on temperature, chemistry and gas concentrations at selected hydrothermal facilities and chloride concentrations in major rivers.

If any volcanic activity should occur in the foreseeable future, it would very probably be a lava flow—but one that would ooze out very slowly over a period of months or years, giving everyone plenty to time to take evasive action. As of 2021, there is no scientific evidence that such a lava flow will begin at any time soon. To get a monthly activity summary, real-time monitoring of seismicity and water flow, and near-real-time monitoring of ground deformation, interested readers can consult the Yellowstone Volcanic Observatory website.

It must not be forgotten that in addition to heat, Yellowstone's geologic wonders equally depend on water, too. This water comes down from the mountains around the Yellowstone Plateau, where snow and cold rain gradually percolate through the layers of permeable rock that are laced with cracks. In the process, some of this cold water runs into the hot brine that has been heated by the magma. Although the temperature of this mixture of water quickly exceeds the boiling point of water, the water always stays in a liquid state because of the great pressure and heavy weight of the overlying water. The net result is superheated water with temperatures above 400 degrees F.

This superheated water is less dense than the colder, heavier water sinking around it. Convection currents are thereby generated that permit the lighter and more buoyant superheated water to begin a journey back to the surface by following the cracks and weak areas of the solidified lava flows. This upward movement is what constitutes the natural "plumbing system" of Yellowstone's hydrothermal activities. Moreover, as the hot water travels through the lava flows, it dissolves some silica. This silica settles into cracks, thus increasing the system's ability to survive the great pressures needed to produce a geyser.

In Old Faithful, for example, the silica coating of the walls of its pressure tube cannot establish a pressure-tight seal, so a great deal of water continues to pour through the silica-lined walls even after an eruption stops. The water pressure in the geyser tube is not maintained by the strength of the wall itself: rather, the water pressure in the tube is maintained by the even greater pressure of the colder water outside of the tube.

At the surface, silica precipitates to form the scalloped edges of hot springs and the dramatic landscapes of the hydrothermal basins. The Norris Geyser Basin is now the hottest of Yellowstone's active hydrothermal areas, with a temperature of 459 degrees F. recorded in a bore hole 1,087 feet deep.

There is always potential danger at the geyser basins. For example, many people have been severely burned—and some have died— after they left the safety of the boardwalks, ventured out onto the thin crust of a geyser basin, and then broke through its fragile surface into the extremely hot water beneath it. Dogs have died there, too, in the same way.

In addition, among many Yellowstone's geological activities, earthquakes are certainly not the least important.[2] This region is one of the most seismically active in the United States: about 700 to 3,000 earthquakes occur there every year, although few of them can be felt by visitors. Yellowstone's earthquakes tend to occur in "swarms," that is, they occur close together both in time and space. They result from the far-reaching network of faults that are integral parts of the volcano itself and the surrounding tectonic features.

The first known photograph of Old Faithful, taken in 1872 by William Jackson (William Jackson, NPS).

Volcanic fluids are transported along these many small breaks in the shallow rocks overlying the magma. In 2017, earthquake data from the University of Utah's Seismographic Stations Network showed that approximately 3,300 tiny earthquakes, much too small to be noticed by humans, occurred in and directly outside of Yellowstone National Park.

Such earthquakes happen along fractures in the crust, where stresses from crustal plate movements and volcanic activity build up to the point where the rocks along these faults begin to slip or break. When this happens, energy is released as seismic waves that travel through the nearby rocks. If and when they reach the surface of the ground, they can be felt and can strongly affect buildings and other human artifacts. The 1959 Hebgen Lake earthquake, for example, caused significant damage to park roads near Gibbon Falls.

These earthquakes support Yellowstone's hydrothermal activity by keeping its "plumbing systems" open. This is essential because mineral deposition might otherwise seal off the many small fractures and channels that carry hot water up to the geysers and hot springs themselves.

Much of Yellowstone has also been shaped by glaciers.[3] They develop when, over a period of many, many years, more snow falls in a given area than can melt there. When the snow gets deep enough, it turns into ice and begins to creep slowly downhill under the tug of gravity and the pressure of its own great weight. In the process, glaciers pick up and carry along with them many rocks of varying weights and sizes that effectively grind down the Earth's surface. They also deposit materials, often leaving in their wake large U-shaped valleys, moraines (ridges of debris), and erratics (out-of-place boulders). During the high point of glaciation, Yellowstone was covered by an ice cap up to 4,000 feet thick. This eventually melted away and between 13,000 to 14,000 years ago most of the Yellowstone Plateau became, and still remains, ice-free.

7

Life in Yellowstone
Under Extreme Conditions

The remarkable hydrothermal features of Yellowstone's microscopic organisms, known collectively as thermophiles (this term comes from Greek "thermo" meaning "heat," and "phile" meaning "a lover of"), merit a brief discussion.[1] Some thermophiles are also extremophiles, that is to say, they thrive only under extreme conditions of such high heat and acidity that they cannot survive at all if these conditions are not met. They are being studied by scientists today in part because they may offer valuable insights into the search for life on other planets.

Thermophiles are responsible for many of the vivid colors on display at Yellowstone's Grand Prismatic Spring, which is located in Midway Geyser Basin. It is the park's largest hot spring, measuring about 370 feet in diameter and is over 121 feet deep. A description of this spring by fur trapper Osborne Russell in 1839 makes it the earliest described thermal feature in Yellowstone that is definitely identifiable today. The spring was also noted by geologists working with the Hayden Geological Survey in 1871, who named it for its magnificent colors. Strikingly, these colors match most of those that can be seen in the rainbow dispersion of white light by an optical prism, namely, red, orange, yellow, green, and blue.

This spring interests scientists today because some of its microbes are similar to the very first life forms on our planet that were capable of photosynthesis, that is to say, they could use sunlight to change water and carbon dioxide into oxygen, sugars, and other critically important by-products. Indeed, it was these life-forms, known as cyanobacteria, which began to create the atmosphere that would eventually support human life. These spring waters were also capable, in 1889, of inspiring the geologist Walter Harvey Weed to write poetically:

The vegetation of the acid waters is seldom a conspicuous feature of the springs. But in the alkaline waters that characterize the geyser basins, and the carbonated, calcareous waters of the Mammoth Hot Springs, the case is otherwise, and the red and yellow tinges of the algae combine with the weird whiteness of the sinter and the varied blue and green of the hot water to form a scene that is, without doubt, one of the most beautiful as well as one of the strangest sights in the world.[2]

The Yellowstone hot springs are important for their diversity of thermophilic bacteria, which have been useful in scientific studies of the evolution of photosynthesis and as sources of thermostable enzymes for molecular biology. The Yellowstone thermophilic communities are just as diverse and varied as human communities. The inhabitants of these heat-loving communities are governed in part by their pH (i.e., hydrogen potential: a scale that classifies how acidic or how basic a solution is) and by water temperatures. For example, these communities can support a wide range of inhabitants, namely, trout, mosses, crustaceans, insects, protozoa, algae, fungi, cynobacteria, and archaea (single-celled microorganisms with nuclei and with membranes different from all other organisms).[3]

In Yellowstone, millions of individual microbes can also connect into long strands called filaments. Some bacteria and algae form thin, delicate structures in fast-moving water, such as the runoff channels seen at hot springs and geysers. In contrast, other microbes develop thick, sturdy structures in slow-moving waters, or in places where chemical precipitates can coat their filaments quickly.

Remarkably, the communities formed by the thermophilic microbes will sustain communities of larger organisms within Yellowstone's hydrothermal areas; in turn, such communities can affect even the more extensive communities of large park mammals. For example, bison and elk look for, and usually find, essential food and warmth along the edges of thermophilic environments during the park's bitter winters. This also encourages coyotes, wolves, and bears to patrol such areas looking for something to eat. They are most successful during the late winter and the early spring, when bison and elk are at their weakest and are most likely to die from predation, ill health, or starvation.

It seems amazing, but is true, that the study of the hydrothermal features of Yellowstone extends all the way to Mars and to the moons of Jupiter. The reason is that if life as we know it on Earth did indeed begin in the extreme conditions believed to have characterized the early years of our planet, then similar life-forms may possibly have arisen on other planets—and still may exist there today.

The chemosynthetic microbes that flourish in Yellowstone's hot springs are able to do so because they can, on their own, metabolize the inorganic chemicals which are sources of energy that do not require sunlight. In fact, such chemical energy sources offer the most likely-habitable niches for some forms of life on Mars, or on Ganymede, Europa, and Callisto—the moons of Jupiter. If groundwater systems exist on Mars or under the icy crusts of Jupiter's moons, there may be some niche habitats for life.

8

An Overview
of Yellowstone's Wildlife

The wildlife of the Greater Yellowstone Ecosystem is so abundant, so diverse, and so unique that a good first step in understanding it is to meet some of the creatures that live there, and find out how well or poorly they are now faring.[1]

Sometimes one picture will be worth a thousand words. A good example is a remarkable photo of a bald eagle and a golden eagle, both surrounded by ravens, landing on the carcass of an elk that had been killed by the Slough Creek wolf pack in Yellowstone National Park near the Lamar River.[2] Slough Creek has been prime wolf territory—and prime *wolf-watching territory*—ever since wolves were reintroduced there in 1995 (see Chapter 11).

There are about 100 different types of mammals in the Greater Yellowstone Ecosystem; about 150 different types of birds; about eight aquatic invasive species; and two different types of amphibians and reptiles. Some of these creatures appear in the list below, which chiefly follows the order and substance of the discussions in the definitive "Ecosystem" and "Wildlife" chapters of the 2019 *Yellowstone Resources and Issues Handbook.*

Bears. There are two species of bears living in this ecosystem: grizzly bears and black bears. The grizzly is bigger, more aggressive, and much more powerful than the black bear. Indeed, its Latin name is *Ursus arctos horribilis*, i.e., "horrible brown bear." Hunters in the 19th century found to their consternation that their single-shot[3] muzzle-loading rifles, which were adequate to kill a bison, the largest land animal in North America (a bull bison weighs up to 2,000 pounds) with one well-placed shot, often failed to stop a charging grizzly bear, despite several well-placed shots.

Even hardened outdoorsmen in the 19th-century Rockies gave

the grizzly bear, to which they accorded the Biblical name of "Caleb," meaning "bold," a very wide berth. In the 1830s, for example, when the artist George Catlin was traveling in these mountains with two trappers, named Bogard and Ba'tiste [Baptiste], their canoe and their personal gear was ransacked by a mother grizzly bear with two cubs. Catlin wanted to kill the mother bear and bring her skin home as a trophy, at the same time capturing the cubs.

The trappers totally refused to comply, and Catlin had to write: "My plans, however, entirely failed, though we were well armed; for Bogard and Ba'tiste both remonstrated with a vehemence that was irresistible; saying that the standing rule in the mountains was 'never to fight Caleb, except in self-defense.' [Bogard told Catlin] 'These darned animals are too much for us, and we had better be off'; at which my courage cooled, and we packed up and reembarked as fast as possible."[4]

The grizzly bear population in the Greater Yellowstone Ecosystem was approximately 712 in the year 2018. Since these bears roam so far—indeed over hundreds of square miles—there is always the possibility their travels will bring them into serious conflicts with human beings. In 2018, for example, for the first time in three years, a bear attack was reported in the park. A family of four hikers had a surprise meeting with an adult female grizzly bear on a trail. The bear, which was apparently protecting her cub, knocked a 10-year-old boy to the ground and bit him on the back and buttocks. Fortunately, his parents had bear spray ready, were able use it immediately to drive off the bear, and the boy survived.

Grizzly bears usually only eat plants, invertebrates, fish, and fungi, but they will also eat human food and garbage when they can get it. For this reason, keeping human foods away from bears is extremely important because it increases the chances of bears and people being able to coexist peacefully in Yellowstone. Visitors must therefore heed the key rule: "A fed bear is a dead bear" (i.e., when a bear gets used to human food, it will try hard to find it and, as a result, it will surely have to be relocated or shot).

The grizzly bear population is doing very well now (2021), successfully rearing cubs in all parts of the ecosystem. These bears are officially still considered a threatened species and scientists will continue to monitor their wellbeing.

The black bear is the most common and widely-distributed bear species in North America, and the Greater Yellowstone Ecosystem is one of the few places south of Canada where black bears can coexist with grizzly bears. Little is known now about the black bear population in the park itself, whether it has been affected by the increase in grizzly numbers and distribution since the 1970s.

The last black bear study in the Greater Yellowstone Ecosystem was conducted many years ago, at a time when black bear behavior was strongly influenced by the then officially-sanctioned policy of letting bears eat human foods from garbage dumps, from non–bear-proof garbage cans, and from handouts from visitors driving along park roads. More recently, a combination of GSP-tracking camera collars and non-invasive DNA samples from hair snares has helped park biologists learn more about the black bears' population size and density; how many elk calves they may be able to kill; and their home range sizes, movements, food habits and use of habitats.

Bison. Yellowstone Park is the only place in the entire United States where bison have lived continuously as a free-ranging population since prehistoric times. Because of their iconic status in the history of the park, it is worth presenting them at some length.[5]

Historically, Yellowstone bison occupied about 7,720 square miles of land in the headwaters of the Yellowstone and Madison rivers. Today, this range has been reduced to Yellowstone National Park itself and to some adjacent areas of Montana. The bison population now lives and breeds in the northern and central northern regions of the park. The northern breeding herd congregates in the Lamar Valley and on the adjacent plateaus for the breeding season. During the rest of the year, these animals use the grasslands, wet meadows, and sage-steppe habitats in the Yellowstone River drainage, which extends 62 miles between Cooke City and the Paradise Valley north of Gardiner, Montana. The northern range is drier and warmer than the rest of the park. It generally has thinner snow, too, so it is rather more "buffalo-friendly."

The central breeding herd lives in the central plateau of the park—from the Pelican and Hayden valleys with a maximum range of 7,875 feet in the east, to the lower and warmer Madison River headwaters in the west. Winters there are often severe, with deep snows and temperatures reaching -44 degrees F. This area contains a high proportion of moist meadows composed of grasses, sedges, and willows, with upland grasses available in drier areas. Bison from the central herd congregate in the Hayden Valley for breeding, but many of them move into other nearby valleys during the rest of the year. Increasing numbers of bison are also traveling to the northern portion of the park and mixing with the northern herd there.

The bison living in and near the park are flourishing now but, in an earlier time, their survival there was very much in doubt. In the 1800s, for example, there was virtually no control over either professional or amateur market hunting, so by 1902 the once-seemingly-endless herds of bison had been whittled down to a tiny total of only 23 animals. Before it was finally too late, the U.S. Army, which administered Yellowstone at the beginning of the 20th century, stepped in and began to protect the remaining handful of bison from further slaughter.

Bison from private herds were then used to establish a herd in northern Yellowstone but, for decades, Yellowstone bison were still being killed because it was believed that, together with elk and pronghorn, they were over-grazing the park. Probably as a result of the growing environmental awareness in the U.S., these herd reductions of bison ceased by 1968.

Because of the ever-increasing numbers of bison and the litigation over their unchecked migration into Montana, bison reductions began again in the 2000s. Some Yellowstone bison are infected with brucellosis, a livestock disease that can be transmitted to wild bison and to elk as well as to cattle through contact with infected fetal tissues.

As a result, conservation of wild bison is now one of the most heated and most complicated of all Yellowstone's resource-use issues. Since 1985, more than 10,000 bison have been legally shot by hunters or have been culled from the bison population, chiefly to protect Montana's cattle industry and to prevent the unlikely transmission of brucellosis from bison to cattle.

What is self-evident is that, in the future, the Yellowstone bison herd needs to be managed very carefully. Thanks to their very high rates of survival and reproduction, bison in Yellowstone increase by 10 percent to 17 percent every year. Unless they are either culled or are allowed to migrate seasonally into surrounding states in the same manner as other wildlife, there will soon come a time in Yellowstone when there will simply be too many bison trying to live in too small a space.

Permitting the Yellowstone bison population to grow ever larger (as of 2018, there were a total of about 4,527 bison in the park itself) will simply force bison migrations and will generate public ill-will outside the park. Hunting in the park is not an option because Yellowstone's enabling legislation explicitly forbids it. The bottom line is that there is now a pressing need for more public tolerance of bison roaming at relative liberty outside the park boundaries. Until that time comes, the bison population can be controlled only by (1) legal hunting outside the park and (2) by capture of bison near the park boundary.

Since captured bison are now transferred to local Native American tribes for slaughter and distribution of their meat and hides to members of these tribes, this is not a long-term solution that pleases all the interested parties. What will ideally be needed is a new set of policies that recognize bison as free-roaming wildlife and gives them the necessary freedom to wander at will over suitable public lands outside the park. Toward this end, Yellowstone bison now have access to 75,000 acres in the Gardiner Basin of Montana; bison are now tolerated year-round outside the west and northern boundaries of the park; the State of Montana is managing a bison hunt on public lands outside the park; and five Native American tribes are conducting bison hunts outside the park, by authority of their respective treaties with the U.S. Government.

A ten-year-long study of bison migration and grazing in the park (conducted jointly by biologists from the National Park Service, the U.S. Geological Survey, and the Universities of Wyoming and Montana) concluded in 2019 that in fact Yellowstone bison have a very positive effect on the landscape.[6] The scientists' findings confirm that wild bison shape vegetation cycles and promote plant growth throughout the summer. With the help of NASA satellites, it was found that areas grazed intensely by larger groups of bison actually "green-up" earlier, more intensely, and for longer periods each year than places that were not grazed by bison.

The findings also show that bison frequently return to the same areas of the park. This keeps the plants there in a growth cycle and provides the most nutritious food for migrating animals. Evidence gathered over the past decade shows that migrating ungulates (hoofed mammals such as bison) follow the wave of spring plant growth. Bison begin their migrations by following the spring green-up, but their slow but intense grazing lets them fall behind the ever-advancing wave of spring. This means that, unlike migratory mule deer who move together with the flush of fresh grass as it advances up the mountains, bison can in effect "make their own fresh grass" by grazing very intensely in big herds. This fact sets them apart from other North American ungulates. It is especially beneficial because these very short, young plants provide the most nutritious food for migrating animals.

Bighorn Sheep. In 2018 there were about 345 bighorn sheep in the northern Yellowstone area, many of them living on the steep terrain along the upper Yellowstone River drainage. Early historical accounts of large numbers of these animals have led to speculation that they were far more numerous before the park was established; indeed, they formed a key part of the diet of the local Native Americans.

Some sport hunting is permitted now outside the park, but the bighorn population is actually far more vulnerable to sudden declines due to disease, habitat loss, and disruption of migratory routes by roads and other human activity. An eye disease (pinkeye) can inflict heavy losses on them because it strongly impairs sheep's vision and can thus result in their death when they sometimes fall from the precipitous slopes where they feed.

Although wolves occasionally prey on bighorn sheep, sheep numbers have in fact increased since wolves were reintroduced to Yellowstone in 1995–1996 (see Chapter 11). Biologists are now studying the relationship between elk abundance and sheep abundance; e.g., do more elk mean fewer bighorn sheep?

Mountain Goats. Today these animals are the descendants of the goats that were first introduced into the Absaroka and Madison mountains ranges during the 1940s and 1950s and that later, in the 1990s, established a population in Yellowstone National Park. There are now 200 to 300 mountain goats in and adjacent to Yellowstone.

Mountain goats are abundant in the northeastern and northwestern parts of the park, but their very success there has caused some minor problems. For example, they can, by intensive use, trample down vegetation cover on the ridges; their urine and feces adversely affect soil chemistry; and, over time, soil rockiness can increase slightly due to their presence. Nevertheless, no large-scale negative effects have been noted to date. Because of dangerous flying conditions for survey aircraft and to budgetary limitations, however, mountain goats have not been surveyed by air in the park since 2014.

Elk. There are now about 30,000 to 40,000 elk living in the Greater Yellowstone Ecosystem.[7] Yellowstone National Park itself provides summer feeding for 10,000 to 20,000 elk. They congregate in six to seven herds, the bulk of which spend the winter at lower elevations outside the park.

These herds offer a great deal of visitor enjoyment and also help to support the local economies: hunters are permitted to hunt elk and some other species outside the park. A Jackson Hole food store assures potential customers that elk meat is lower in fat and higher in protein than beef or chicken, and is an excellent source of iron, phosphorus and zinc.

As Yellowstone's most abundant large mammal, elk comprise about 85 percent of the winter wolf kills. They are an important food source for bears, mountain lions, and at least 12 scavenger species, including bald eagles and coyotes. Changes in elk abundance over space and time can change the plant and animal communities of Yellowstone. Competition with elk influences the diet, habitat selection, and demography of bighorn sheep, bison, moose, mule deer, and pronghorn. Moreover, elk browsing also affects vegetative production, soil fertility, and plant diversity.

Thanks to their enormous antlers, bull elk are perhaps the most-photographed animals in Yellowstone. The antlers of a typical healthy bull are up to 60 inches long, nearly six feet wide, and can weigh about 30 pounds a pair. They begin growing in the spring and usually drop off in March or April of the next year. Antlers only rarely occur on females.

In the park itself, many of the elk winter at lower elevations outside the park near Jackson, Wyoming. The timing and routes of the Northern Yellowstone elk migration closely follow the times of seasonal vegetation growth and of changes in the depth of the snow. After winters with high snowpack, elk delay their migration to the lowlands; in years with lower snowpack and earlier vegetation growth, they move sooner. Yellowstone's biggest elk herd winters in the area of the Lamar and Yellowstone river valleys from Soda Butte to Gardiner, Montana. Some elk migrate outside the park into the Custer National Forest and onto private lands.

Calves are born in May and June. Since they are brown with white spots and have very little scent, it is not easy for predators to see or smell them. Nevertheless, up to two-thirds of each year's calves are killed by predators—black bears, grizzly bears, wolves, coyotes, cougars and golden eagles. There have now been many decades of arguments about elk on the Northern Range. Because the issues involved these debates are both interesting and complex, the Northern Range is the subject of Chapter 10.

Moose. The largest members of the deer family in Yellowstone, an adult bull can weigh close to 1,000 pounds, stand 5½ to 7½ feet high at the shoulder, and has heavy antlers which it usually sheds in late November or December. Moose have very long legs that let them wade deep into rivers and travel through very heavy snow; they can also swim fast and run fast. Despite its great size, a moose can slip through the woodlands without making a sound. Visitors must remember that moose—especially cows with calves—are quite unpredictable and have chased people in the park.

An adult moose eats about 10 to 12 pounds of food per day in the winter, and about 22 to 26 pounds in the summer. Marshy areas of meadows, lake shores, and near riverbanks are their favorite areas. They were rare in Yellowstone until the latter half of the 1800s and in Jackson Hole until the early 1900s. Their numbers then began to increase through predator control programs, forest fire suppression, and restrictions on moose hunting. The moose population in Yellowstone tumbled after the extensive fires of 1988, which burned mature fir forests, and it fell further during the severe winter of 1988–1989 that followed the fires. There are now fewer than 200 moose left in Yellowstone. The State of Montana has taken note of a state-wide decline in its moose populations, and has limited hunting as a result. Yellowstone National Park is also conducting a study of moose populations using non-invasive methods.

Deer. There are mule deer and white-tailed deer in the Greater Yellowstone Ecosystem. Both are subject to regulated hunting in the autumn but not, of course, in the park itself. Their natural predators include wolves, coyotes, mountain lions, and bears.

Widely dispersed throughout the park during the summer, mule deer migrate seasonally, and about 400 members of the 1,850-to-1,900 mule deer herd spend their winters north of the park, i.e., in the Northern Range. Although the white-tailed deer is the most common deer species in North America, it has always been scarce in Yellowstone, possibly because it is not well-suited to the habitat and elevation of the Northern Range, or because of the competition from other hoofed mammals. Its numbers are not being monitored now.

Wolves. In the early days of the United States, wolf packs roamed freely from the Arctic tundra south into Mexico, but by the early 1900s the accelerated loss of their habitat and the widespread extermination programs targeted on them eradicated them throughout most of the country. In 1973, the U.S. Fish and Wildlife Service listed the northern Rocky Mountain wolf as an endangered species and designated the Greater Yellowstone region as one of its three wolf-recovery areas.

The upshot was that between 1995 and 1997, there were 41 wild wolves from Canada and northwest Montana released in Yellowstone National Park. As was hoped for and, indeed, as was expected, the wolf population soon began to grow and soon "colonized" new territories outside the park where they are not protected from human hunting. At the same time, the park protects the wolves' long-term viability in the Yellowstone region, and also provides a place for continuing research on how the wolves can affect many other aspects of the ecosystem. As of 2015, there were about 528 wolves in the Greater Yellowstone Ecosystem and, in 2019, about 109 wolves in the park itself.

Packs of wolves play a key role in the Greater Yellowstone Ecosystem because, by hunting together, they can efficiently bring down large prey that other predators usually cannot kill. In the park itself, 90 percent of their winter prey consists of elk. Ten to 15 percent of their summer prey is deer, and they can also kill bison.

Secretary of the Interior Bruce Babbit and others carry a crated wolf for release in Yellowstone National Park in January 1995 (Jim Peaco, NPS).

The biology of wolves places strict limits on their capacity to kill large animals by themselves. Wolves do not have skulls that are mechanically configured to deliver a killing bite, nor do wolves have retractable claws and strong forelimbs designed to grapple closely with their prey. It is precisely these biological limits that prevent an individual wolf from ever becoming what has been jokingly called a "runway killing machine."[8]

Many other animals profit from wolf kills. Shortly after a pack of wolves kills an elk, ravens arrive to pick up scraps. Next come the coyotes, which wait patiently until the wolves have eaten their fill. Bears will then often try to chase the wolves away, and are usually successful. Last but by no means least, many other creatures, ranging from magpies to invertebrates, queue up to polish off the remains.

The leading cause of death for wolves within the park is predation by other wolves; outside the park, it is usually human-caused death by hunting. Although no hunting of any kind is allowed in the park itself, Montana, Idaho, and Wyoming all permit regulated hunting outside the park. Since wolves do not recognize political boundaries and often move between different jurisdictions, some wolves that live within the park for most of the year may at times move outside the park. They are then subject to being shot by legal hunters.

On the other hand, 65 percent of the collared wolves, i.e., wolves that have been captured, fitted with radio-tracking collars, and then released back into the wild, are ultimately killed in the wild by rival packs of wolves.

Preliminary results from studies of wolf reintroduction show that this will probably lead to greater biodiversity throughout the Greater Yellowstone Ecosystem—a very positive result. Packs of wolves have preyed chiefly on elk, and these large carcasses provide food for a variety of other animals, especially scavengers.

Increasingly, packs of wolves are preying on bison, too, especially late in the winter when other foods are scarce and when bison are relatively weak. Grizzly bears, in turn, have usurped wolf kills nearly at will, so these kills are an important source of protein for bears in low food years. Moreover, wolf aggression toward coyotes found in wolf territories initially reduced the number of coyotes, which may have given smaller predators and rodents marginally longer leases on life.

At this writing, there is no shortage of wolves. Indeed, they can now be hunted legally in Montana, Wyoming (but not in Yellowstone Park), and Idaho during the regulated hunting seasons. The future of wolves in the Greater Yellowstone region will ultimately depend chiefly on how the issues of wolf-kills of livestock, on one hand, and the hunting of wolves outside the park, on the other, are handled by human beings.

Moreover, wolf populations will also continue to be affected by the availability of elk, deer, and bison. These can fluctuate in response to any changes in public interest in hunting; in hunting quotas themselves; in the severity of winters; and in health issues among the animals themselves.

Wolves are not normally dangerous to humans unless they become used to associating humans with food. No wolf is known to have attacked a human in Yellowstone Park, but a few attacks have occurred in other places. To date, eight wolves in the park have become too habituated to humans, and two of the animals have had to be killed.

Coyotes. Jokingly known as "song dogs" because they communicate with each other by a range of long-distance vocalizations by howling at dawn and at dusk, coyotes are quite abundant in Yellowstone. They are intelligent, adaptable, and face very few predators. Indeed, at present they thrive not only in the wilderness but also in the cities.

Like many other predators, coyotes were heavily hunted in the early 1900s because sometimes they ate livestock. They survived this assault in part by a stroke of good luck. During the 1900s, the elimination of wolves led to a boom in the coyote population. The increasing absence of wolves opened up an environmental niche that coyotes were ideally-suited to fill, and fill it they did.

Until wolves were reintroduced in Yellowstone in 1995–1996, coyotes had very few predators there except for mountain lions, which will try to kill any coyotes they find feeding on mountain lion kills. When the wolves returned to the Northern Range, the coyote population initially fell by about 50 percent as a result of competition with wolves for food, attacks by wolves, and loss of territory to them. More recently, the coyote population has rebounded in the Lamar Valley of the Northern Range. Coyotes do, however, face threats from people because coyotes quickly learn the ease and attractions of roadside feeding. This can lead to aggressive behavior on their part when they expect food but do not receive it. In the process, moreover, they also risk being hit by a passing car or truck. The best solution is that visitors must realize that coyotes and other wild animals are potentially dangerous and should never be fed or approached.

Red Foxes. At least two subpopulations of these foxes live in the Greater Yellowstone Ecosystem, but they are not seen often because they are nocturnal, usually forage alone, and try to avoid open spaces by traveling along the edges of forests or wet meadows.

Most of the foxes in the lower 48 states, especially those in eastern areas and the plains states, are a subspecies of the European foxes that were introduced into the eastern United States in the 1700s and 1800s for fox hunting and for fur farms. Some of the animals that survived these hunts or escaped from the fur farms proliferated and headed westward. In Yellowstone, they can sometimes be seen in the Hayden and Pelican valleys and in the Canyon Village area.

Foxes can quickly become used to human beings if they are fed by them. For example, in 1997, one fox was trapped and was relocated from the Tower Falls parking area because visitors gave it human food. After being relocated twice between 10 and 60 miles away, it returned twice. Finally, it turned up in Mammoth, where it was fed again. The end result was that this fox had to be killed; it is Yellowstone's policy that if any potentially dangerous animal gets so used to human food that it returns to its human food source after being relocated, it must be killed.

Mountain Lions (Also Known as Cougars). Many years ago, one of the authors (Hunt Janin) took a camping trip with some friends into Los Padres National Forest, not far from the town Jolon, close to the central coastal mountains of California. There he roasted a pork loin by means of a "Hawaiian oven," which is made by digging a hole in the ground; building a small fire in the hole; putting some rocks into the fire to get them very hot; placing the pork loin (well-oiled, well-seasoned, and carefully wrapped in layers in aluminum foil) on top of the rocks; refilling the hole with dirt and tamping it down; and, finally, waiting patiently for about one hour while it slowly cooks.

This pork loin was a great culinary success, not only for the hungry campers themselves but also for a hungry mountain lion. Late that night, the campers heard something moving the empty tin cans near the ashes of their extinguished campfire. Emerging from their tent with a flashlight in hand, they were just in time to see a big, beautiful mountain lion leap away from the campfire and vanish into the nearby bushes. This was a rare treat indeed, because very few campers ever see a mountain lion in the wild.

During the predator-removal campaigns of the early 1900s, all the mountain lions were probably killed off in Yellowstone itself, but they survived elsewhere in the West because of their secretive nature, excellent camouflage, and strong preferences for inaccessible rocky, rugged lands where they are impossible to track without dogs. Indeed, to find them at all, licensed hunters must use well-trained dogs, which force the mountain lions to take refuge high in the branches of trees, where they can easily be shot.

There are now about 25 to 35 mountain lions living in the Northern Range. Others come to the park seasonally, but none of them is easy to see. The Northern Range is ideal mountain-lion country because there is not much snow there, and tasty prey is always readily available—primarily elk (mostly calves) and mule deer, but also smaller mammals such as marmots.

A mountain lion can bound up to 40 feet horizontally when running, and can also leap 15 feet up a tree. They usually attack their prey by first silently stalking the animal; leaping onto the animal's back; and, finally, killing it nearly instantly with a fierce bite to the base of the skull or to the throat. A mountain lion then eats its fill and hides the carcass under fallen leaves or branches until its next meal. It spends an average of three to four days consuming a carcass and then devotes the next four to five days to making another kill. Very few mountain lion–human conflicts have occurred in Yellowstone, but any sightings of mountain lions close to areas of human use or residence should be reported immediately.

Canada Lynx and Bobcats. There are very few lynx (*Lynx canadensis*) but many bobcats (*Lynx rufus*) in the Greater Yellowstone Ecosystem. Both are solitary and they are difficult at any considerable distance to tell apart, but bobcats have different markings on their tails, shorter ear tufts, and make smaller tracks in the snow. The lynx has wider paws with fur in and around the pads, which allow it to run very easily across the snow. Both animals can eat a variety of other creatures—hares, rabbits, voles, rodents, birds, red squirrels, and perhaps sometimes even deer and pronghorn as well.

Bats. There are 13 species of bats in the Greater Yellowstone Ecosystem, all of them insect-eaters. They use an echolocation system to find their way and to find their food in the dark: these echoes provide bats with an accurate sonic picture of the environment they are flying in, including the movements of their potential prey.

To save energy, bats can lower their metabolic rate and body temperature, going into a condition known as "torpor" that can last for months. This is a seasonal response to low temperatures or food shortages. When at rest, bats roost head-down, which makes them less vulnerable to predators and makes it easier for them to resume flight.

Beavers. Some of Yellowstone's beavers managed to escape the very intensive trapping that occurred in the Rocky Mountains during the 1800s, first because of Yellowstone's relative inaccessibility, and second because of changing men's fashions, which in the 1830s began to favor silk hats rather than hats made from beaver fur. The eventual upshot was that, by 2015, about 100 colonies of beavers were living in Yellowstone National Park. A colony can include from two to 14 beavers, which are usually related; 6 beavers is the usual average.

They are very efficient and tireless dam builders, a skill that does not endear them to the ranchers and other property owners who are living outside the park—where beavers are not protected and are frequently trapped. Some of these people privately joke that the only way to deal with beavers whose dams flood their lands is an effective but illegal solution: "Shoot, shovel, and shut up!"

In the Yellowstone area, beavers like to live in the southeast (Yellowstone River delta), the southwest (Bechler), and the northwest (Madison and Gallatin rivers). These regions attract beavers because of their suitable waterways, wet meadows, and the abundance of such preferred foods as willow, aspen, and cottonwood. Interestingly, beavers do not shun areas that are also very popular with humans: in fact, several beaver lodges are located close to well-used backcountry campsites and trails.

Pikas. Small mammals that are the size of a guinea pig (about eight inches long and weighing six ounces), pikas are abundant in Yellowstone and often prefer rocky alpine or sub-alpine zones in the Tower and Mammoth areas. Pikas are likely to disappear eventually from some of the lower elevations and warmer sites in Yellowstone because of global warming. Active year-round, they much prefer the cooler times of the day. They are easily stressed by a number of factors—winter cold, summer heat, and variations in site habitat quality.

White-Tailed Jackrabbits and Snowshoe Hares. These jackrabbits are common in lower elevations in Yellowstone. Most of the park is too forested or has too much snow to appeal to them, but in lower elevations of the Northern Range they can dine on sagebrush, rabbitbrush, and other shrubs during the winter. White-tailed jackrabbits are extremely prolific, having one to four litters per year, each with one to 15 offspring. Those offspring who do manage to survive the bobcats, coyotes, wolves, hawks, eagles, and owls of the park will be able to run up to 50 miles per hour, cover up to 10 feet with each bound, and swim when being chased by predators.

Snowshoe hares, for their part, are common in some parts of Yellowstone, notably in the Norris Geyser Basin. Their large hind feet make it easy for them to travel on snow, while their white winter coats and their summer coats blend in very well with the changing seasons. During the breeding season, they chase each other, drum on the ground with their hind legs, leap into the air, and occasionally fight each other. Mostly nocturnal, their presence in the winter is visibly shown by their abundant tracks, which skiers and hikers can easily spot in the snow. They are preyed upon by lynx, bobcats, coyotes, foxes, weasels, hawks, and great horned owls.

Wolverines. These fierce, tenacious carnivores are members of the weasel family and can weigh up to 31 pounds and be 47 inches long. They are now very rare in the Yellowstone region: between 2006 and 2009, only seven of them (two females and five males) were documented by scientists in eastern Yellowstone and its adjoining national forests. By the 1930s, commercial trapping and predation control efforts had substantially reduced the wolverine population in the lower 48 states. Since then, their numbers have increased somewhat but this species has not been documented recently in most of its historic cold, snowy, high mountain environments.

Wolverines can consume a wide range of foods and have even been known to eat animals much bigger than themselves, notably deer, elk, and even moose. The likely impact of climate change on wolverine habitats, especially declines in the high elevation snowpacks needed by denning females, constitutes the chief threats to this species. Montana now has the largest wolverine population and, in recent years, licensed trappers there have been authorized to harvest only a very small number—five wolverines per year.

Other Small Mammals. A basic source for this chapter (the "Wildlife" chapter of the 2019 *Yellowstone Resources and Issues Handbook*) provides brief reports on 12 of these small animals. In the interest of brevity, only a few of the points the *Handbook* makes are given below for each animal below.

> *Badger*: Short, strong, stout, and an excellent digger, a badger needs to eat about two ground squirrels or pocket gophers a day in order to maintain its own weight.
>
> *Golden-Mantled Ground Squirrel*: Found throughout Yellowstone at all elevations, this squirrel is preyed upon by coyotes, weasels, badgers, hawks, and grizzly bears.
>
> *Red Squirrel*: One of the park's most territorial animals (i.e., it strongly defends its own territory), the red squirrel cuts cones from trees and hides them in middens; grizzlies later raid the middens in whitebark pine and limber pine habitats to get these fatty and nutritious nuts.
>
> *Unita Ground Squirrel*: During the winter, the squirrels that hibernate near Mammoth Hot Springs, but are also active then, may have been roused from their long sleep by hydrothermal activity.
>
> *Least Chipmunk*: This small chipmunk can be identified by its quick darting movements and carries its tail vertically.
>
> *Short-Tailed Weasel*: In summer, its fur is light brown and white. In winter; it is all white, except for its black-tipped tail, and is then known as an ermine.
>
> *Long-Tailed Weasel*: Eats voles, pocket gophers, mice, ground and tree squirrels, rabbits, and sometimes birds, eggs, snakes, frogs, and insects.
>
> *Marten*: Active throughout the year; hunts mostly on the ground.
>
> *Mountain Vole*: Probably the most important small prey species in the park, it is eaten by coyotes, raptors (birds of prey), grizzly bears, and other animals.
>
> *Pocket Gopher*: Transports food in cheek pouches to an underground cache, which grizzly bears sometimes dig up— along with an unsuspecting gopher.
>
> *River Otter*: Can swim underwater at up to 6 miles per hour and

for 2 to 3 minutes at a time; when hopping and sliding on snow or ice, it can reach speeds of 15 miles per hour.

Yellow-Bellied Marmot: One of the largest rodents in Yellowstone, they were called "whistle pigs" by the early settlers because of the loud whistle they give when alarmed by seeing a predator.

Birds. Yellowstone has maintained records of bird sightings since its establishment in 1872. These records document nearly 300 species of birds, of which about 150 nest in the park itself. Yellowstone National Park now monitors golden eagles, wetland birds, songbirds, and woodpeckers. Species of concern include the trumpeter swan, the golden eagle and the common loon.

Raptors. The Yellowstone Raptor Program was a five-year (2011–2015) enterprise designed to provide baseline information on golden eagles, red-tailed hawks, Swainson's hawks, American kestrels, prairie falcons, and owls. Surveys show that at least 17 species of raptors use the Hayden Valley in the Northern Range as a migration corridor.

Bald Eagles: Named by Congress in 1782 as the national symbol of the United States, the bald eagle is found near open water from Mexico to Alaska. In 2018, park staff monitored 32 bald eagle territories, finding that of 16 active nests, nine (56 percent), successfully fledged young. Since human presence can disturb eagle nesting and foraging, some nest areas in Yellowstone and other national parks may be closed to visitors on a case-by-case basis.

Golden Eagles: In response to wide-spread concerns about the long-term prospects for golden eagles, Wyoming has set up a golden eagle working group; the U.S. Fish and Wildlife Service is studying them, too. Surveys have located 28 golden eagle territories within the park, 20 of them within the Northern Range alone.

Osprey: Like many other birds of prey, osprey populations declined in the mid–1990s and then, after the banning of pesticides such as DDT, rebounded in the latter part of the century. Yellowstone's osprey population on and around Yellowstone Lake has declined, probably because of the decline in cutthroat trout there. It is hoped that a planned increase in cutthroat trout production will help the osprey, too.

Peregrine Falcons: These are the fastest birds in the world, capable of flying at 55 miles per hour, and striking their prey in a mid-air dive of more than 200 miles per hour. They were so badly affected by the widespread use of DDT and other toxins that in 1970 they were listed as endangered. In the 1980s, Yellowstone National Park was a site for peregrine reintroductions. These were halted when the use of harmful toxins abated; since then, the falcons have made a full comeback on much of their former range and were delisted in 1999.

Wetland Birds: About 30 percent of the bird species that breed in Yellowstone depend largely on wetlands. Because wetlands are expected to shrink because of climate change, scientists are now concerned about these species, some of which are discussed very briefly below.

Common Loons: In Yellowstone, the common loon is listed as a "Species of Special Concern" because of its limited range, its small population (there are only 45 loons there), its sensitivity to human disturbance, and the loss of its breeding habitat outside of Yellowstone. The number of loons has declined significantly since the mid–2000s. Recent studies suggest that, for reasons that are not yet understood, the number of loons in the park can vary widely from one year to another. Given the tiny size and the isolation of Wyoming's breeding loon population, there is a high probability that it will become extinct before too long.

Trumpeter Swans: With wingspans of up to eight feet, the numbers of these big birds are increasing in the Rocky Mountains, are stable in the Greater Yellowstone Ecosystem, but are declining in Yellowstone National Park itself. The basic reason for this decline in the park seems to be that Yellowstone offers only very marginal conditions for swan nesting. The 24 swans that do live there now may, for some unknown reason, have been forced out of a more favorable environment elsewhere. Scientists are studying this matter.

Songbirds and Woodpeckers: These species constitute the majority of birds in Yellowstone National Park. They are monitored in a number of different ways. These include counts in stands of willows; in recently-burned forests, where birds are among the first returning vertebrates; in old growth forests; and in grassland and sagebrush steppes. They are also studied in the North American Breeding Bird Survey, the fall migration surveys, and summer-early fall banding stations.

Other Notable Birds: American Dippers, Ravens and Sandhill Cranes.

Also called the water ouzel, the dipper's thick downy feathers, waterproofed by oil from a preen gland, enables it to survive and flourish in very cold mountain waters. Ravens are very intelligent birds that are quite able to link cause and effect. They follow wolves to elk kills and then wait for the wolves to rip open the thick skin of elk carcasses. Ravens have even learned how to unzip and unsnap hikers' backpacks to find any food hidden in them. Yellowstone has an on-going raven study which has marked 55 birds.

At a distance, sandhill cranes are often mistaken for standing human beings: they are about 4 feet tall and have a wingspan of 6.5 feet.

Fish. There are now 11 native species and five non-native species of fish in Yellowstone.[9] For thousands of years, Native Americans harvested some of them for food. Although hunting has always been banned in the park itself ever since the park's founding more than 100 years ago a major attraction for many visitors has been the fishing. In fact, about 50,000 of the park's four million visitors now fish each year.

What is most remarkable is that, historically, in what is now Yellowstone National Park, any widespread distribution of native fish was originally prevented by waterfalls and watershed divides there. The result was that when the park was established in 1872, about 40 percent of its waters—including Lewis Lake, Shoshone Lake and the Firehole River above Firehole Falls—did not contain any fish at all.

Early park managers actively encouraged fishing by stocking fishless park waters with fish; by rearing fish in hatcheries and transporting them to streams; and, finally, by introducing a wide variety of non-native fish. These latter included lake trout, brook trout, brown trout, rainbow trout, and other species. In retrospect, this policy turned out to be a mixed blessing.

On the one hand, there were now many more fish in Yellowstone's waters. On the other, the ranges and densities of the native trout and ling were substantially affected. The non-native species tended to displace the park's native fish by competing for food and habitat, by eating them, and by degrading their genetic integrity through hybridization.

In response, park managers developed a formal stocking policy and discontinued stocking any non-native fish. Stocking of the Yellowstone cutthroat trout continued, both within and beyond its native range. Indeed, historically, from the early 1880s to the mid–1950s, a total of more than 300 million fish were stocked throughout Yellowstone. Today, there are fish in about 40 lakes there: the other lakes were either never stocked at all or have now reverted to their original fishless condition.

Yellowstone Lake and the Yellowstone River, taken together, hold the largest inland population of cutthroat trout in the world. Ironically, although the Yellowstone cutthroat trout is a *Pacific drainage* species, it has managed—without any human help—to travel east over the Continental Divide and to find a new home in the Atlantic drainage.

In the Yellowstone area, one likely passageway for this travel is Two Ocean Pass, which is located in the Teton Wilderness south of the park. This pass separates the headwaters of Pacific Creek, which flows west into the Pacific Ocean, and Atlantic Creek, which flows east into the Atlantic Ocean. In the summer of 1860, the famous trapper Jim Bridger, who was leading a U.S. Army surveying party into this remote, uninhabited region when deep snow forced him to make a long detour, said of this area: "A bird wouldn't fly over there without taking a supply of grub along."[10]

Nevertheless, in a marshy part of Two Ocean Pass, adjacent to an unusual hydrographic site known as the Parting of the Waters, some water actually does cover the Continental Divide. This means that a fish can, with no difficulty, swim from the Pacific Ocean drainage to the Atlantic Ocean drainage.

Fish habitat conditions within the park itself are still excellent, but non-native fish continue to pose a serious threat to native fish. In Yellowstone Lake, for example, the voracious lake trout—which can live up to 25 years, can reach 50 pounds in weight, and can eat up to 41 cutthroat trout every year—are real threats to cutthroat trout. Brown trout, brook trout, and rainbow trout also compete with the cutthroats for food and habitat. A further problem is that rainbow trout can hybridize with cutthroat trout. And finally, since there are no physical barriers to fish movements in the lower reaches of most drainages, the non-native fish have been moving upstream and threaten to replace the native cutthroat there.

With the very limited technology and manpower now at hand—that is to say, nets, electrofishing, angling, traps, other mechanical methods, and piscicides (toxins that can kill fish in habitats where the above procedures cannot safely be used), the lake trout probably cannot ever be eliminated entirely from Yellowstone Lake. Continuing use of suppression efforts until at least 2025 may at least reduce the ravenous lake trout population to a more tolerable level where it will have only a modest impact on the cutthroat population. Given the very high reproductive potential of lake trout, however, they will at once begin to increase again if suppression efforts are ever abandoned.

Amphibians and Reptiles. Amphibians form an important part of Yellowstone's aquatic and terrestrial ecosystems. There are five species of amphibians in the park; none of them is now listed as threatened or endangered. They are important because many of Yellowstone's reptiles, birds, mammals, and fish prey on larval and adult amphibians. These, in turn, eat a wide variety of vertebrate and invertebrate species.

There are six species of reptiles in Yellowstone (five snakes and one lizard), and none of them is considered threatened or endangered. The only dangerously venomous snake in the park is the prairie rattlesnake, but it is usually defensive, and is not aggressive. In fact, only two snake bites are known to have occurred in the history of the park.

9

Implications of Climate Change in the Yellowstone Region

By far the most important step when studying the effects of climate change is to rely only on well-documented and peer-reviewed scientific facts. Despite the overwhelming preponderance of scientific evidence on the realities of climate change, some highly conservative politicians and media outlets, especially those in the United States with very strong in-group loyalties, will still try to present climate change as an unresolved controversy that requires much more study before any significant decisions can possibly be made. All the information used in this chapter (and, indeed, everywhere else in this book) comes from reputable scientific sources.

What is most evident is that, as Dr. Ann Rodman, who is the "Climate Program Lead" at the Yellowstone Center for Resources, wrote in 2015:

> Although there is some variation in the end result of climate change projections used by the IPCC [the Intergovernmental Panel on Climate Change], there is no doubt that the planet's climate is being altered by human activities. The math and physics involved in climate change are indisputable. Sea level rises, increasing temperatures, extreme weather events, and declining snow and ice are occurring now and will continue into the future. The extent and intensity of these results may vary by greenhouse emissions scenarios, but the trajectory of outcomes is clear. Humans will need to adapt, as will wildlife and ecosystems.
>
> Climate change is generally not an easy or pleasant conversation piece. However, it is a conversation that we need to have, and a process we must continue to study.... Through better understanding, we may arrive at more informed decisions to help conserve and adapt to our changing environment.[1]

Scientists are now conducting more research to better understand the likely effects of climate change on Yellowstone National Park itself. For example, the Greater Yellowstone Inventory and Monitoring

Network undertakes natural resource monitoring and collects data to track changes as they occur. It is part of the National Park Service's High Elevation Climate Change Response Monitoring Program which, together with the Rocky Mountain Network and the Upper Columbia River Network, measures the effects of climate change.[2]

The global climate system is so complex that probably there will never be a single "best model" to use when trying to predict the future climate everywhere on Earth. Scientists will therefore always have to use a range of different models, some of which will be better than others in predicting different parts of the answers.

The real issue here will not be the mathematical pros and cons of the models themselves, but rather the underlying question of *what human beings will actually do—or not do*—about dangerous and well-recognized problems such as the need to limit greenhouse gas emissions. The best guess of the authors is that both some wise actions, and some damaging steps, will inevitably be taken in the years ahead.

In any case, there is now compelling evidence that the climate has changed in the last century. It will continue to change into the foreseeable future. Researchers looking at average annual temperature report an increase of 0.31 degrees F/decade for this area, an increase that is consistent with the continuing upward trend in global temperatures.[3]

Conditions are also becoming significantly drier at elevations below 6,500 feet. Remarkably, the rise in minimum temperatures in the last decades actually exceeds those of the 1930s Dust Bowl in the United States. A warmer, drier future for the Greater Yellowstone Ecosystem now appears to be highly likely in the coming decades.

By the latter part of this century, the hot, dry conditions that resulted in the great fires of 1988 will probably become more common. Indeed, in the long run, the Yellowstone region may be heading toward the more arid climate that is now predominant in the southwestern United States.[4] The shift to drier conditions, which will result in more wildfires and to changes in plant community composition, is not because of less precipitation. Instead, the increasingly warmer temperatures will speed up the rates of transpiration, so that as it gets hotter plants will get less and less water, even if precipitation stays the same or increases. This will result in drought conditions for the plants.[5]

Much of the snow that falls in Yellowstone ultimately melts and runs into the American rivers that eventually thread their ways into the Gulf of Mexico or into the Pacific Ocean. Significant changes in snowfall are now being recorded, not only in the amount of snow actually hitting the ground but also in the intensity and timing of the spring runoff itself.

The bottom line is that although studying climate is quite complicated and the future impacts of climate change are very hard to predict, Yellowstone's temperatures are certain to continue to rise over the next century. Indeed, four important changes have already taken place:

1. Average temperatures in the park are now higher than they were 50 years ago, especially during the spring; nighttime temperatures now seem to be rising more rapidly than daytime temperatures.

2. In some areas of the park, in the last 50 years the growing season (i.e., the time between the last freeze of spring and the first freeze of fall) has increased by roughly 30 days.

3. At the northeast entrance to the park, there are now 60 more days per year above freezing than there were in the mid–1960s.

4. There are now about 30 fewer days per year with snow on the ground than there were in the 1960s.[6]

Rising temperatures will certainly alter Yellowstone's ecosystem, and in ways that may not be possible to predict very far in advance. The mix of plants and animals throughout the park will change. Much of the forest that now covers about 80 percent of the park may eventually dwindle. Some reasonable forecasts are as follows:

- Changes in the amount and timing of spring snowmelt will affect water levels; the growth of plants; and the movements of wildlife, ranging from the migrations of bison to the spawning of trout and the arrival of pollinators.
- Moreover, any significant changes in the rivers flowing out of Yellowstone's water basins are certain to affect many downstream users, too—ranchers, farmers, town dwellers, and city inhabitants alike.
- There could also be more fires and more intense fires, plus a longer fire-season.
- Climate change may well cause some of Yellowstone's birds to shift their range and migratory patterns. It may also interfere with their reproduction.

The men and women of Yellowstone National Park will, of course, continue to safeguard the park's biodiversity, natural processes, cultural resources, as well as all the trails and infrastructure that encourage so many visitors to enjoy this unique place. As the effects of climate change become evident, both the park staff and the visitors will need to be much more attentive to how nature and people are adjusting to these slow-moving but important developments.[7]

What must be kept firmly in mind is that recent studies consistently indicate that the climate of the Yellowstone region will change markedly. Rapid temperature rise can result in substantial reductions in snowpack and stream runoff, as well as changes in stream temperatures, fire frequencies, and the deaths of dominant tree species.

One possibility in the future of the Yellowstone region is that it may shift gears into a new reality marked by very little summer snow; very low stream flows; and very frequent severe forest fires. Taken collectively, these changes could slowly usher in a transition from today's forest-dominated vegetation to a new, more desert-like, scrub vegetation.[8] Experts are now confident that the long-term forecast for the Yellowstone area is for much less snow. There may be some decades-long ups and downs in this process, but the net result will be that people who are now living downstream and who thus rely heavily on water that begins as snow in the mountains of Yellowstone, must be aware that there will be less water in the future, and must plan accordingly.[9]

Yellowstone's mountain snow is extremely important because its influence stretches so far beyond the park's own boundaries. For example, the Yellowstone River, the Snake River, and the Green River all have their sources in the high mountains near the park. These rivers are, in turn, the biggest tributaries of the Missouri, Columbia, and Colorado rivers. If much less snow falls on the Yellowstone region, the consequences can be far-reaching, for example: much less water downstream for agriculture, human consumption, recreation, energy production, and wildlife.[10]

Other recent studies suggest that climate suitability for the forests of the Greater Yellowstone Ecosystem will change substantially in the coming century. For example, warming temperatures, less springtime snowpack, and less late-season soil moisture will result in a longer, warmer, and drier growing season than exists at present. The likely result will be that sagebrush and juniper communities will expand from the valley bottoms where they now thrive and will move "up slope" in elevation—i.e., into the lower forest zone and the Yellowstone plateau which occupies the central portion of the park. At the same time, the climate will become less hospitable to the dense and productive forests of Douglas fir and aspen that now carpet the lower forest zone. Moreover, Ponderosa pine—a species not currently found in this ecosystem—will find a welcome habitat there by the end of the century.[11]

The Intergovernmental Panel on Climate Change (IPCC) has organized research groups to project possible future climates under well-defined greenhouse gas emissions scenarios. The three main IPCC greenhouse gas emissions scenarios focus on lower emissions, on medium emissions, and on higher emissions. Today, actual global emissions are on a path *far above* the higher emissions scenario. A general circulation model (GCM) is a type of climate model that uses a mathematical model of the general circulation of a planetary atmosphere or ocean. Such models are used for weather forecasting, understanding the climate, and predicting further climate changes. For the three main IPCC emissions scenarios above, the general circulation models of the atmosphere project an increase in 21st-century temperature seven to 11 times greater than the amount of historical 20th-century warming in Yellowstone National Park. Moreover, precipitation could also increase under all three emissions scenarios.

Modeling of potential shifts in mammal species in the park due to climate change also suggests that a number of shifts may occur. For example, with fewer elk dying in deep winter snows as climate change reduces heavy snowfalls, the carrion from other wolf kills may help to compensate for any loss of food for small scavengers. At the same time, there may be more rodents. Potential changes in fish habitat may include losses in trout habitat in the Greater Yellowstone Ecosystem, with cutthroat trout being especially vulnerable in the park itself.[12]

Summarizing the likely effects of climate change on the Greater Yellowstone region is never easy, and different forecasts are often made in very similar but not identical terms. What is most certain is that both ecological and man-made changes will continue to be the norm there, not the exceptions. Some of these changes have been forecast in a study that makes the following predictions:

> The upper treeline in the Greater Yellowstone Ecosystem is likely to move [upward] toward higher elevations in response to increased temperatures, regardless of the direction and magnitude of the changes in precipitation and water use efficiency, and the distribution of Douglas fir is likely to expand.
>
> Concomitantly, the alpine and whitebark pine zones [will] decrease in extent and become more fragmented under all scenarios considered here. Thus, it appears that under these climate scenarios, several or many species and communities that are restricted to the alpine zone are likely to become locally extinct within Yellowstone Park and possibly the Greater Yellowstone Ecosystem during the next few centuries.
>
> However, the total number of species within [the ecosystem and the park] may actually change little. Semi-desert vegetation, which is currently rare and restricted to specialized habitats, may expand in lower-elevation portions of the [ecosystem], especially under the warm, dry scenario.[13]

10

Yellowstone's Northern Range

One of the most interesting areas of the Greater Yellowstone Eco-system—but one that is probably not familiar to most readers of this book—is its north-eastern sector, which is known as the Northern Range.[1] It has been mentioned before in this book, but it is a living, complex, colorful, and ever-changing wildlife hub, and needs a more thorough discussion.

The Northern Range lies both inside the park (65 percent of it) and outside the park (35 percent) and covers a total of about 600 square miles along the Lamar and Yellowstone river basins. This is the only area of Yellowstone Park that is accessible year-round by car: a 57-mile road, plowed in winter, links the Montana communities of Gardiner at the park's North entrance and Cooke City outside the Northeast entrance.

This region is often hailed as of the best and easiest places in the world to see wolves and other free-roaming animals. It constitutes only 10 percent of Yellowstone Park itself and stretches into neighboring Montana, but from a wildlife point of view it has the deepest and best-documented history of any part of the Greater Yellowstone region.

Moreover, the Northern Range has been the cockpit of slow-moving but major changes in both the human perceptions of wildlife there and the ecological relationships among elk, bison, wolves, grizzly bears, beavers, willows, and other forms of plant life. The most dramatic of these changes was the reintroduction of wolves into the Northern Range and elsewhere in the Greater Yellowstone Ecosystem. This remarkable process is discussed in the next chapter.

Taken as a whole, the Northern Range is a poster-child of the Yellowstone ecosystem. Indeed, it is often considered to be America's answer to Tanzania's Serengeti Plains in Eastern Africa because of the large numbers of hoofed mammals living there. The daily life-or-death struggles of these creatures, coupled with their extensive seasonal migrations and vivid photogenic qualities, strongly appeal to environmentalists and visitors alike.

The Northern Range embraces the broad rolling grasslands that border both the Yellowstone River and the Lamar River Valley (this latter river is a 40-mile-long tributary of the Yellowstone) and that stretch into Montana itself. The Lamar River Valley is one of the most popular places in Yellowstone to see "big" wildlife, especially grizzly bears, wolves, and elk. It is a focal point of the animal migrations that can be described as follows.[2]

The high mountains overlooking this valley create a large water catchment area, which in turn gives rise to a wide range of different climate zones. These include boreal forests; open rolling hills; and, last but not least, the game-rich sagebrush and grasslands covering the Lamar River Valley floor itself. In all these zones, the animals follow an endless and naturally-choreographed cycle of seasonal travels.

For example, as winter descends on the Yellowstone region, the deer, elk, moose, bighorn sheep, and bear all drift away from the snowy high mountains where nutritious grazing is no longer possible, and make their way down into the comparatively lower and warmer elevation of the Lamar Valley. This offers much better winter forage than the high country because it gets less snow, more sun, and the prevailing winds prevent deep drifts from building up on the south-facing hillsides.

It is this somewhat sheltered habitat that gives animals a much better chance of surviving the fierce winter storms, during which temperatures can fall to minus 45 degrees Fahrenheit and where winds gust at more than 30 miles per hour. These winter extremes play a major role in further weakening any elk or other prey that have injuries, are old, or are just in poor health.

The immediate beneficiaries of such weaknesses are the major predators, chiefly the wolves, which are waiting patiently in the wings until they can make an easy kill with little or no risk to themselves. For a wolf, getting kicked or gored by an elk or a bison can easily be fatal, either at once or soon thereafter. While waiting, they carefully "test" their prey to determine, in some way that is not evident to human observers, whether there is anything sufficiently "wrong" with a given animal to justify the risk of attacking it. Even so, because the majority of wolf attacks are *not* successful, repeated tests and repeated pursuits of their prey are needed to bring meat to the wolf pack.

In 2015, there were about 528 wolves living in the Greater Yellowstone Ecosystem. The Northern Range is an ideal place for them to pull down young or weakened elk and bison during the winter months; to gorge themselves then; and, afterwards, to abandon the meaty carcasses to the always-hungry bears, coyotes, ravens, and smaller creatures who are next in line at such a feast. For a very short time after the wolves kill a large animal, there is more than enough food to go around.

The winter does not last forever and when temperatures do begin to rise in the spring, the snow melts on the valley floor and the rivers and other waterways become ice-free. As soon as the grass begins to grow again, the fair-weather residents, notably trumpeter swans, sandhill cranes, pronghorns, and grizzly bears (the latter just emerging from their mountain hibernations), all return to the valley floor. From May to mid–June the Lamar Valley is at its glorious best. The calving season is now in high gear. The birth of so many very vulnerable offspring, all at about the same time, means that now, for grizzly bears, wolves, mountain lions, and coyotes, "the livin' is easy."

By June, the melting snow pack has also revealed new food resources in the higher mountains, which attract the deer and the elk. As they migrate, these animals are shadowed by their predators, chiefly wolves. Prey and predator alike, all will remain foraging in the high pastures until the first snows begin in the autumn. At this point, the familiar migration cycle slips into high gear again by gently tugging these animals downhill back toward the Lamar Valley.

The Northern Range thus supports one of the biggest and most diverse communities of free-roaming large animals that can be seen on any continent. As a result of the relative integrity of its ecosystem, its sparse vegetation, and its year-round road access, it has long offered scientists and visitors alike some unparalleled opportunities both to see native species in action and to study the ecological processes that sustain them. An historical example can be used here.

Since the 1930s, there have been many heated scientific debates over whether, in terms of grazing or overgrazing, there have been too many elk on the Northern Range, too few, or just about the right number.[3] This is an important issue because elk are the most abundant ungulates on the Northern Range and they compose most of the wolf kills. Even today, the Yellowstone-Montana aerial elk count is far from exact. Only those animals that can actually be seen from low-flying aircraft are tallied, and it is believed that the airborne pilots or observers who are counting them manage to record only about three-fifths of the elk that are actually living there.

The earliest counts of elk in the Northern Range are not now believed to have been entirely reliable. By the early 1930s, scientists and park managers had concluded that although a combination of overgrazing, overbrowsing, and drought-related effects on animal pregnancy and survival rates had significantly reduced the carrying capacity of the Northern Range, nevertheless, twice as many elk were on the range in 1932 as had been there in 1914. This meant that there were then too many.

As a result, between 1935 and the late 1960s, large numbers of elk, bison, and pronghorn were removed from the Northern Range by culling (shooting) or trapping them. For example, more than 26,000 elk were culled or shipped out of the park in order to limit their numbers and to repopulate the areas where over-harvesting or poaching had previously eliminated them. In addition, legal hunting outside the boundaries of the park also removed another 45,000 elk during this period. In total, it is estimated that these removals reduced the annual elk counts in the Northern Range from about 12,000 elk counted per year down to fewer than 4,000 per year.[4]

Due in part to growing pressure from the public, there was eventually a fundamental change in the management philosophy of the National Park Service in Yellowstone. After 1968, the new policy, known as "natural regulation," was to avoid human intervention in controlling animal populations, and simply let them fluctuate on their own accord in response to competition from other animals, forage availability, legal hunting, predation, and the weather.

In theory, natural regulation means "free of direct human intervention": the theoretical intent is to allow biological and physical processes within the park to function entirely on their own. A more precise definition of this process, as actually practiced by the National Park Service, is simply is *to minimize human impacts on the natural systems of the park.* This is easier said than done. Every year the National Park Service must deal with millions of visitors and must do its utmost to control the naturally-ignited fires that, if not dealt with promptly, could easily endanger human lives and buildings and, of course, wildlife as well.

Although the natural regulation policy involves very little direct National Park Service intervention within the park itself, the ongoing ecological processes there (chiefly due to climate change) can be also profoundly affected by human-caused activities. No ecosystem on earth is entirely unaffected by such activities.

Still, as the National Park Service puts it, the goal now is to have "natural environments evolving through natural processes minimally influenced by human actions."[5] That said, concern has been expressed about the long-term prospects for the health of the ecosystem of the Northern Range, especially the possible effects of natural regulation on the populations of hoofed animals and on vegetation there.[6] One reason is that, in the past, without any controls inside in the park itself, annual elk counts there had soared to about 12,000 elk by the mid–1970s; to 16,000 by 1982; and, remarkably, to 19,000 elk by 1988. All told, there are now about 10,000 to 20,000 elk in the park during the summer, and about 4,000 during the winter. This has stimulated further debates on the likely long-term effects on the Northern Range of both elk and bison grazing there.

In addition, such debates also raised another controversial matter, namely, the impact of the reintroduced wolves on the Greater Yellowstone Ecosystem. This is discussed in the next chapter.

11

The Return of the Wolf
to the Yellowstone Ecosystem

This chapter is a summary of a much longer and more complicated story about how the wolves in the Greater Yellowstone Ecosystem were first destroyed—and were then officially reintroduced.[1] Today, the wolves are doing very well, although their reintroduction and management remain a topic of debate.

It is not known how many wolves there were in this ecosystem when Yellowstone National Park was founded. One educated guess is that there may have been 300 to 400. They coexisted very well with the local Native Americans, who may have viewed them as sacred animals.

As settlers moved into the area in and around Yellowstone, domesticated animals such as cattle and sheep began to outnumber the dwindling number of bison, which market hunters were then killing in very large numbers. When wolves began to prey on the domesticated animals, farmers, ranchers, biologists, and average citizens all viewed the wolves with great hostility and demanded that organized programs of extermination be directed against these predators.

Wolves were then believed to kill elk and deer purely "wantonly"— that is, without any valid reason. Moreover, elk and deer were the very animals cherished by hunters, writers, filmmakers, and, ultimately, by tourists alike. The result was that by 1926, acting legally and with explicit Congressional approval, Yellowstone Park Service hunters had killed 136 wolves, thus virtually eliminating them from the park.

The last wolf pack in Yellowstone was destroyed in 1926, although reports of individual wolves traveling through the region continued to be received. During the 1960s, the Federal government, responding to pro-environment shifts in American public opinion and to concomitant changes in American laws, began to think about reversing its anti-wolf policy. An intensive survey in the 1970s found no evidence of any resident wolf population in Yellowstone. In 1974, the wolf was officially listed as endangered and its recovery was mandated under the Endangered Species Act of 1973. The long process to bring the wolves back to Yellowstone had begun.

In 1991, Congress appropriated money for an Environmental Impact Statement (EIS) for wolf recovery. In 1994, a report was completed for wolf reintroduction in Yellowstone and central Idaho. This EIS generated more than 160,000 comments from the public—the largest number of public comments on any Federal proposal up to that time. The result was that, in 1995 and 1996, a total of 31 wolves from western Canada were captured and were relocated to and released in Yellowstone.

Initially, a U.S. District Court judge ordered the removal of the reintroduced wolves in Yellowstone, but stayed his order pending an appeal. The judge's order was reversed in 2000.

Quite quickly following its reintroduction, the wolf population in Yellowstone began to increase. During the first years after the release of the wolves into the wild, their numbers grew rapidly because newly-formed packs had plenty of elk to eat and could easily expand into any lands that offered them sufficient prey. Having expanded their numbers and their ranges, wolves are now found throughout the entire Greater Yellowstone Ecosystem. In 2005, responsibility for wolf management was officially transferred from the Federal government to the neighboring states.

In 2008, the wolf populations in Montana, Idaho, and Wyoming were removed from the endangered species list but they were later returned to it. The next year, the U.S. Fish and Wildlife Service again delisted (as endangered) wolf populations in Montana and Idaho, but not in Wyoming. A legal challenge resulted in the Rocky Mountain wolf population being returned to the endangered species list. In 2011, wolf populations were again delisted in Montana and Idaho by an act of Congress, and the U.S. Fish and Wildlife Service proposed delisting wolves in Wyoming, which resulted in a Congressional directive of 2012 delisting wolves in Wyoming. Two years later, wolves were once again relisted in Wyoming following litigation over the management plan.

Finally, in 2017, wolves were delisted in Wyoming, and the Northern Rocky Mountain District wolf population was no longer listed. The upshot was that, as of April 26, 2017, wolves were no longer on the endangered species list in Montana, Idaho, and Wyoming. They can thus legally be hunted in these states during regulated hunting seasons.

There have been three primary benefits to the reintroduction of wolves in Yellowstone. In an interview with senior wolf biologist Doug Smith, he described the first benefit as being *ethical* or *philosophical*:

namely, that a species that had been totally eliminated by man from a portion of the United States has now been returned to the wild.[2] It took a National Park to do this, plus the tireless efforts of park staff, administrators, and countless advocates devoted to restoring and protecting nature.

Second, from an ecological point of view, the presence of wolves restored *the original balance* found in nature. An ecosystem cannot function efficiently in the absence of its top predator—a fact that will be discussed in more detail in the following pages.

Third, the extensive body of scientific information about wolf behavior in Yellowstone has not only benefited wolf-science worldwide, but has also proved to be a good example of the merits of reintroducing an endangered species. Because of Yellowstone's worldwide appeal, information about wolves in the park catches headlines and promotes wolf popularity. Indeed, the presence of wolves in the park strongly draws tourists and generates park revenues of about $35 million annually.

The wolves reproduced so easily after reintroduction that by 2020 it was estimated that there were about 350 to 400 wolves living in the Greater Yellowstone Ecosystem, with at least 109 living in 11 packs in the park itself. In general, since 2009, wolf numbers in the park have fluctuated from about 83 to 109 wolves.

Surprisingly, the average lifespan for adult wolves living within the park is four to five years, but their average lifespan outside the park is much less: only two to three years. The leading cause of death for adult wolves within the park is death inflicted by other wolves, usually because of territorial disputes or competition for carcasses. The leading cause of death for wolves outside the park is human beings, either by regulated hunting or by cars or trucks.

Wolves are intelligent and highly social animals that live in packs averaging about ten individuals. Each pack is a complex family, with older members—often an alpha (dominant) male and an alpha female— with their own personality traits and mutually-supporting roles within the pack. Packs are territorial and actively defend their own territory against any invading pack, both by howling loudly and by scent-marking with their urine.

Wolves eat a wide range of prey, large and small. One of their most remarkable traits is that, due to their teamwork and the power of the pack, they can successfully hunt and bring down much bigger prey that other predators are not able to kill. For example, although a male wolf weighs only about 100 to 130 pounds and a female wolf 80 to 110 pounds, in Yellowstone 96 percent of their winter prey is elk, which can weigh about 700 pounds each. In summer, the majority of their prey continues to be elk (85 percent), with about 14 percent being bison—an animal that can weigh up to 2,000 pounds. Adult bison are known to form a protective ring around a young bison to protect it during a wolf attack.

Although wolves are often unsuccessful in killing their prey, they do not give up easily or quickly. By working together as a pack, sometimes over a period of several days, these resourceful animals can bring down elk and bison greatly in excess of their own size. The British writer Rudyard Kipling was not mistaken when he wrote, in 1894 in *The Jungle Book*, his famous line: "For the strength of the wolf is the Pack, and the strength of the Pack is the wolf."

A great many other creatures also benefit, directly and indirectly, from wolf kills. For example, as soon as wolves bring down an elk, the ravens arrive. Coyotes turn up soon thereafter, but have to wait near the carcass until the wolves have eaten their fill. The next diners are likely to be grizzly bears, which because of their much greater size and strength will chase the wolves away and monopolize the kill as long as they like. Many other creatures, too, ranging from magpies to invertebrates, are waiting patiently for their own turns to join the feast.

Wolves, grizzly bears, cougars, lynx, and birds of prey are "apex species," which means that they are all key predators at the top of various food chains. They are important in our understanding of the environment because they play an important role, namely, keeping numerous prey populations firmly in check, thus helping to assure ecological stability by preventing any given creature from becoming so numerous that it begins to unbalance an entire ecosystem.

In Yellowstone, the reintroduction of the wolf in 1995 and 1996 gave researchers a unique opportunity to study what is technically known as a "trophic cascade" (i.e., a "feeding cascade"). This ecological concept is mostly settled science today, but there are still a few dissenters. It refers to how the presence of an apex predator (the wolf) can influence the behavior of its plant-eating prey (the elk), and how this in turn can influence both the plants themselves and other animals as well.

Wolves are now thought to be causing a remarkable cascade—or perhaps, more modestly, a remarkable *trickle-down*—of feeding changes in Yellowstone. These include slowly increasing the beaver population by restoring the aspen, willows, and other vegetation that had been heavily impacted by so many elk.

The trophic cascade theory was initially advanced by the path-breaking naturalist and author Aldo Leopold. He based it on his own observations that some mountain slopes were being overgrazed by deer soon after human hunters had killed off all the local wolves, which had kept the deer numbers in check.

Trophic ecology can be very briefly defined here as "the study of the feeding relationships among the different organisms in an ecosystem." These relationships are usually described as being food webs or food chains. The idea is this: natural processes that begin by a change at the top of a food chain can gradually work their way down into lower trophic levels. Indeed, these processes can eventually rebalance the relationships of very different species.

When the wolf was reintroduced into the Greater Yellowstone Ecosystem in 1995, for example, there was only one beaver colony in the park itself, though there were many more living in the Northern Range. The very numerous elk had pushed the limits of Yellowstone's carrying capacity by eating much of the vegetation.

Moreover, during the winter months the elk did not move around a great deal, but tended to stay put in one area and browse heavily on the young willow, aspen, and cottonwood plants they found there. This may have been good for the elk, but it made life hard indeed for the beavers, who need to eat willows in order to survive the winter.

After the wolves were reintroduced, they not only reduced the number of elk by eating some of them (there were other factors at play here, too, that reduced the elk population) but also, by the very threat the wolves presented by their presence, may possibly have helped to keep the elk on the move and thus less inclined to "stay put" in their browsing. If so, this has been favorable for the beavers. The park is now home to nine beaver colonies, with the hope of more to come. A flourishing beaver population may thus be one of the unexpected but welcome spin-offs of wolf reintroduction.

As the beavers spread out and build new dams and ponds, the trophic cascade effect continues because beaver dams have multiple effects on stream hydrology. They smooth out the seasonal pulses of runoff; store water for recharging the water table; provide shaded water for fish; and even encourage songbirds to live in the branches of the now-robust willow stands.

Concerning the elk themselves, after many decades of debates over whether the Northern Range was in fact being overgrazed by high elk numbers before wolves were reintroduced there, the pendulum of public opinion has now swung toward equally-acute worries that the elk herd there is now too small.

In 2003, the winter elk count, which totaled about 17,000 when the wolves were reintroduced, had tumbled to fewer than 10,000. It then fluctuated to between 6,000 and 7,000 elk, as the wolf population itself on the Northern Range slipped from about 94 in 2007 to about 50 by the end of 2015. By early 2013, the elk count had dropped to 3,915, which was the lowest figure since culling ended in the park.

Because counting elk is a difficult and inexact process, the resulting elk estimates are very likely to be understated. An aerial survey in January 2018 found that there were then more than 7,579 elk on the Northern Range. This was 29 percent higher than the 2017 survey of 5,349 elk, and was 48 percent higher than the 2013 low point. The 2018 estimate therefore suggested that the size of the elk herd on this range is now increasing.

The reasons for its earlier decline are not known at this point, but it may have been due to the cumulative results of the recovery of the large elk-eating carnivores such as wolves, grizzly bears, and mountain lions; more successful hunter harvests (that is, when human hunters kill more elk than usual); or reduced elk pregnancy and survival rates due to drought. In any case, Montana responded by reducing the number of hunting permits issued for Yellowstone's largest elk herd, i.e., the herd that winters in the Northern Range along and north of the park's northern boundary. This should mean that, in the future, elk hunting by humans there will have only a modest impact on the size of the herd, so there should still be enough elk for wolves and scavengers alike.

What are the challenges currently facing the wolves of Yellowstone? According to Doug Smith, one important challenge is the need to continue educating people about wolves. If this is not done, people may otherwise "make up their own stories," which could cast wolves in an unjustified negative light. Thus the need to study wolves and to become their advocates in ecological terms will always be a work-in-progress.

A second important challenge is that there are now increasing pressures from human-related developments surrounding the park itself. The underlying problem here is that wolves need many thousands of acres upon which to live; even Yellowstone Park itself, taken alone, is not big enough to host a viable wolf population.

In this way, elk/deer hunters and wolf advocates alike all have the same goals: namely, to preserve large areas of still-intact nature. As Doug Smith points out, "The news about nature is not very good. The news about the environment is not very good, either. To have wolves, you must preserve the habitat. To have elk and deer, you also must preserve the habitat. If you lose nature, you can't ever get it back. We thus all have the same goal."[3]

The story of the reintroduction of wolves in Yellowstone is complex and engaging. It is also an excellent example of the need for all species—including human beings—to understand and maintain the ecological balance of Yellowstone Park.

12

A Miscellany
of Yellowstone Events

This chapter highlights a range of noteworthy historical events, most of which are first-rate human-interest stories, too. They are first identified in chronological order as briefly as possible, and are then discussed in the following pages.

They address the following events:

- The settlement of Bozeman, Montana, in 1864.
- The U.S Army takes charge of Yellowstone in 1886.
- The first of many later "boiling water fatalities" occurs in 1890.
- The Lacey Act (named after its sponsor, Congressman John Lacey of Iowa) establishes, in 1894, the legal basis for protecting the park.
- The great naturalist John Muir publishes a widely-read essay on Yellowstone in 1898.
- The 1963 Leopold Report, written by the environmentalist A. Starker Leopold, son of the ecologist Aldo Leopold, fundamentally changes National Park Service strategy.
- A new bear-management plan eliminates the Yellowstone open garbage pits in 1970.
- The horrific "Summer of Fire" in 1988 has only short-term effects.
- Yellowstone Park's administrative offices expand in the late 1990s and early 2000s to centralize the park's science and resource management functions.

The Settlement of Bozeman

John Merin Bozeman (1837–1867) was an American pioneer, frontiersman, and merchant who in the early 1860s blazed the Bozeman

Trail through Wyoming Territory into the gold fields of southwestern Montana territory. He also founded the city of Bozeman, Montana, in 1864, which still bears his name. Having failed as a gold prospector, Bozeman decided that he could do much better by "mining the miners" than by looking for gold himself. He therefore teamed up with another unsuccessful prospector, John Jacobs, to find a new and shorter route into Montana Territory from the east.

In 1863, he and Jacobs successfully blazed the Bozeman Trail—a new route from the Oregon Trail in Wyoming to Bannack, Montana— and guided prospective miners through the Gallatin Valley. Bozeman himself settled in the valley, at a site that he is said to have chosen as "standing right in the gate of the mountains, ready to swallow up all the tenderfeet that would reach the territory from the east, with their golden fleeces ready to be taken care of."[1]

Bozeman was murdered in 1867 while traveling along the Yellowstone River, about 40 miles east of what is now the city of Bozeman. His killer was never found. Thomas Cover, Bozeman's traveling companion, survived the fracas with a bullet wound in his shoulder. Cover claimed that he and Bozeman had been suddenly attacked by a group of Blackfeet Indians. His story did not convince the local residents, who thought it much more likely that Cover had killed Bozeman and then made up the Native American attack story. Another possibility is that Bozeman was instead killed by an accomplice of the pioneer Montana rancher Nelson Story.

In any case, after Bozeman's death, the local residents petitioned the U.S. Government to build a fort in the Gallatin Valley to protect them from the allegedly hostile Native Americans. As a result, during the summer of 1867, Fort Ellis was built in the valley. The officers and cavalrymen of Fort Ellis participated in some of the early exploration of Yellowstone, notably the Washburn expedition of 1870–1871. This venture contributed to the creation of Yellowstone as a National Park in 1872.

Bozeman's close proximity to Yellowstone continued to make it an excellent jumping-off point for explorers and tourists alike. It was one of the closest larger towns north of the park, and people could count on finding hotel rooms there and being able to buy supplies for their trips into the park. This, remarkably, is still true today.[2]

The U.S. Army Takes Charge of Yellowstone

When the park was set up in 1872, the National Park Service did not exist. Moreover, there were no military instruction manuals or standing orders to tell the Army how to preserve and manage it.[3] In

1886, Congress refused to appropriate any more money for the ineffective administration of the park. This meant that there was no legal way to punish either the Caucasian poachers or the Native American (Eastern Shoshone and Bannock) "trespassers."

The result was that, during its earliest years, the park came under serious threat from people who could, with impunity, kill its game and exploit its resources. Since no law enforcement procedures were in place, poachers shot the animals; souvenir hunters broke off large pieces of the incrustations around the geysers and hot springs; and developers set up tourist camps near the hot springs, complete with soapy bathing and laundry facilities that were located within the hot springs themselves.

Since the fledgling administrative structure of the park did not have the legal authority, experience, manpower, or funds to deal with these severe problems, the U.S. Army was called in by the Secretary of the Interior to save the park. On 20 August 1886, under the command of Captain Moses Harris, a company of cavalrymen from Fort Custer in Montana Territory began what would come to be a 32-year U.S. military presence in the park.

The Army strengthened, posted, and enforced regulations in the park. Soldiers guarded the major attractions, threw out troublemakers, and either cavalrymen or ski patrolmen kept a quiet eye on some of the vast unpopulated interior regions of the park. In short, the Army carried out many of the same duties that park law enforcement rangers still undertake today.

In 1890, Congress finally appropriated $50,000 for a permanent Army post, to be known as Fort Yellowstone, which was finished by late 1891. In 1910, at the height of the Army's presence in Yellowstone, there were 324 soldiers stationed here. In 1916, when Congress created the National Park Service, the Army turned Fort Yellowstone over to this new agency. When local political resistance made a smooth transition impossible, the Army had to return in 1917. In 1918, the park was at last fully under National Park Service control, and the Army was able to leave.

"Boiling water fatalities"

About four million people come to Yellowstone every year to see "nature in the raw." Probably all of those who visit the backcountry are well-aware of the potential dangers there posed by grizzly bears, bison, elk, or wolves, but relatively few of the many more numerous visitors who come to the park's geyser basins and other geothermal features understand that they will be in mortal peril if they ever wander off the protective boardwalks there.

Yellowstone has more than 10,000 assorted geysers, mudpots, steamvents, and hot springs. People who get too close to them are sure to suffer always-painful and sometimes fatal burns.[4] During the 1870 Washburn Expedition exploring the region, for example, the explorer Truman Everts was separated from his party for 37 days and severely burned his hip while seeking warmth at hot springs at Heart Lake. The first known fatality was a seven-year-old boy from Livingston, Montana, whose family reported that he died after falling into a hot spring in 1890.

According to a 1995 compilation, National Park Service records identify 19 human fatalities caused by people tumbling into thermal features. The victims included seven young children who slipped away from their parents; teenagers who fell through the thin surface crust; fishermen who waded into the hot springs near Yellowstone Lake; and park concession employees who illegally and foolishly took swims in thermal pools. One of the most horrible deaths occurred in 2000, when, at night and not carrying a flashlight, a 20-year-old park concession employee tripped and fell into the ten-foot-deep boiling waters of Cavern Springs. She went completely underwater and, after being hospitalized, died several hours later from third-degree burns that covered her entire body.

More recently, in 2020, a woman entered Yellowstone National Park illegally when it was closed because of coronavirus fears. While taking pictures, she fell into a thermal feature in the Old Faithful area, and had to be airlifted to Idaho Falls for burns treatment.

The Lacey Act of 1894

In 1894, Congressman John Lacey told the House Committee on Public Lands that:

> There has been for some years a necessity for a law to punish crimes in the Yellowstone National Park. Various crimes have been committed and the perpetrators have escaped all punishment for want of the necessary legislation.
>
> The bill reported [i.e., the Lacey Act] attaches the park to the United States district of Wyoming and enacts the criminal statues of Wyoming and gives them full force in the park....
>
> The U.S. Government has set apart this park as a pleasure ground for the people of the United States perpetually, and has directed the preservation of the wild beasts and birds of the park. But no laws to carry out the purpose of protecting the game and birds of the park are now in force, and wanton and

cruel slaughter of the buffalo and other wild animals in the park have been reported, and the Secretary of the Interior has found himself powerless to prevent it.

Of the vast herds of millions of buffaloes [bison] that used to course the plains of America a few hundred only remain, and they are now all in the Yellowstone Park, and one of the purposes of setting aside this park has been to preserve this little herd. A few days ago poachers entered the park and commenced the slaughter of these animals. Prompt action is necessary or this last remaining herd of buffalo will be destroyed.[5]

The National Park Protection Act of 1894 (the Lacey Act) became the cornerstone of all later law enforcement efforts to protect wildlife in the park. It was the result of a number of expeditions from 1869 to 1890 that not only contributed to the creation of Yellowstone Park itself but also generated a much wider scientific, public, and even international understanding of its resources and marvels. The Act provided, among other things,

That all hunting, or killing or wounding, or capturing at any time of any bird or wild animal, except dangerous animals, when necessary to prevent them from destroying human life or inflicting an injury, is prohibited within the limits of said park; nor shall any fish be taken out of the waters of the park by means of seines, nets, traps, or by use of drugs or any explosive substances or compounds, or in any other way other than by hook and line....[6]

The well-known bison poacher Ed Howell was the first person to be arrested and punished under this Act for slaughtering bison in the park's Pelican Valley. In February 1894, Howell and his partner dragged a heavy sled into the park.[7] It was bulging with all the supplies they needed to deal with all bison they hoped to kill, such as axes to cut off their heads (with horns attached) and ropes to hang the heads from trees until spring. The poachers also made arrangements to return with pack-horses and to deliver the bison heads to taxidermists, who would pay up to $300 for each one. (In 1894, $300 was the equivalent of about $8,000 in 2021.) Howell then got into an argument with his partner, ordered him to leave, and settled down in his own tipi to wait for morning and the easy chance to kill some bison.

When Captain George Anderson, the park superintendent, heard about Howell's sled trail heading into the park, Anderson sent out Sergeant Troike and a civilian scout, Felix Burgess, to investigate. On long skis, these two outdoorsmen followed the poachers' snowshoe tracks and soon came upon six bloody bison heads hanging from a tree.

They quickly slid to a stop when they heard gunshots up ahead; 400 yards ahead of them, they saw a man shoot a bison and then begin to hack off its head with an axe. The man had a dog with him and was armed with a powerful repeating rifle, very likely a Winchester. The only weapon they themselves had with them was a Colt .45 caliber six-shot Single Action Army revolver. This was an excellent close-range weapon, but it was quite useless at 400 yards. They therefore considered what do to next.

On the one hand, they realized that if they continued to ski but broke through any patches of crusty snow, the poacher would surely hear them coming and could easily open fire on them with his rifle. Moreover, much earlier, his dog might begin to bark as soon as it saw or smelled them, and thus alert him. On the other hand, their job was to follow Captain Anderson's orders and to protect the animals of the park, which meant confronting the poacher directly—regardless of any risk they might run themselves. They decided to take action.

Burgess therefore carried the Colt in one hand (photos show that in Yellowstone at that time, skiers used only one wooden pole, not two, so a skier could carry a weapon in his free hand), and the two began moving carefully across the 400 yards of snow that separated them from Howell. Their luck held: the snow was very quiet, the dog did not bark, and How-ell was concentrating on the task of decapitating the bison he had killed. Indeed, he did not even notice them until they were only 15 to 20 feet away—i.e., within very easy killing range for any revolver marksman.

As soon as Howell saw them, he dropped his knife and tried to get his rifle to his shoulder. Burgess then cocked the revolver and shouted at Howell to drop the rifle and to surrender or be killed. Howell had the good sense to surrender, and Burgess and Troike would later receive official commendations for their bravery. Howell was the first person prosecuted under the provisions of the Lacey Act.

John Muir on Yellowstone in 1898

After the great environmentalist John Muir died in 1914, President Theodore Roosevelt wrote of him: "He was a dauntless soul. Not only are his books delightful ... but he was also—what few nature-lovers are—a man able to influence contemporary thought and action on the subject to which he had devoted his life."[8]

In 1898, Muir described the park in these warm, accurate, and poetic words:

> However orderly your excursions, or aimless, again and again amid the calmest, stillest scenery you will be brought to a standstill hushed and awe-stricken before phenomena wholly new to you. Boiling springs and huge deep pools of purest green and azure water, thousands of them, are plashing

and heaving in these high, cool mountains as if a fierce furnace fire were burning beneath each one of them; and a hundred geysers, white torrents of boiling water and steam, like inverted waterfalls, are ever and anon rushing up out of the hot, black underworld.[9]

Regarding Yellowstone Lake itself, Muir had this to say:

Yellowstone Lake ... lies at a height of nearly 8,000 [feet] above the level of the sea, amid dense black forests and snowy mountains. Around its winding, wavering shores, closely forested and picturesquely varied with promontories and bays, the distance is more than 100 miles....

No other lake in North America of equal area lies so high as the Yellowstone, or gives birth to so noble a river.... In calm weather it is a magnificent mirror for the woods and mountains and sky, now pattered with hail and rain, now roughened with sudden storms that send waves to fringe the shores and its borders of sand and gravel.

The Absaroka Mountains and the Wind River Plateau on the east and south pour their gathered waters into it, and the river issues from the north side in a broad, smooth, stately current, silently gliding with such serene majesty that one fancies it knows the vast journey of four thousand miles that lies before it.[10]

The Muir Woods National Monument was established in northern California in 1908, and John Muir has been honored ever since as the father of the modern environmental movement in North America.

The 1963 Leopold Report

This report, officially entitled *Wildlife Management in the National Parks*, reviewed a complex and controversial subject very carefully and made a number of recommendations for change that have stood the test of time.[11] The Leopold Report's recommendations were upheld in 2002 by the National Academy of Sciences[12] report, entitled *Ecological Dynamics on Yellowstone's Northern Range.* Since both the summary and the findings of this report are still considered by experts to be valid today, they are cited in this book.

The basic concept of this creative and well-received report was that wildlife in the park must be managed not by culling (i.e., by killing) or by otherwise directly controlling animal populations, but instead by relying on "natural regulation." This policy is also known today known as ecological management. It means, in most cases, simply letting nature take its own course and thus allowing animal populations to find their own levels, no matter whether these levels are above or below the present levels.

The Leopold Report also broke new ground in environmental thinking by holding out an ambitious and idealistic national park ideal. It is worth citing this at some length. The report famously alludes to the goal of recreating an unaltered national park landscape:

> As a primary goal, we would recommend that the biotic associations [i.e., the relationships between different species] within each park be maintained, or where necessary recreated, as nearly as possible in the condition that prevailed when the area was first visited by the white man. A national park should represent a vignette of primitive America.
>
> Restoring the primitive scene is not easily done nor can it be done completely.... Some species are extinct.... Exotic plants, animals, and diseases are here to stay. All these limitations we fully realize.
>
> Yet, if the goal cannot be fully achieved it can be approached. A reasonable illusion of primitive America could be recreated, using the utmost in skill, judgment, and ecologic sensitivity. This in our opinion should be the objective of every national park and monument.[13]

In a book on *Ecological Dynamics on Yellowstone's Northern Range* that was published in 2002, the National Academies Press added the following caveat:

> The underlying belief that national parks should, to the maximum extent possible, harbor natural ecosystems has fostered extensive debates about how to react to ecosystem changes in the parks and how to determine when such change is caused by humans....
>
> The problem of differentiating human-caused from natural change is complex because no ecosystem on earth is entirely unaffected by human activity. Thus, defining "natural" is difficult.
>
> In view of the profound changes that have occurred within the GYE [Greater Yellowstone Ecosystem], such as increased development of roads and housing adjacent to the park, it is no longer possible to have an ecosystem that is truly natural—that is, containing the same numbers and distributions of all the species of plants and animals that were there before European settlement, let alone before Native American populations arrived. YNP [Yellowstone National Park] may contain many of the same species, but they can no longer respond to change as they used to by dispersal and migration.[14]

Since the Leopold Report, times have changed a great deal and there have been a number of new, widespread, volatile, and potentially far-reaching developments. These include biodiversity loss, climate change, habitat fragmentation, expanded land uses, groundwater withdrawals, invasive species, as well as air, noise, and light pollution.

The parks, national forests, and other outdoor areas held in trust for the pubic that in earlier years may have slumbered quietly for many decades in wild or lightly-populated rural areas now find themselves surrounded by accelerating human demands, ranging from recreational uses to energy developments.

At the same time, changing political priorities in the United States have limited public funding for these lands held in public trust. It now seems unlikely that these spending constraints will be lifted anytime soon.

What is perhaps most evident today is that the overarching goals for the National Park Service must be (1) to husband its limited resources in order to cope with environmental changes that are not yet well understood but are certain to be far-reaching, and (2) to preserve the ecological integrity and historical authenticity of Yellowstone Park itself.[15]

Bear-Management Closes the Garbage Pits in 1970

Bears have lived in the Yellowstone area for thousands of years but they were never fed by human beings, although the first Native Americans and, much later, the first Caucasians saw them frequently. The men of the Hayden Geological Survey encountered the Yellowstone bears in 1871, and several members of that party relished bear meat during their trip. Geologist Albert Charles Peale, for example, reported that it "tasted deliciously."[16]

Nevertheless, at that time, the region's bears were, at best, simply tolerated, not encouraged. The early park superintendent Philetus W. Norris reported shooting some of them, and it is thought others may have been killed by poisoned carcasses laid out to eradicate wolves and other scavengers. It appears that the bear population in Yellowstone toward the end of the 19th century was noticeable but was not any cause for any anti-bear policies.

The idea of feeding bears garbage from the Yellowstone hotels arose more or less by accident. In the late 1880s, hotels were built around the park, and bears started feeding at the garbage dumps there. Indeed, by 1900, according to the historian Paul Schullery, "the bear replaced Old Faithful as the most recognizable symbol of the park," and that bear feeding sites sprang up across the park, rising with the growing number of visitors.

Tourists really loved seeing the bears eat, and the end result was a public relations triumph (for the people, that is, if not for the bears). At night, under the watchful eye of an armed ranger, hundreds of visitors watched crowds of grizzly bears paw through heaps of hotel garbage. An occasional additional thrill for viewers were the loud, spectacular fights between big bears attracted to the same delicacies.

According to Horace M. Albright, the superintendent of Yellowstone in the 1920s and later the second director of the National Park Service, bears now began spending a lot more time along the roads, realizing that, if they did, people might well stop and throw food to them. Some of the most intrepid black bears even became known to the rangers as "beggar bears" or as "hold-up bears" because they would stand on the edges of roads until the drivers stopped and gave them some food.

But not all the bear feedings took place at the big garbage dumps. Many bears learned to loiter near the roads and then to wander up the lines of slow-moving wagons (and, later, of cars), expecting to be fed. Many visitors were only too happy to oblige. Albright told visitors that

> These black bears were not vicious, but they were big and powerful, and could be dangerous if provoked, and we constantly warned visitors that the bears were wild animals and should be treated with caution. But visitors would often hold out food with their hand, hoping to get a bear to rise up on its hind legs and reach. Occasionally the bear would bite or scratch the visitor in trying to reach the food. Then, of course, we would get an impassioned complaint about the "vicious" bear.[17]

Yellowstone's officially-tolerated large-scale food handouts lasted far too long—namely, until 1970, when the open-pit garbage dumps in Yellowstone were finally closed. These dumps had weaned bears away from their natural foods and gave rise to many incidents between ignorant people and hungry bears, which often resulted in "problem bears" having to be relocated or killed.

According to the Yellowstone Park Foundation, in the years between 1931 and 1969, there was an estimated total of 48 bear-related injuries to visitors in the park, and over 100 cases of property damage resulting from bears trying to get at food in cars or tearing down the thin wooden fences that stood between them and a free meal.

Today, feeding table scraps to bears or giving them access to any garbage pits is forbidden and is quite unthinkable. The path to environmental wisdom now consists simply of letting bears (and all other wildlife) live in Yellowstone as unfettered and as unsupervised as possible.

For the record, since 1979 Yellowstone has hosted over 118 million visits. During this time, 44 people were injured by grizzly bears in the park. For all park visitors combined, the chances of being injured by a grizzly bear are approximately 1 in 2.7 million visits. The risk is significantly lower for people who do not leave the highly developed areas, and higher for anyone hiking in the remote backcountry.[18]

The 1988 "Summer of Fire"[19]

Fire is one of the key factors in the ecology of the Greater Yellowstone Ecosystem. Native plant species have adapted so that they can survive and, indeed, in some cases even *flourish* after periodic fires. The National Park Service's goal is to restore fire as a natural and desirable process whenever and wherever this is safely feasible.

Fire encourages habitat diversity by removing the forest overstory (i.e., the trees in a forest whose crowns constitute this layer), thus allowing different plant communities to become established. At the same time, fire prevents the trees from taking over and choking off open grasslands.

Fire also increases the speed in which nutrients can become available to plants by releasing them from the leaves and litter of the forest floor, and by hastening the decomposition of minerals in the soil. Indeed, without frequent small fires and occasional big fires, leaf litter and deadfalls will build up much faster than they can decay, and will thus be unable to return their nutrients to the soil.

Moreover, trees in Greater Yellowstone are unusually well-adapted to fire. The cones of the lodgepole pine tree, for example, will never release their seeds until the resin sealing them has melted at a temperature of at least 113 degrees F. This trigger-mechanism helps to make sure that the seeds do not spread out into the wider world until fire has already created the best possible conditions for their survival, namely, less litter on the forest floor, and plenty of sunlight streaming in through an open canopy of trees.

For 14,000 years, fires have been key factors in shaping the Greater Yellowstone Ecosystem. Historically, the very long (100 to 300–year) intervals between major fires always gave trees the chance to mature and to build up their seed banks. Lightning strikes may ignite dozens of forest fires during a single summer, but most of them go out naturally after burning less than half an acre. On rare occasions, wind-driven fires can destroy very large areas of forest.

During the "Summer of Fire" in 1988, uncontrollable forest fires started by more than 18 lightning strikes torched about 1.4 million acres in the Greater Yellowstone Ecosystem—the result of extremely warm, dry, and very windy weather, coupled with an extensive and highly-flammable forest cover. It was not until September 1988 that only light rain and snow could finally stop the inexorable advance of the flames.

Contrary to media reports and public speculation, these huge fires killed very few park animals. Out of an estimated 40,000 to 50,000 elk, for example, only about 345 of them died. Other animal losses were modest, too: 36 deer, 12 moose, six black bears, and nine bison. Since 1988, in the wake of the fires, tiny seeds have become young trees; young trees have become new forests; and, on balance, it is now certain that no lasting damage has been done to Yellowstone's ecology by these fierce fires.

In summary, it can therefore be said that what the fires of 1988 did was to create *a mosaic of deeply-burned, partially-burned, and unburned areas.* These soon became natural firebreaks and can now support a greater variety of plant and animal life than before. Vegetation capable of feeding another major fire is expected to be rare for decades to come—except for any extraordinary and unforeseen situations brought about by severe climate change or other unique situations.

Yellowstone's Administrative and Research Offices

The Office of the Superintendent is located at park headquarters in Mammoth Hot Springs. The Superintendent has been in Mammoth ever since the second Superintendent, Philetus Norris, arrived in 1877. (The first Superintendent came to the park only a couple of times.) The Superintendent has the responsibility of managing the 2.2 million–acre park with its staff of 800 National Park Service employees and a budget of approximately $33 million.[20] Some of the other key park units include the following:

The Yellowstone Center for Resources, located in Mammoth, was created in 1993 to centralize the park's science and resource management functions.[21] Its goals are to gather, manage, and analyze data in order to conserve the park's natural and cultural resources; to understand and mitigate the environmental and historic consequences of park management; to preserve and curate rare, sensitive, and valuable natural and cultural resources; to work with partners to meet resource management needs; and, last but by no means least, to promote the transfer of knowledge both to other park staff members and to visitors to the park.

To pursue these goals, the Center for Resources has five branches, which focus on Wildlife and Aquatic Resources, Physical Resources and Climate Science, Vegetation and Resources, Cultural Resources (e.g., Native American culture), and Environmental Compliance and Science Coordination.

Yellowstone's Heritage and Research Center opened in Gardiner, Montana (near the north entrance to the park), in 2005.[22] Its historic collections present the cultural and natural history of the world's first national park and the present conditions of its resources. The collections reflect the history and sciences of the park; changes in perception and meanings over time; and the interactions between people and nature. Specimens range from geology and natural history, on the one hand, to tribal and European and American cultural items, on the other.

The collections storage facility also houses the park's herbarium and archeology lab, and features small rotating exhibits in the lobby. A U.S. National Park Service historian is based at the Center and is a useful source of information on the history of the park. The collections play key roles in resource management, research, and educational programs. They also serve as baseline databases for the park's natural, archeological and cultural assets.

With several million park records and many other historical items now in its keeping, Yellowstone has one of the largest collections in the U.S. National Park Service. Researchers must complete their preliminary research at other archives, libraries, or museum collections first. The Research Center itself has only a very limited reference staff, and all research must be done on-site in the museum reference room or in the library reading room.

"Yellowstone Forever" is a nonprofit partner of Yellowstone National Park and was the result of a merger in 2009 of two closely-related environmental bodies, namely, the Yellowstone Association and the Yellowstone Foundation. The Yellowstone Forever Institute, which provides educational programs in the field, has introduced thousands of visitors to the park's natural wonders. Programs have ranged from one day to three weeks in length, and highlight the park's wildlife, geothermal sights, history, and wilderness areas.

13

Winter: Animal
and Human Uses

In the first part of this chapter, it will be the wild animals of the Yellowstone area that merit attention; in the second part, it will be the human uses of winter in Yellowstone. Winters in Yellowstone National Park will always mean much smaller crowds and an abundance of crisp, snowy days and nights.[1] The park itself is always open (except in the rare case of a medical emergency, such as a potentially-lethal virus), but when the park roads themselves are closed due to snow, the park is then accessible only to hardy oversnow travelers.

Overland transportation is then reduced to the adventures offered by skis, snowshoes, snowmobiles, and even snowcoaches (described later). Staying warm in a guided snowcoach in midwinter in the high mountains, in the company of other like-minded visitors, is in its own way a modest adventure for young or old travelers who are unable or unwilling to spend time outdoors in the snow.

It is often mentioned by the park staff who live year-round in Yellowstone that winter is their own favorite season. Many park visitors who choose a winter trip to Yellowstone will come back for more in later years. It is extremely important for all winter visitors to keep in mind this prudent advice from the National Park Service:

> Yellowstone has miles of trails for the adventuresome skier and snow-shoer. Although track is set only on a few trails (i.e., only a few trails have cross-country tracks groomed into them), all unplowed roads and trails are open to cross-country skiing and snowshoeing.
>
> Whether you are skiing a groomed trail in a developed area or venturing into the backcountry, remember that you are traveling in wilderness with all its dangers: unpredictable wildlife, changing weather conditions, hydro-thermal areas, deep snow, open streams, and avalanches. *Your safety is not guaranteed.* Be prepared for any situation and know the limits of your ability.[2]

For wild animals, winter in Yellowstone is always a time and a place of great vulnerability.[3] Average winter highs there are 20–30 degrees F; average lows are 0–9 degrees F. The record low of -66 degrees F was reached at the Riverside Ranger Station, near the park's West Entrance, in 1933. Annual parkwide snowfall tends to be around 150 inches, but higher elevations can receive as much as 200 to 400 inches. Since Yellowstone is at a high elevation and is very affected by alpine weather systems, it is critical for human visitors to be very well-prepared when visiting or traveling there during the winter.

In winter-time, the animals must be able to endure extremes of cold and wind, and the absence of ready and familiar foods. Their tracks through deep snows are silent but powerful testimonies to their tenacious, but often unsuccessful, struggles to stay alive throughout the long, lean winter. All those that perish will soon become food for other creatures, great or small.

Winter in the Greater Yellowstone Ecosystem is always marked by cold temperatures, deep snow, and short days. Not surprisingly, the plants and animals living there are extremely well-adapted to these arduous conditions. For example, conifers keep their needles during the winter; this extends their ability to photosynthesize (use sunlight to synthesize nutrients from carbon dioxide and water).

Aspens and cottonwoods contain chlorophyll in their bark, which lets them photosynthesize before they produce any leaves. Bison, for their part, have elongated vertebrae to which their very strong neck muscles are attached. These permit them to sweep their huge heads from side to side and scrape off up to three feet of snow in order to graze on the grass beneath.

The National Park Service records some of the creative solutions that animals have developed over many thousands of years to cope with the Yellowstone winter. These are so interesting it is worth listing them here[4]:

- Both beavers and red squirrels cache food, i.e., they hide it, before the winter begins. The squirrels sometimes forget where they have buried their nuts: when this happens, the nuts grow into trees.
- To conserve heat, some birds roost with their heads tucked well into their back feathers.
- Deer mice huddle closely together to stay warm.
- Deer, elk, and bison prefer to follow each other through the deep snow in order to save their energy.
- By living *under the snow*, small mammals can find insulation,

protection from predators, and easier travel by moving through their little tunnels there.

- Grouse roost overnight by burrowing into the snow for insulation.
- Bison, elk, geese, and other animals find food, warmth, and safety in numbers by spending time in hydrothermal areas.
- Mammals molt their fur in late spring to early summer. The incoming guard hairs are longer and serve to protect the underfur. Extra underfur grows each fall, consisting of short, thick, and often wavy hairs designed to trap air.
- In addition, a sebaceous (oil) gland next to each air canal secretes oil which waterproofs the fur. Mammals also have muscular control of their fur: they can fluff it up to trap air when they are cold, and can sleek it down to remove the air when they get warm.
- The fur of river otters contains long guard hairs with interlocking spikes. These hairs protect the underfur, which is very wavy and dense in order to trap insulating air. Oil secreted from sebaceous glands stops water from contacting the otter's skin. When otters leave the water, they expel the air in their fur by rolling in the snow and then shaking their wet fur dry.
- Snowshoe hares, white-tailed jackrabbits, long-tailed weasels, and short-tailed weasels all turn white for the winter. This not only provides good camouflage in the snow, but the white color may also have evolved to keep these animals warm: these white hairs are hollow and contain insulating air rather than just pigment.
- Snowshoe hares have big, broad feet to spread their weight more evenly over the snow. Martens and lynx grow additional fur between their toes, which effectively gives them larger feet.
- Moose have special joints that allow them to swing their legs over the snow, rather than having to force their way through deep snow, as the elk must do.
- Chickadees' half-inch-thick layers of feathers keep them up to 100 degrees warmer than the outside temperature.

On the biochemical and physiological fronts, many other evolutionary small changes are evident, too:

- Mammals and waterfowl have counter-current heat exchange in their limbs that lets them stand in very cold water: cold temperatures cause the surface blood vessels to constrict, effectively shunting blood into the deeper veins that lie close to arteries. The cooled blood that returns from extremities is warmed by arterial blood traveling towards the extremities, thus conserving heat.

- At night, the body temperature of a chickadee drops from 108 degrees F to 88 degrees F. This lessens the sharp gradient between the temperature of their bodies and the external temperature. The net result is a 23 percent decrease in the amount of fat burned each night.
- Chorus frogs tolerate freezing by becoming severely diabetic in response to cold temperatures and to the formation of ice within their bodies. Their liver quickly converts glycogen to glucose, which enters the blood stream and serves as antifreeze. Within eight hours, the blood sugar level rises 200-fold. Remarkably, when a frog's internal ice content reaches 60–65 percent, the frog's heart and its breathing both stop. Within one hour of thawing, the frog's heart begins to beat again.

After this review of Yellowstone's animals during the winter, it is now time to discuss the human situation.[5] The first step is to understand that, in terms of winter use, the National Park Service is required to follow two mandates that sometimes contradict each other. The first is to preserve and safeguard Yellowstone's resources for future generations; the second is to make sure that the park is available and accessible for immediate public use and enjoyment. It is not easy to square this circle. In fact, as the National Park Service puts it so well, "Winter use planning is one of the most contentious issues for park managers and visitors, with the debate spanning *more than 80 years*."[6] This book's Appendix 4, which addresses the litigation and planning history of winter use in Yellowstone, offers a short summary of some of the key legal and administrative events of this long-running saga.

In the meantime, a few examples showing the inherent complexity of the issues involved in this debate may be of interest here[7]: A fundamental National Park Service Regulation prohibits snowmobile use in national parks when there is no specific rule authorizing their use. This is known as the "closed unless open rule." It means that without a specific rule, oversnow vehicles would be prohibited from entering Yellowstone.

The National Park Service has seven Winter Use Management Goals. In essence, these involve offering a high-quality, safe, and educational winter experience for visitors; providing for visitor and employee health and safety; protecting wilderness character and values; preserving pristine air quality; preserving natural soundscapes; mitigating impacts on wildlife; and coordinating with partners and gateway communities.

At the same time, the National Park Service must also focus on nine "Concerns Raised by the Public." Lightly edited, these concerns include the following:

> Overcrowding, i.e., too many people and/or machines; adverse visitor impacts on natural resources; noise and air pollution; availability of facilities and services for visitors; restrictions on the use of snowmobiles, now that trained guides are required; the importance to the local and regional economies of winter visitation; the use of groomed roads by wildlife as well as by oversnow vehicles; the problems inherent in displacing wildlife by an increasing number of human activities; and, last but by no means least, health and human safety.

In 2013, a final Winter Use Plan/Supplemental EIS (Environmental Impact Statement) to guide the future of winter use in Yellowstone National Park was signed. This document introduced the concept of managing oversnow vehicles by "transportation events." Since a group of snowmobiles traveling together is comparable to one snowcoach in terms of environmental impact, a transportation event is defined as a group of up to 10 snowmobiles, averaging 7 seasonally, or 1 snowcoach.

The town of West Yellowstone, Montana, may now be the snowmobile capital of the region.[8] These machines were first ridden in Yellowstone in 1963 but had become very controversial by the next decade. In fact, they were then officially banned from use in Glacier National Park because of the noise they made. In that era, the superintendent of the Yellowstone park was advocating the use of snowmobiles and snowcoaches (these latter are the multi-passenger, heated, tracked vehicles that protect winter travelers from the frigid winter air and are driven by trained guides) as safe ways for non-skiers to enjoy the park in relative comfort during the winter. He also maintained that the road-grooming required for snowmobiles was less expensive than trying to use big plows to keep the roads open for two-wheel-drive traffic. Perhaps as a result, in May 1974, all of Yellowstone's roads south of Mammoth Hot Springs were designated as official snowmobile routes.

In the late 1980s, the many negative traits of snowmobiles—noise, air pollution, disturbance of wildlife and vegetation—were being studied by park managers. At that time, winter visits to the park were in high gear, and West Yellowstone, together with other gateway communities, was very heavily invested in snowmobiling. During the next ten years, up to 70,000 snowmobiles entered Yellowstone each winter.

A Federal ban on these machines was proposed, but the hopes for, or the fears of, such a measure both faded when the political winds in

Washington, D.C., changed. The ban was never enacted. In 2002, Yellowstone broke into the news on this issue when the Yellowstone park rangers at the West Entrance donned respirators in order to dramatize the very high pollution levels caused by the exhaust of the snowmobiles lined up and waiting to enter the park.

More recently, the National Park Service has allowed a total of 720 snowmobiles, equipped with modern emissions and sound controls, per day—but only with a commercially-guided tour. An interesting development is that snowcoaches appear to be overtaking snowmobiles in terms of their popularity: far fewer than the allowed number of snowmobiles are now said to enter the park each day.

14

Conflicts of Interest

*The Old West vs. the New West—
a "Super-Wicked" Problem*

In recent years, the population of the 20 counties in the Greater Yellowstone Ecosystem has grown explosively. Data compiled by the Greater Yellowstone Inventory and Monitoring Network, for example, show that, in the 20 years from 1990 to 2010, the population in and near the Greater Yellowstone Ecosystem increased nearly 50 percent, i.e., from about 220,000 people to 323,000.[1]

As part of this still-accelerating process, a profound social and economic change is taking place in the region. Perhaps the best way to explore this change is, first, to think about the differences between the "Old West" (the long-term residents) and the "New West" (the newcomers) as a "super-wicked" problem, and, second, to flag some of the key factors in the long-running disputes over uses of the Greater Yellowstone Area. In condensed form, the following meanings are used here:

In 1973, a treatise defined a "wicked" problem as an intractable social planning problem that is difficult or impossible to solve because of its incomplete, contradictory, or ever-changing requirements. As a result, by definition, *a wicked problem does not have any single solution.*[2] Later, in a 2012 article, this insight was broadened to include "super-wicked" problems. These have four special characteristics, namely: (1) time is running out; (2) there is no central authority involved; (3) those who are trying to solve the problem are also the ones who are causing it; and (4) any possible positive or encouraging developments in the future are not being adequately considered.[3] Global climate change is therefore a classic example of such a "super-wicked" problem.

Historically, the mythic narrative of the Old West evokes cattle drives, vast open spaces, and cowboys-and-Indians frontiers. It is now remembered as a time of tough, self-made, and self-reliant men and women. Today, their Old West descendants are the rural men and women who are often politically and socially very conservative and whose small communities are largely based on the resource extraction and commodity production industries, such as forestry, ranching, mining, and fisheries, as well as tourism.[4] Organizations speaking for the Old West school of thought include the Blue Ribbon Coalition, a pro-motorized recreation group that advocates increasing use of off-road vehicles.

One of the fundamental conflicts of interest between the partisans of the Old West and those of the New West is, not surprisingly, *money*. A local Old West fisherman living in the Jackson Hole area, for example, joked with us that the established millionaires of that region have now been surpassed by the New West *billionaires*. The New West thus coexists, sometimes uneasily, with the Old West.

The New West population tends to be younger, more liberal, better educated, and probably more familiar with world events outside the United States. They emphasize the importance of environmentally-sensitive and people-sensitive economic development that is ultimately subject to regulation by the Federal government. Organizations such as the Greater Yellowstone Coalition are the advocates of the New West, calling for better protection of the lands, waters, and wildlife of the 20-million-acre Greater Yellowstone Ecosystem.

One thing that partisans of both the Old West and the New West do have in common is a love of world-class outdoor recreation set in magnificent surroundings. The Greater Yellowstone region is, fortunately, one of the very best places in the world for them to pursue these interests.

It is worth adding a bit more here about these two Wests. The resource-extraction economies and the "anything goes" economic development policies of the Old West—the industrial and agricultural West before the 1960s—frequently used and abused Western lands and waters without any regard for the environmental fallout. These policies involved such undertakings as hydraulic and open pit mining; clear-cut logging; extensive cattle and sheep grazing; intensive farming; heavy pesticide use; gas and oil production; road-building; the expansion of highways, towns and cities; and excessive use of scarce water resources. Not surprisingly, these projects often harmed the land, the air, the waters, and the wildlife.

Many of these activities rested on a philosophical foundation of very conservative political doctrines which elevate the importance of individual freedom. Still very popular in the Rocky Mountain West (and elsewhere, of course, in the United States) today, these doctrines stress the primacy of private property rights and the need for only a very minimalist (if any) role of the Federal government in regional, state, local or personal affairs. As one professional environmentalist describes in a 2020 email to the authors, "There is now so much 'stakeholder fatigue' from New West listening sessions and surveys that most Old West landowners are nauseated."

In the distant past, because of local residents' then-deeply-held anti-park convictions, there was a great deal of local opposition to Yellowstone Park during its earliest years. Some residents, for example, believed that strict Federal prohibitions against developing natural resources and allowing human settlements in the park would surely throttle any future economic development in their whole region and would thus impoverish them. They therefore wanted to reduce the size of the park and to encourage mining, hunting, and logging there. As a result, numerous bills were introduced into Congress, usually by Montana representatives, who tried, unsuccessfully, to remove what they considered to be the onerous Federal land-use restrictions.

The liberal, pro-environment, post–1990 economies of the New West, on the other hand, have largely been designed to avoid environmental damage. Two modest examples are, rather than automatically clear-cutting huge tracts of forest lands, smaller-scale and more selective logging, which is much easier on the land, is now often used instead.

Many communities in the Greater Yellowstone Area are now looking for better ways to cultivate their growing economies and, at the same time, to preserve the splendid natural landscapes that draw so many people to live, work, and play there. In fact, there is truly no easy way to do both at the same time. Indeed, this is a classic example of a "super-wicked" problem.

There are a few positive straws in the wind on this issue. A few years ago in Teton County, Wyoming, then–Commissioner Luther Propst gave an interview to the *High Country News* as he was stepping down from the helm of the organization he had founded, the Sonoran Institute, which is still devoted to highlighting the intersections of economy and ecology, especially by calling attention to the many ways in which wise landscape stewardship can deliver dividends for the quality of life, including better prospects for the creatures that depend on human protection. Commissioner Propst said:

> The problem is that the Lords of Yesteryear [the established financial interests of the region] never disappeared as we were promised and the challenges of the New West are far worse than we were promised. I don't want a West of man-camps and gas field booms, nor a West of precious tourist

towns that exist to feed a global cowboy/mountain-man/Disney/ski-resort/ New-Age fantasy, surrounded by busted towns that are ghettos for workers.[5]

In a 2019 interview, the environmentalist Dennis Glick, who had previously worked at the Sonoran Institute under Commissioner Propst, had some insights into the conflicting interests and challenges at play in the Greater Yellowstone Ecosystem. Lightly edited, this is the gist of what he wrote[6]:

- Bozeman, Montana, which forms the urban crown of the Greater Yellowstone Area and which affects, directly or indirectly, all the smaller communities around it, is one of the fastest-growing regions of the United States. It is expected to double in size in less than 20 years to a total of almost a quarter of a million people. At Big Sky, Montana, only 44 miles from Bozeman, about $1 billion worth of new construction and infrastructure improvements is now underway—on top of the considerable infrastructure that already exists there.
- The significant growth and transformation of areas around Yellowstone has made it very hard for local residents to live and work there, and has greatly—and adversely—affected the local wilderness and wildlife. Newcomers bring with them a raft of local problems that lightly-staffed local official offices may not be equipped to handle.
- Teton County, Wyoming, is now one of the richest counties in the United States, so living there can easily be well beyond the reach of people earning only middle-class incomes.
- Local farms and ranchlands in Greater Yellowstone are rapidly becoming subdivisions or second-home sites for former city-dwellers. One result is that many rural towns that were once "joined at the hip" with the agricultural economy continue to wither as the agricultural economy is being transformed into a service economy.

A final point that Glick made bears repeating: "Welcome to the New West. It's not the environmental paradise we had all imagined. And while it does have its bright side, if we don't do a better job of conserving those things that we love about this place, its dark side will become ever more apparent."[7]

An important step in trying to bridge the economic, political, and cultural rural-urban divide is to encourage a dialogue between the Old West, who are now or who can become good stewards of the land, and the broader New West conservation community.

In a similar vein, writing for the *National Geographic* magazine in a 2016 issue entitled "Yellowstone: The Battle for the American West," journalist David Quammen warned his readers that "there are ways in which Yellowstone is in danger of being loved to death."[8] He also made the following points (shortened and edited here):

Although about four million tourists are visiting Yellowstone each year, it is actually *the purchase of private lands* around the park that poses a much bigger threat. As more and more people buy more and more property around Yellowstone, they put up cabins, build roads, keep predatory animals (dogs and cats), and gradually transform the wild landscape, with its open pastures, wet meadows, and forest land, into a human-dominated landscape. This poses enormous problems for the migrating bears and elk that formerly could move, unhindered, throughout the region.

Because the animals in Yellowstone often need to migrate outside the park in winter, the lands in the Greater Yellowstone Ecosystem will play a very important role in the park's continued existence. The fundamental reason is this:

> Yellowstone Park is not an island: it is part of this larger system, this larger body of wild landscape, and it needs the rest of this wild landscape just as the rest of the wild landscape needs it. If the elk can't migrate into the park, then this creates problems for the wolves, for the grizzlies, and for a lot of other creatures. These things all fit together. The elk are the most abundant large herbivores in the Yellowstone ecosystem; there are thousands and thousands of them; they migrate in and out, so these migration routes need to stay open.[9]

In more general terms, three major themes now dominate the literature which outlines the distinctions between Old West and the New West groups in the Greater Yellowstone Area. These themes—federalism, science, and the relationship between people and nature—are discussed below.[10]

Federalism (National vs. Local Control) and Yellowstone Politics

Different, and sharply-conflicting, theories of American politics play pivotal roles in the Yellowstone region. Old West groups think that the issues of Greater Yellowstone are the ones that affect local citizens the most. For this reason, they believe that locally-elected officials, such as Congressmen and Congresswomen from Idaho, Montana, and Wyoming, plus local interest groups, should alone have all the power they need to make political decisions affecting their own region.

New West groups, on the other hand, believe that Yellowstone is a region of national or even international concern. For this reason, they think that the best policy-mix consists of elected national officials from outside the tri-state Yellowstone area; of members of national-based interest groups; and of concerned citizens and residents, no matter where in the world they may live.

Science and Yellowstone Politics

In theory, science might become a useful bridge between the two Wests, but it seems highly unlikely at this time. Three reasons are: Men and women in the New West camp tend to support "natural," i.e., hands-off, environmental management. By the same token, they also call for better ecosystem protection and for more biodiversity through the safeguarding of rare and endangered species. They believe that science is the most reliable guide for making wise environmental choices.

Old West groups, on the other hand, tend to argue that environmental problems should be resolved instead, chiefly by using better technology. Their view of science is "human-centered": they believe that nature should be managed and directed by local experts, who in the process will, in their view, also increase the productive use of natural resources. Moreover, Old West supporters tend to be rurally-based, not highly educated, and to have a utilitarian, provincial, and skeptical view of science. They are especially said to distrust much of New West science as being "too mystical and New Age."

The Relationship Between People and Nature

The keystone in the arch of New West philosophy is the hands-off approach to ecosystem management. According to this school of thought, which is now the policy of Yellowstone National Park, human involvement in natural processes should be held to a minimum. The extraction of natural resources is judged to be much less important than maintaining or increasing a region's biodiversity.

Conversely, the Old West's philosophy is based on the importance of active resource use and management by locally-based residents. Such residents are inclined to believe that only they, and not "ignorant outsiders," are by far the best judges of their own destinies.

From a broad perspective, given the significant differences of opinion between the partisans of the two Wests, it is not surprising that many of the major policy disputes in the Greater Yellowstone Area are still very far from being resolved.[11] It now seems reasonable to conclude that the very mind-sets which participants bring with them into discussions of these disputes all but guarantee that little, if any, progress will be made in resolving them any time soon.

Typically, proposed solutions to "super-wicked" environmental problems are accepted by some, but by no means all, of the interested parties involved. The results are often protracted lawsuits, lengthy administrative delays, complicated rule-making, intense and conflicting public relations appeals, and bad feelings all around.

This outcome seems to be common, no matter what solutions are involved. Proposed solutions can be technical, scientific, economic, or some combination thereof. Unhappily, none of them usually end any policy conflicts. Some examples:

- In Yellowstone, efforts by New West supporters to stop snowmobiling in the park spurred snowmobile makers to propose snowmobile access to the park by cleaner-burning four-stroke snowmobiles. Critics then complained that the new, cleaner snowmobiles still stressed the winter wildlife by forcing animals off the groomed snow trails and into the deeper unplowed snow.
- Although for more than two decades, ecological science had advocated the merits of returning wolves to Yellowstone, the success of this policy after the reintroduction of wolves in 1995–1996 did not end criticism from Old West supporters, many of whom continue to be anti-wolf.
- Ranchers are now compensated for the loss of their livestock to wolves, but these payments have not reduced the intensity of the fight over wolf restoration.[12] In Idaho, for example, anti-wolf groups attacked the compensation program as "nothing more than a publicity tool" for pro-wolf New West supporters. In 2004, the Idaho Anti-Wolf Coalition even claimed that ranchers would never be compensated for 90 percent of the livestock that is lost to wolves but is never officially recorded.

Moving beyond the "official" positions of the two Wests, it is notable that, given the increasing highly-mobile population and the greater cultural diversity of the Greater Yellowstone region, the individual freedoms of one citizen may well conflict with the individual freedoms of another citizen.[13] For example, one person may be able to drive his 4-wheel-drive vehicle off-road through the mountains, but another person may want to enjoy some peace and quiet during a hiking trip with her young children.

There is no way to resolve this dilemma other than by calling for maximum tolerance, restraint, and good fellowship on all sides. This is fundamentally necessary because neither the partisans of the Old West nor those of the New West can be said to have a monopoly on truth.

Historically, the Old West has often shrugged off the human casualties and environmental costs of its own outdoor policies by tacitly appealing to an old French saying that translates as: "If you are going to make an omelet, you have to break eggs."

The New West, for its part, often turns a blind eye to the downside of its own policies. For example, its desire for a very wide range of housing, food, drink, travel, entertainment, and leisure-time activities has contributed to increasing pollution, soaring land and house prices, and pockets of working-class poverty in a sea of urban-generated middle-class wealth.

15

Monitoring Vital Signs
The Health of the Ecosystem Today

Monitoring vital signs in the Greater Yellowstone Ecosystem is essential to define a "safe operating zone," namely, the natural or historical range of variations from which any departure can be detected as soon as possible and for which remedial measures, if feasible, can quickly be considered. Writing in 2019 in the National Park Service's report on "Vital Signs: Monitoring Yellowstone's Ecosystem Health," Andrew M. Ray of the Greater Yellowstone Inventory and Monitoring Network had this to say:

> While early proponents [of the park] helped establish the management boundaries that define and protect the diverse habitats that together form Yellowstone, these boundaries and the added protections of neighboring public lands that make up the Greater Yellowstone Ecosystem *will not shelter the park from outside forces that are changing the health of its ecosystems (e.g., climate change, non-native species, wildlife disease, and land-use change on areas bordering the park).*
>
> Temperatures on earth are rising, droughts and extreme weather events are becoming increasingly common, and biodiversity declines are widespread … a monitoring program analogous to that used in human health [therefore] offers a meaningful strategy for assessing and tracking the health of Yellowstone's ecosystems….
>
> Fortunately, the National Park Service has been championing the monitoring of select vital signs in Yellowstone and neighboring public lands for more than a decade….
>
> [Three themes have emerged from this effort:] (1) the need for increasing the number of vital signs monitored; (2) the importance of expanding monitoring program across the [whole ecosystem]; and (3) the value of regular communication of trends in vital signs to decision makers and the public.[1]

Broad-based monitoring at the ecosystem or regional levels now makes it possible to study environmental events that cannot be handled by small-scale laboratory or field experiments. Two good examples here are (1) our current state of knowledge about the lives of antelope, mule deer, elk, grizzly bears, and other animals; and (2) our estimates of the future of the snowpack in the Yellowstone region.

Our knowledge of the first point comes from monitoring the movements of the animals during their annual migrations across the vast Yellowstone ecosystem. For example, coordinated long-term modeling of grizzly bears and of one of their important food sources—whitebark pine trees—has given ecologists important insights into the status of populations of these iconic species.

Programs to monitor vital signs are now in place at the park, regional and national levels. They can indicate if environmental events are still within the natural range of present or historic variation, or whether they are instead now nearing the limits that should not be crossed. For example, when non-native lake trout were detected in the food chain of Yellowstone Lake, action had to be taken quickly to prevent this ecosystem from tipping into an undesirable and potentially unrecoverable state in which the large, voracious lake trout would soon wipe out the native cutthroat trout. These cutthroat trout are important to the Yellowstone region on both ecological and recreational grounds.

Global warming changes the snow and the ice cover of the land by increasing the amount of precipitation that falls as rain rather than as snow, and by speeding up snowmelt. Climate scientists have already noted these trends in the American West and believe that atmospheric circulation may also be leading to an overall decrease in the amount of precipitation. (Atmospheric precipitation is the large-scale movement of air which, together with the circulation of the oceans, redistributes thermal energy over the surface of the Earth.)

In much of the western United States, snowpacks have declined substantially since the 1980s, but there is still a lot of snow in and near Yellowstone. For example, the average seasonal snowfall is about 13.5 feet at Lake Yellowstone, 8.2 feet at the Lamar Ranger Station, 5.9 feet at Mammoth, 15 feet at Old Faithful, 8 feet at Tower Falls, and nearly 24 feet at one site along the Snake River.

All this is important because winter recreation in Yellowstone, such as oversnow travel on the park roads, skiing, and snowshoeing, now contribute significantly to the local economy. Long-term vital signs monitoring of precipitation and temperatures can contribute significantly to the quality of snowpack forecasts. These signs also support other predictions of future changes in patterns of snowfall, namely, that under the warmer climate change conditions that are now forecast, there will be less snow in the Yellowstone mountains—and therefore, in the years ahead, less water running downstream into lower elevations for human and other uses there.

The bottom line is that winters are now getting shorter in the Yellowstone area. Indeed, it is estimated that, in 30 years or less, the snowpack will retreat from West Yellowstone, Montana, by mid–April, i.e., up to three weeks earlier than it does now. If so, the popular road to Old Faithful will be able to support snowmobiles and snowcoaches only 40 percent of the current winter-season days.

Any report card on the Yellowstone region must, to be useful, include creatures both great and small. In 2005, for example, the presence of amphibians was chosen as one of the 12 vital signs for the region. Perhaps the smallest (one inch long at maturity) but by far the loudest amphibian in Yellowstone is the male boreal chorus frog. These frogs reproduce in very shallow seasonal wetlands that are subject to annual weather-driven changes, e.g., the melting snowpack. Less snowpack moisture corresponds to fewer wetlands available for breeding and, therefore, a reduction in chorus frog breeding. For these reasons, in Yellowstone and Grand Teton parks, the boreal frog has thus become one of the ecologists' touchstones for the seasonal wetlands with their teeming biological diversity.

The need to monitor the health of wild fish populations was first understood in 1996 after a parasite almost destroyed the trout in the Madison River of Montana. This fish-kill suggested that continuous monitoring of wild fish health might be necessary.

The mass mortality of mountain whitefish along the Yellowstone River south of Livingston, Montana, in 2016 underscored the importance of understanding such fish mortalities. This die-off was caused by Proliferative Kidney Disease (PKD), which develops only when water temperatures exceed 59 degrees F for several weeks or longer. Further studies of PKD kills are needed to understand what factors cause these losses.

Insects are of course a vital sign in the Greater Yellowstone Ecosystem. It is certain that as a result of the endless co-evolution of plants and insects, they are dependent on each other for survival. Insects pollinate most flowering plants: in many cases their relationships are so close that without its pollinator a plant simply cannot reproduce. The opposite side of the coin is that without its food source an insect simply cannot survive.

Insects also provide an essential connection between plants and invertebrates. Indeed, without insects, many food chains would simply collapse. For example, during the hot dry summer months when higher-quality foods become scarcer and Yellowstone grizzly bears are thus stressed for food, insects such as bees, wasps, and army cutworm moths become an alternative and usually reliable food source.

Insects also play important roles in the crucial process of nutrient recycling by moving soil, consuming carrion, and decomposing organic matter. Despite the importance of insects in the Yellowstone region, however, there is currently no park-wide or region-wide program in place to monitor insect populations or communities. In this region, which has such a large population of big animals, the unsung carrion beetle is especially important in the process of decomposition. In fact, more than 50 species of carrion beetle are present in the Northern Range, where they are heavily dependent on the carcasses of the many hoofed mammals that die there each year.[2]

Large, readily visible plants are technically known as macrophytes. Of the 41 vital signs selected for Yellowstone National Park, nearly two of every five (that is, 40 percent) are connected to macrophytes. Like amphibians, they can also provide clues of distressed aquatic populations and habitats. The potential for invasive macrophytes to make their way into the Greater Yellowstone Ecosystem was identified in 2019 by the National Park Service as

> a looming formidable concern for the conservation and management of regional aquatic ecosystems. Continued research and monitoring will improve our understanding of the role and importance of macrophytes in aquatic ecosystems and will alert park managers to the unwelcome arrival of invasive species.[3]

When invasive species are introduced into a native plant community, there can be numerous negative effects. For this reason, long-term monitoring of vegetation communities helps to develop both a "present model" showing the current situation, and a "transition model" that identifies any new situation in which a change in species composition or abundance has been generated by fire, beetles or other external events.

Whitebark pine trees are both a keystone and a foundation species that has a strong impact on the biodiversity and productivity of high-elevation and subalpine communities in the Yellowstone area.[4] (A keystone species is one that has a disproportionate impact on its ecosystem when compared to its abundance. A foundation species is usually a primary producer that dominates an ecosystem in abundance and influence.)

Because of these qualities and due to the many threats it faces, the whitebark pine has been chosen by the Bureau of Land Management, the National Park Service, and the U.S. Forest Service as an important regional and cross-jurisdictional vital sign. Perhaps the greatest threat this tree now has to face is a native insect, the mountain pine beetle.

This is one of the most aggressive and damaging creatures in the western pine forests. Its behavior is directly tied to temperature: the 2006–2009 warming period, for example, was at first combined with an abundant food supply. It generated a "perfect storm" in the eruption of these beetles at epidemic levels across the whitebark pine forests of the Greater Yellowstone Ecosystem. By 2009, however, the onset of cold weather early in the winter killed many mountain pine beetle larvae before they could adjust to the cold. The result was that in many areas the beetle populations returned to their pre-warming levels. The bad news was that the three-year mountain pine beetle outbreak killed many larger, reproducing whitebark pine trees, but left the smaller-size, and typically *non-reproducing*, trees more or less intact.

Subsequent ecological studies showed this outbreak was unusual because it lay well outside the historic range of variability of mountain pine beetle attacks. This fact suggests that a constantly-warming climate may, thanks to these beetles, result in heavy losses in some of the whitebark pine forests.[5] Moreover, these trees have had to face not only beetles but also blister rust, wildfires, and climate-change-induced drought. For some regional and local populations of trees, a tipping point may be near, so continued monitoring is essential.

In an attempt to summarize the present but rather complicated status of the ecological health of the Greater Yellowstone Ecosystem, the following points can usefully be considered.[6]

Species declines and extinctions are now going on in the world at rates unprecedented in both human and geological history, often due to human-caused factors. In this 22 million–acre ecosystem, however, almost two-thirds of the lands are managed by United States Federal agencies, which use well-tested approaches to achieve and to maintain the health of these lands for the benefit of future generations. The successes of this policy are matters of record.

For example, grizzly bear populations have grown from about 150 bears in 1975 to more than 700 bears today. Wolves, wiped out by the 1930s, were reintroduced into the ecosystem between 1995 and 1997; despite some human-caused mortalities (due chiefly to state-licensed hunters), wolves are now widespread there. Efforts are being made to protect cutthroat trout through programs designed to eradicate or at least reduce non-native species. Finally, protection for the antelope, elk, and mule deer migration corridors is now being studied.

Not all of the news here is positive. Some threats still stem from the misuse of these lands which occurred before the park was setup.

Pollution from mining activities of the past is the best example here, but there are numerous modern stressors, too. These include climate change, exurban growth, increased recreation, invasive species, wildlife diseases, and very heavy visitation in the park itself.

To get a better grip on these matters, monitoring of vital signs in the Greater Yellowstone Ecosystem must be tailored to its unique needs. For example, an integrated, cross-organizational, and ecosystem-wide program for monitoring, documenting, and assessing vital signs would be an excellent idea. The overall goal would be to help environmental managers, politicians, scholars, and interested citizens alike become aware of problems at an early stage and well before they become unmanageable. At the same time, more attention should be paid to the merits of highly advanced technology by using satellites to study the patterns of "primary production" and ecological drought in Yellowstone.[7] These factors are discussed below.

To begin with, photosynthesis converts sunlight into energy, which is stored in the millions upon millions of leaves, flowers, seeds, and trees that form the complex web of life in the Greater Yellowstone Ecosystem. This transformation of energy fixes carbon, provides organic matter to soils, and creates the potential fuel for wildfires. As the first link in the food chain, new plant biomass is known as primary production. It basically provides the energy needed by wildlife and other consumers. In winter, Yellowstone is a high-mountain environment with very deep snows, but summer wildfires prove that the park can dry out a great deal once the snow is gone.

This annual dryness increases the chances for big fires (as occurred in 1988 and 2016) and also affects primary production and the food chain. In the future, because of global warming, droughts will play an even greater role in changing the structure and the composition of the ecosystem's vegetation. Drought in Yellowstone has been studied for many years, but the key scientific indicators of drought were not formally defined until 2017. Today, a very promising way to approach this issue is to measure, first, how the vegetation is impacted negatively by drought, and then how it is affected positively by more favorable climatic conditions (rain or snow) when the drought finally breaks. The endless ballet of drought-stressed conditions on the one hand, followed by damp pro-growth conditions, on the other, will become more important in Yellowstone as climate change takes a firmer hold there and temperatures rise.

In the past, monitoring primary production and vegetation changes in wildland settings was very time-and-resource intensive, involving such traditional ground-based techniques as cutting and then weighing vegetation biomass. More recently, these traditional methods have been augmented by monitoring primary production via satellite. For example, measurements of solar radiation reflectance in both visible and near-infrared wavelengths can show primary production at frequent intervals by means of the Moderate Resolution Imaging Spectrometer (MODIS) on satellites operated by the National Aeronautics and Space Administration (NASA).

The Greater Yellowstone Inventory and Monitoring Network is responsible for natural-resource monitoring and is charged with collecting data tracking any relevant changes in resources. It uses these data to track primary production across Yellowstone over time. By linking these changes to vegetation types, soils, and climates, scientists are better able to understand how, where, and when changes in production have already occurred and are likely to occur in the future.

16

Management Challenges

These challenges have many complicated facets, both ecological and human. There are several issues involved:

- Impacts of climate change on the park's ecology
- Problems of excessive visitor use
- Questions of long-term sustainability, i.e., the capacity of the biosphere and human civilization to coexist
- Strategic priorities for the park
- Systematic planning for the major irreplaceable and potentially vulnerable sites of the Greater Yellowstone Ecosystem, considered as a whole.

We begin on the ecological front with the views of Dr. Ann Rodman, the senior Climate Program officer in the Yellowstone Center for Resources. In 2020, she kindly sent to the authors of this book a very useful email. Lightly edited, her comments ran along the following lines:

She noted that one of the most visible but little-known near-term threats from climate change (in addition to the many other major climate change problems mentioned elsewhere in this book) is the increasing populations of early-season invasive annual plants. One of these is cheatgrass, which is a winter annual grass native to some other parts of world but now invading the native plant communities of the Northern Range. In the lower elevations around Gardiner, Montana, cheatgrass and desert allium have already completely replaced large areas of the native grasslands.

The changes that Dr. Rodman and her colleagues were observing (longer growing season; earlier spring snowmelt; and hotter, drier summers) are all conducive to the spread of cheatgrass. This is seen now both in the higher reaches of the Northern Range (in the Mammoth and Tower areas) and out into the lower Lamar Valley.

In high densities, cured cheatgrass (that is to say, sun-and-wind-dried cheatgrass) is flammable and, once ignited, will easily support fire.

This fact can lead to shorter fire-return intervals in Yellowstone, which will eventually eliminate native grasses and shrubs entirely, resulting in a mono-culture consisting only of cheatgrass. This is *not*, of course, what park managers want to see happen in the region! In summary, then, cheatgrass is a very real and current threat to the Yellowstone ecosystem but there is no easy way to deal with this problem: cheatgrass now infests more than 100 million acres in at least 49 states.

The U.S. Department of Agriculture, for its part, mentions four possible management options. Depending on local conditions, they are identified as physical methods, cultural methods, biological methods, and/or chemical methods. Without going into the details, it can safely be said that none of them is suitable for widespread use in the extensive wilderness areas of Yellowstone.

Turning now to the problems of excessive visitor use, the National Park Service offers the following comments, which have been lightly edited and compressed here.[1] Yellowstone is famous for being a place where people today can get a glimpse of North America as it must have been before so many humans arrived. It is a unique and relatively unspoiled part of the American West where we can share open landscapes with thousands of wild animals, including bison, bears, elk, wolves, and a few mountain lions. It is also a place where volcanic powers always generate multi-colored hot springs, mudpots, and geysers. And as if all this were not enough, visitors can also see these sights in great safety and ease from their own cars, thanks to a well-maintained road system that connects five park entrances with many popular tourist destinations.

All this is fine, but there is some bad news, too. More and more visitors want to see these wonders with their own eyes. Since 2008, annual visits to Yellowstone in the summer have risen by more than 40 percent—such a sharp increase that it has caused traffic jams, roadside soil erosion, trampling of local vegetation, and unsanitary conditions around overused public restrooms.

Half of this surge in visits occurred in only two years (2014 to 2016). They were associated with a steep rise in motor vehicle accidents, additional calls for ambulances, and more search-and-rescue efforts. At the same time, National Park Service staffing levels and funding have remained flat over the last ten years.

The National Park Service is required to provide visitors with every opportunity to enjoy Yellowstone—but, at the same time, to accomplish this without permitting such enjoyment to destroy, damage, or in any major way diminish the very attractions these visitors have some so far to see. This raises a number of difficult questions, the chief one of which is that most visitors want to keep their cake and eat it, too. In other words, they want a park with far fewer people and much less vehicle traffic but they do *not* want strict limits on their own right to visit the park or on their own use of private vehicles there.

Numerous difficulties are posed by the very high levels of summer visitation, coupled with changes in the composition of the visitors themselves: today, many visitors will have had very little—if any—previous outdoor experience in a large park. This flood-tide of visitors can affect not only the park and its employees, but also all the nearby gateway communities as well. These communities are the homes or workplaces of many different individuals or institutions that have long-standing economic, political or other ties to the region.

The National Park Service therefore believes that difficult decisions lie ahead, and that all interested parties should try to work together closely and harmoniously to balance the need to protect Yellowstone's finite resources, on the one hand, with the widespread public national and international interest in visiting and enjoying the world's first national park, on the other.

Toward these ends, Yellowstone is now laying the factual groundwork for an eventual planning process to manage the high levels of visitor use. New projects will include working to understand the impacts of greater visitation on park resources and on park staffing, operations and resources. In addition, park managers also want to know what visitors have to say about their own experiences in the park, and what the gateway communities think.

In the short term, the park is focusing on how it can improve its operations in order to protect the park's limited resources and how it can give visitors a much better experience in the most scenic areas, which are now very congested. In the longer term, if visitation continues to rise in the coming years, as seems very possible, future management strategies will include but are not necessarily limited to: park operational and staffing changes; better communication and traffic management systems; shuttles or other transportation alternatives that will get visitors out of their cars and trucks; and setting up advance reservation or timed-entry systems at locations where demand often exceeds capacity.

Some examples of research the park has undertaken in recent years to address such issues[2] are:

PILOT PROJECTS. The park continues to test a range of pilot projects, such as changing traffic flows, parking, visitor flow configurations, and adding staff to improve resource protection, safety, operations, and visitor experiences.

Visitor use studies. Park researchers can solicit visitors' opinions about possible scenarios that might be used to manage the flow of visitors more efficiently in the future. Visitors can also be invited to consider the pros and cons of various trade-offs, such as which scenarios they would prefer if a local shuttle service became available. In 2017, for example, the park began a continuing monitoring partnership with Oregon State University and with the Youth Conservation Corps (YCC) to better understand visitor volumes and visitor behavior at sites that are very heavily used.

YCC crews have monitored the numbers and density of visitors to these sites, have studied how they use these areas, and have noted any instances of adverse impacts on park resources. This monitoring has occurred at Norris Geyser Basin, Lower Geyser Basin, Midway Geyser, the Fairy Falls Trail to the Grand Prismatic Overlook, Canyon (Artist Point), Old Faithful, and Artists' Paintpots.

Transportation studies. These studies have collected data on traffic, parking, vehicle capacity, and visitor flow patterns throughout the park, for example, on the West Yellowstone to Old Faithful Corridor. A feasibility study of a shuttle system between West Yellowstone and Old Faithful has also been conducted.

Wildlife–people jams. Park employees have worked with University of Montana students to better understand how humans and large animals interact with one another at these jams along park roads.

Visitor and employee safety. Graduate students from the National Park Service (NPS) Business Plan Internship program have worked in the park to study the relationship between increasing visitation, human safety, and impacts on employees and operations in the park's Resource and Visitor Protection Division. In addition, park employees also monitor the creation and expansion of "social trails," i.e., the informal, unofficial, and unwanted trails that are made by visitors and that damage the soil and plants of the park.

Imbalance between visitors and employees. A chart drawn up by the National Park Service shows that, counting from the year 2000, annual park visits have soared from about 2.75 million people at that time to over 4 million people by 2018. The number of full-time park employees has remained relatively constant in that same period, averaging only about 550 people.

Questions of long-term sustainability are easily asked, but are not so easily answered. It is to them that we now turn.

Yellowstone has always been in the forefront of environmental protection. Today the joint assignments of the park's managers and staff are to continue this legacy of environmental stewardship in their own operations—and in all the visitor services that they supply. Support and direction for environmental stewardship is deeply embedded in both the National Park Service's missions and in Yellowstone's own international significance. The park's sustainability program extends this commitment to conservation and protection to cover the likely environmental impacts of the park's own operations. The park was established in 1872 as the first National Park in the world, and since then it has been further "promoted" by becoming a biosphere reserve and World Heritage Site. At present, it remains a world example for excellence in environmental management.

Now one of its main challenges is to show world-class leadership in sustainability and in adapting to climate change by running its operations in a prudent manner that will preserve the park's resources for this and for all future generations. In this context, sustainability can most simply be defined as *the process through which human beings can make the fullest use of their environments without destroying them.* A firm commitment to sustainability has now been made even more essential due to the increasing pace of climate change in the world and its increasing impact on local and global natural resources. A good deal has already been done: Federal legislation in the United States now requires U.S. Government agencies to protect natural resources through good planning for the future.

A National Park Service "Green Parks Plan," for example, provides further impetus for environmental stewardship and has led to widespread support for Yellowstone's role in this process. One component of this plan is the Climate Friendly Park Program, of which Yellowstone is a member. More than 120 member parks are included in the Plan, and will use its resources to help educate both park staff and the public about the realities of climate change.

A recent National Park Service Sustainability Report spells out an ethic for environmental stewardship. The park's Environmental Coordinating Committee (YECC), for example, has embraced the National Park Service Green Parks Plan and now works to ensure a comprehensive approach to sustainability in Yellowstone. This team consists of representatives from such committed activist agencies as the National Park Service itself, Zanterra, Delaware North, Medcor, Yellowstone Park Service Stations, and Yellowstone Forever.

These men and women work hard to develop the most sustainable practices and to reduce their own footprint. The YECC compiles an annual Sustainability Report and shares data on the park's uses of energy, fuel, water, and waste diversion. Some of the issues they have focused on include the recycling of used, expired or unwanted bear spray canisters; a portable solar array to power the Bechler Ranger Station with energy from the sun; establishing a network of charging opportunities for electric and plug-in hybrid vehicles; promoting "idle-free" driving for users of internal combustion vehicles; updating irrigation controls in Mammoth Hot Springs Historic District; installing more efficient road lamps in that same District; and reintroducing hydro-electric power (i.e., water-generated) in the Mammoth area.

Such creative projects invite thinking about the most suitable strategic priorities.[3] The National Park Service lists five of them, which were developed by Park Superintendent Cameron Sholly, with significant inputs from field staff around the park. This ambitious shopping list has been edited and shortened (although it is still choked with bureaucratic jargon). The key points are:

Focus on the Core Duties

...by improving employee housing; work conditions; health and wellness; team spirit; interdivisional respect and collaboration; accountability; professional development; hiring processes; and internal communications.

Improve financial management practices by priority-setting processes; project formulation; and workforce performance.

Develop more efficient arrangements to improve the sharing of limited resources, communications, and operational performance.

Strengthen the Ecosystem and Its Resources

Understand and respond more effectively to climate change impacts; advance and sustain wildlife management and large-scale landscape conservation efforts; identify new cooperative conservation opportunities with states and partners (for example, work on setting up wildlife corridors); continue building scientific capacity to improve decision-making for the ecosystem; and improve environmental sustainability.

Improve the conditions of historic buildings; protect archeological sites, collections, and archives; and promote American Indian tribal heritage and collaboration.

Deliver a World-Class Visitor Experience

Develop an effective visitor use strategy that focuses on protecting park resources; strengthening staffing and infrastructure; improving visitor recreation opportunities; and working closely with gateway communities.

Provide a high level of law enforcement, resource protection, and emergency responses.

Build world-class interpretative experiences and programs by using new technology; youth and community outreach; and helpful citizen services.

Improve accessibility, recreational opportunities, and sustainable practices.

Invest in Infrastructure

Set up an effective framework of forward planning and funding priorities.
Improve the physical condition and capacity of housing for park employees.
Improve the transportation infrastructure.
Improve the historic structures, visitor services, and public health facilities.

Build Coalitions and Partnerships

Build trust with gateway communities; honor Indian tribal legacies and heritage; cultivate relationships with elected local officials, environmental and recreation groups; and build global partnerships.

There is now some worthwhile thinking about creative but possibly too-idealistic "systematic planning" ideas for protecting the major irreparable and potentially vulnerable sites of the Greater Yellowstone Ecosystem, considered as a whole.[4] To set the stage, it is important to understand that systematic planning on a regional scale has now become the standard approach of most conservation organizations and agencies all over the world.

The Greater Yellowstone Ecosystem was initially defined as the minimum amount of wilderness needed to sustain the Yellowstone population of grizzly bears. It shows that systematic conservation planning is much better than mere chance—or than politically-based approaches can hope to be. It focuses on specific goals, on quantitative targets, and on well-tested ways to protect the environment.

Although the Greater Yellowstone Ecosystem is not a "troubled spot" on a global or continental scale, it does have a singular quality that most troubled spots do not enjoy. It continues to present to researchers and scientists a nearly-unique opportunity to help conserve a large ecosystem *that is still relatively intact today.* This is the plus side of the present situation. Perhaps unavoidably, however, this region has become so attractive that its human population is growing very rapidly—perhaps to such an extent that the negative impacts of this growth may now even exceed the earlier damage caused by timbering, mining, and other resource-extraction industries.

Population-growth rates for the 20 counties within the Greater Yellowstone Ecosystem have risen sharply. This area lies in such close proximity to a highly mobile, prosperous, and adventuresome population that is willing—indeed, even *eager*—to make an enormous effort to get away from the cities and the suburbs in order to be close to world-class outdoor recreation and to nature.

Studies have shown that about 27 percent of this ecosystem is now under some form of environmental protection. However, this coverage is very patchy at best, and there is much room for further improvement. One future-oriented study has even assigned "irreplaceability scores" to 43 "megasites," which were defined as large aggregations of environmental planning units. It concluded that if all these theoretical megasites were somehow fully protected by law, such a new environmentally-safeguarded area of the Greater Yellowstone Ecosystem would expand by 71 percent the protection of species there that are now held to be imperiled.[5]

If ever established (the costs, politics, and other factors involved in this process will make this approach highly unlikely for the foreseeable future), such an ambitious conservation policy would go very far toward protecting the habitats of the creatures that need the most room to roam—for example, the grizzly bears, wolves, mountain lions, and wolverines.

17

Prospects for the Future

A great deal, both pro and con, can be said about the likely prospects for Yellowstone's future, but the brief points of view summarized in this chapter may be good starting points for any discussions that readers themselves may wish to undertake.[1]

A key point to understand here is that the biodiversity of the Greater Yellowstone Ecosystem can never fully be guaranteed. There are now many threats facing this unique area. These include climate change, population growth in the region, land development, increased recreation, habitat fragmentation, and the encroachment of invasive and non-native species.

Many of the ecosystem's plant and animal species are rare, threatened, endangered, or at some level of sustainability risk. Thus, in order to meet the park's mandate to preserve its resources and values for the public over the very long run, park managers must do their utmost *now* to keep the park itself in tip-top condition. Keeping Yellowstone healthy now also has the great advantage of improving the quality of life for people living outside the park. They can certainly profit from such "free" park resources as clean air, clean water, flourishing wildlife populations and vegetation communities, and sound long-term management practices.

A number of factors will impact the Greater Yellowstone Ecosystem, for better or for worse. This enormous ecosystem extends across different climate and vegetation zones, and different state and local legal jurisdictions. It is now the last remaining big and relatively-intact native ecosystem in the contiguous United States. Because of its beauty and relatively unspoiled qualities, it also attracts a growing number of people who want to live there permanently. When they do, they inevitably take up more and more space in this region. Such ever-increasing habitat modification can pose serious threats to the biodiversity and thus to the smooth functioning of the ecosystem.

For example, when homes are built close to the boundaries of any

Greater Yellowstone wilderness, they inevitably fragment the animals' familiar ranges; isolate local and diverse populations of plants and animals; short-circuit the natural processes which have been responsible for their very survival; and, ultimately, encourage other "land-hungry" buyers to want to move into this scenic region, too.

Yellowstone National Park came into being before most of the surrounding states existed. This makes its relationships with them somewhat different from those of other national parks. For example, this park has legal jurisdiction over all the wildlife within the limits of the park. As a result, wildlife management there responds to National Park Service and Federal directives, not to state wildlife management goals.

In practice, the National Park Service certainly understands that natural (i.e., ecological) boundaries are not the same as the political, economic or social boundaries that gave birth to the park and to other protected areas. Park managers must therefore establish and maintain good relations with neighboring agencies in order to coordinate policies that are sometimes very different on different sides of the park boundary. On a positive side, park managers generally work well with the states, even on such thorny issues as wolf management and bison movements.

Experienced managers face problems by looking, early on, at the whole ecosystem, by trying to understand its individual components and their sometimes complex inter-relationships. This approach is much wiser than simply waiting until environmental problems become so acute they simply demand emergency action.

No matter how good they may be by themselves, effective managers also need experienced partners. Fortunately, several management and research partnerships already exist between state, Federal, and tribal agencies to focus on problem-solving and limited resources.

Academic and nonprofit institutions are often involved as well. The National Park Service mentions at least four of them in a recent report,[2] but there must be many others, too:

- The Greater Yellowstone Network (GRYN), which was set up by the National Park Service in 2000 to support the stewardship and management of natural resources in Bighorn Canyon National Recreation Area, Grand Teton National Park (including the John D. Rockefeller, Jr., Memorial Parkway), and Yellowstone National Park. The GRYN is one of 32 units nationwide that group about 270 national parks into networks based on geographic similarities, common natural resources, and resource protection problems.

- The Rocky Mountain Cooperative Ecosystem Studies Unit (CESU) conducts research, educational programs, and technical assistance on agency-specific issues and on issues involving public-private and other mixed ownerships. This information is made available to those who need it most—the land managers and the political and industry leaders.
- The Greater Yellowstone Coordinating Committee (GYCC) was formed in 1964 by the managers of the national parks and national forests in the Greater Yellowstone Ecosystem. It now includes managers from two national parks; five national forests; two national wildlife refuges; and the Bureau of Land Management offices in Montana, Idaho, and Wyoming.

It is not a regional decision-making body but is instead designed to share information and to help streamline administrative procedures on a voluntary basis. Current priorities include ecosystem health, namely air and water quality; management of invasive species and other species that are "on the brink," such as bears, cutthroat trout, whitebark pine; adapting to climate changes; wildlife migrations; and what further steps are feasible to help "connect people to the land."

The 10 GYCC Subcommittees are: Fire Management, Hydrology, Terrestrial Invasive Species, Clean Air Partnership, Whitebark Pine, Sustainable Operations, Aquatic Invasive Species, Native Fisheries, Climate Change Adaptation, and Wildlife.

- The Great Northern Landscape Conservation Cooperative, for its part, is an alliance of conservation partners who share the goal of increasing ecosystem resilience within the Great Northern geographic area. This region includes the Columbia River Basin, the Rocky Mountains, and the Sage Steppe of the Interior West in both the United States and in Canada.

Peering into her crystal ball showing Yellowstone's possible future 20 to 50 years from now, a Wilderness Education and Management Specialist in Montana, who has 40 years of experience in these matters, kindly gave the authors some of her considered judgments on likely future developments in Yellowstone National Park and in the similar lands near it. Lightly edited here, she made the following comments in 2019:

– There will be an increase in the ethnic diversity of visitors, who will have different interests and desires for a wilderness experience compared to today's visitors. They will want wildlands that are closer to urban areas, and public transportation to get them there and back home again.

– There will be an increasing need for commercial services, such as fully-outfitted trips, because people will no longer have the necessary skills of self-reliance, backpacking, orienteering, and overnight camping. They may not understand, either, that in outdoor living the forces of nature are much stronger than we are. In short, in order to "get along" in the outdoors, we must "go along" with these forces.

– The number of people allowed into wildlands will have to be limited and managed in order to protect biological and cultural features. There will therefore have to be many more enforceable regulations on where you can hike or camp and on how long you can stay in one site. Stricter wildlife viewing regulations will become necessary, too, in order to prevent wildlife disturbance and displacement.

– There will be an increased need for education and interpretation to help people understand the contrast between the civilized world where they themselves live, and the importance to society of having large tracts of road-free and trail-free areas at the same time. People must understand, as well, the ecological role that fire plays in wild ecosystems; the importance of apex species; and the effects of climate change on the flora and fauna of the wilderness.

One of the international institutions that is working for the conservation of nature and for the sustainable use of natural resources is the International Union for the Conservation of Nature and Natural Resources, usually referred to as the IUCN. It was established in 1948 and based in Gland, Switzerland.

The IUCN is perhaps best known to the environmentally-literate public for its work in compiling and publishing the IUCN "Red List of Threatened Species." Rather than simply trying to mobilize public support for nature conservation, the IUCN aims at actively influencing governments, businesses, and other key stakeholders by providing accurate information and advice to them and by building environmental partnerships. An excellent example of this process is the IUCN's "Conservation Outlook on Yellowstone National Park," which is the source of much of the information used here.[3]

The IUCN's report card on Yellowstone is that of four possibilities. They are (1) "Critical"; (2) "Significant Concern"; (3) "Good with Some Concerns"; or (4) "Good," the park earns, overall, a rating of "Good with Some Concerns." The park, suggests the IUCN, now offers six "World Heritage Values." Lightly edited, these can be described as follows:

- Yellowstone is a foremost site for the study of the evolutionary history of the Earth. There is visible evidence of 55 million years of extensive volcanism; volcanic dispositions preserving 27 layers of fossilized forests; a variety of lava flows; the world's foremost collection of active geysers and hot springs; and, last but not least, intense and continuing earthquake activity.

- As noted repeatedly in this book, the park is also one of the few remaining large ecosystems left in the northern temperate zone of the Earth. Yellowstone's ecological communities thus provide unparalleled opportunities for the conservation, study, and appreciation of its large-scale living and dead wildlife. (This last point is important because winter-killed or otherwise deceased animals are a significant source of food for Yellowstone's surviving creatures.) A significant improvement in ecological wholeness has been the reintroduction of wolves.
- The extraordinary scenic treasures of Yellowstone include the world's largest collection of geysers; the Grand Canyon of the Yellowstone River (never to be confused with the far-bigger Grand Canyon of Arizona); and great herds of wildlife. The volcanic history of the region has left the legacy of an incised and scenic landscape that is punctuated by about 350 small waterfalls.
- The park is one of North America's foremost refuges for rare plant and animal species. At the micro-level, the hydrothermal features create habitats for the microbes that are offering links to primal life.
- Because of its high elevation, the Greater Yellowstone Ecosystem can also serve as a refuge for plant and animal species that will be adversely affected by climate change.
- Thanks to its leadership in ecosystem management, Yellowstone has become a world center for information-sharing about natural-area conservation. It is perhaps the world's leading laboratory for experiments in the values and ideas that drive modern conservation. As the world's first national park, Yellowstone has inspired conservation elsewhere in the world.

The points made above by the IUCN are the most favorable news about the park; happily, there is not in fact much negative news. The IUCN does list numerous "Current Threats" to the park, but notes that most of them are beyond the direct control of the park managers because they lie outside the park itself or are related to international climate change. The IUCN judges that, with cooperation and support from external sources—but with one important exception—these threats should be manageable. The sole exception is the outbreak of beetles, which the IUCN lists as a "High Threat."

The IUCN also examines, in passing, these other threats:

- There is a possibility of gold exploration on private land near the Yellowstone River, which would disfigure the land and would almost certainly pollute this river or other waterways.

- The type, scale and rapid pace of commercial developments in the communities that are not far from the entrances to the park have the potential to affect adversely both the natural beauty of the park itself and the movements of animals between the park and the surrounding Greater Yellowstone Ecosystem.
- Grizzly bears have expanded their range in recent years into smaller areas of more secure habitat. Barriers to the free movement of these bears can prevent the infusion of genes from other populations of grizzlies, and would reduce the viability of the surviving Yellowstone population if it should suffer a decline for some reason.
- Bison are indeed an iconic feature of Yellowstone, but they can be infected with the bacterium *Brucella abortus*, the causative agent of brucellosis—a disease that causes abortion in cattle and is thus of significant economic and political concern to ranchers.

In addition, real and perceived bison-related conflicts (competition for grasses, public safety, property damage) have all combined to reduce rancher and public tolerance of bison that wander outside the limits of the park.

- Beetles are an endemic species that experience cyclical population outbreaks. There is evidence that recent outbreaks are more severe and more widespread than those in the past and are exacerbated by warming temperatures. Beetles attack a number of pine species, particularly lodgepole pine and whitebark pine. Because whitebark pine is an important grizzly bear food, the beetle infestations may have long-reaching impacts on grizzlies. The infestations can also increase the risk of catastrophic wildfires.
- Fish from outside the park, including non-native species such as brook trout and lake trout which compete with the native species, were introduced in 1890. Lake trout were discovered in Yellowstone Lake in 1994. They competed so effectively with the native cutthroat trout that the latter declined while the former increased greatly. Measures to control lake trout began in 1995; their numbers have been reduced, but total eradication is virtually impossible because they reproduce so quickly.
- Since wildlife has no understanding of park boundaries, wolves, grizzlies, elk, and other mammals can easily fall prey to legal hunting conducted outside of park boundaries. Yellowstone officials must therefore continue to work with neighboring states and associated foundations to minimize any such wildlife losses.

In terms of the long process of learning about the park, worth mentioning here is the now-largely-forgotten Jones Expedition of 1873, a fact-finding survey chiefly designed to locate a usable wagon route between the Union Pacific Railroad in the southern part of the Wyoming Territory, on the one hand, and Yellowstone National Park, on the other.

This well-equipped expedition was led by Captain William A. Jones and included prominent scientists of the era. It was transported by eight wagons and 66 mules and was supported by numerous Native American guides, cowboys and cooks. This outing was quite successful, in that it documented many little-known physical features of western Wyoming, including Togwotee Pass in the Jackson Hole Valley.

Among the scientists was the geologist Theodore Comstock who, though forgotten today, was able immediately to grasp Yellowstone's future scientific importance. For example, he wrote:

> There is one young but active science—microscopy—which has as yet scarcely entered this field, but which, I firmly believe, will discover within the limits of the Park most valuable treasures. The act of Congress providing for this reservation [i.e., the park itself] insures [*sic*] the preservation of the greater portion of whatever may be available for this purpose.
>
> Among the most interesting objects for the microscope, will be found in the colloidal and filamentous products of the hot springs, the minute vegetable and animal life of both hot and cold springs, the animal and vegetable parasites, and the numerous crystalline deposits of the hot springs and geysers.[4]

Conclusions

The future of Yellowstone will ultimately be determined by the collective ability of the interested parties to protect and preserve this wondrous ecosystem from the impacts of human beings, including but not limited to climate change, increased development surrounding the park, greater tourism (i.e., the danger of Yellowstone being "loved to death"), and conflicting views on animal management. In all cases, new legislation mandating wilderness status for some parts of the park and the nearby national forests would help to protect this region in perpetuity in a manner that will best preserve its natural state.

In researching this book, the authors made a point of asking Yellowstone experts what they think needs to be done *now* to improve conditions in the park. Some of the best answers, lightly edited here, ran along the following lines:

- More Federal funding is needed—not only for Yellowstone alone, but also for all the U.S. Government-funded parks and national forests. Importantly, the Great American Outdoors Act was signed into law in August 2020, and will provide $1.9 billion per year for five years to fund deferred maintenance projects identified by the National Park Service, the U.S. Forest Service, the U.S. Fish and Wildlife Service, the Bureau of Land Management, and the Bureau of Indian Education.
- Increasing visitation numbers are a problem. They can cause severe crowding, which can overwhelm both the infrastructure and the staff capabilities, and can also generate conflicts with the wildlife.
- Work is needed on interagency cooperation on the most complicated issues, such as bison and grizzly bear management; wildlife migration into and out of the park; and social and economic pressures to reopen the park if access to it has to be reduced, or if the park has to be closed entirely , for virus-control reasons.

- Efforts should be made to assure that Yellowstone is a safe, welcoming, and inclusive destination for people of color.

The following is perhaps the best recent summary we have seen of the past and likely future of the Greater Yellowstone Ecosystem. Written in 2020 by Robert B. Keiter, the Wallace Stegner Professor of Law at the University of Utah, it is lightly edited, annotated, and summarized as follows[1]:

By about 1990, the concept of the Greater Yellowstone Ecosystem, and the best ways to manage and preserve it, had surfaced as keys to preserving these public lands and the wildlife living on them. At that time, however, Yellowstone grizzly bear numbers were in sharp decline. There were no wolves left, and bison and elk management issues needed more attention. The National Forest lands of the ecosystem were being subjected to extensive logging and other commercial activities that threatened the region's ecological integrity. Moreover, a high-profile U.S. Government "Vision" effort to improve resource management practices had collapsed under intense political pressures.

Since the 1990s, however, intensive development activities in the ecosystem have mostly been held at bay, and most of the wildlife populations there are in better shape now than they were 30 years ago. The bottom line is that the Greater Yellowstone Ecosystem concept itself is now widely accepted, but the related *ecosystem management principles* have yet to be fully embraced by the responsible agencies.

Looking forward, the Keiter article identifies several difficult new problems now confronting this ecosystem. These include escalating park visitation; mounting recreation pressures; private land development; chronic wasting disease (a contagious neurological disease affecting the brains of infected deer, elk, and moose, leading to their death); and climate change.

Professor Keiter recommends that, to address these looming problems, ecosystem management efforts must be expanded and better coordinated. If they are not, then the prospects of litigation and political intervention will still lurk in the background, as has in fact always been the case over the past 30 years.

Yellowstone embodies a unique American identity as a place where nature, largely untouched and unmanaged, is allowed to flourish. Our continent can boast of something envied by countries around the world: a multitude of national parks for enjoyment, solitude, freedom and exploration—of which Yellowstone is the crown jewel. So many people before us have bravely explored, passionately envisioned, and ardently fought to preserve this cultural asset that has now become a haven for generations to come. Truly, it is an American dream.

A Chronology

Pre–18th century: For thousands of years before the coming of any non–Native American travelers, at least 26 Native American tribes use Yellowstone for hunting, fishing, vision-quests, prayer-making, and ceremonial exchanges of gifts.

1728-1797: The British explorer and geographer David Thompson translates a Minnetaree Indian phrase as meaning "Yellow Stone River."

1804–1806: Lewis and Clark explore large parts of the western mountains of what is now the United States.

1807–1808: The explorer John Colter is probably the first non–Native American to get a close look at the Yellowstone region.

1818: The War Department chooses Stephen H. Long to lead an expedition into the Rockies. His erroneous description of the Great Plains as nothing more than a "Great American Desert" discourages farmers from settling there.

1823: The traders Andrew Henry and William H. Ashley set up the Rocky Mountain Fur Company and advertise in the Missouri newspapers for adventuresome trappers eager to open up the Rocky Mountains to the fur-trapping business.

1827: A letter to a national newspaper from a then-unknown correspondent, who later turns out to be the trapper Daniel T. Potts, gives a very detailed and reasonably accurate account of Yellowstone's wonders.

About 1829: Joe Meek, a 19-year-old fur trapper, is separated from his party by an attack by a Native American, survives alone in the wilderness, and explores the Norris Geyser basin of Yellowstone.

Late 1820s: "Davy" Jackson traps beaver in the Jackson, Wyoming, area.

1830: The famous explorer and mountain man Jim Bridger visits Yellowstone geysers in 1830 but finds that his colleagues do not believe what they consider to be his "tall tales."

1830–1836: The visual "Indian Gallery" of Native American portraits by the artist George Catlin is very well-received in the United States and in London, Paris and Brussels. He begins the two-volume report of his travels with these words: "Mouth of the Yellow Stone. Upper Missouri. 1832: I arrived at this place yesterday in the steamer *Yellow Stone*, after a voyage of nearly three months from St. Louis, a distance of two thousand miles, the greater part of which has never before been navigated by steam."[1]

1833–1834: German Prince Maximilian and the young artist Karl Bodmer travel to the headwaters of the Missouri and produce a masterful written and pictorial record of Native American tribes there.

1834: A clerk of the American Fur Company, Warren Angus Ferris, writes the first factual firsthand account Yellowstone's Firehole River.

1835–1839: The fur trapper Osborne Russell visits the Yellowstone area three times and is one of the very few early explorers to leave any written record of his thoughts and travels.

1856: Together with his Native American "mother," as a boy Nick Wilson visits, and later writes about, an extensive Native American encampment held in the Big Hole Basin of the Snake River.

1859: Captain William F. Raynolds, a U.S. Army surveyor, sets out on a two-year survey of the northern Rocky Mountains.

1860s–1870s: The outdoorsman "Beaver Dick" Leigh becomes a guide for the hunting parties that begin to trickle into the Rocky Mountains.

1869: The first formal and well-organized—but still unofficial—expedition into the Yellowstone region is the privately-funded Folsom-Cook-Peterson expedition.

1870: The first official expedition into Yellowstone is undertaken by Washburn, Langford, Hedges, and Doane. They decide to christen one particular geyser "Old Faithful" because of its regular eruptions. Washburn, the oldest member of the expedition, becomes separated from the party; is soon hopelessly lost; and finally survives, chiefly by eating the roots of thistles, after spending 37 days alone in the wilderness.

1871: The Ferdinand V. Hayden Geological Survey of 1871 marks the beginning of the scientific exploration of Yellowstone.

1871: The first intrepid "pioneer tourists" begin to visit Yellowstone: the writer Calvin Clawson records the details of the trip in his book on Yellowstone's "infernal regions."

1872: President Ulysses S. Grant signs the Yellowstone National Park Protection Act, thereby creating the world's first national park.

1876: Led by over-eager and inept Army Lieutenant Doane, the Snake River expedition nearly starves to death before he and his men finally manage to reach a trapper's cabin on the Snake River. Doane is recalled to Fort Ellis in disgrace.

1882: William Adolph Baillie-Grohman was a prolific writer; an excellent shot, big game hunter, and mountaineer; and a pioneer in British Columbia. His 1882 book on *Camps in the Rockies* contains accurate and sympathetic passages describing the Native Americans and the local customs.

1883: When the Northern Pacific Railroad was completed in 1883, it was now much easier for tourists from the East to travel to Yellowstone. The railroad soon became the dominant local political power, but the naturalist and publisher George Bird Grinnell takes the lead to stop what he terms "The Park Grab" of Yellowstone by the railroad.

1883: Heavily burdened by the pressure of his office, President Chester A. Arthur takes a holiday trip to the new national park of Yellowstone in 1883. His chief assistant is Senator George Vest of Missouri, who later helps bring Yellowstone to such wider public attention that conservationists hail him as "the self-appointed protector of Yellowstone National Park."

1883–1889: The Hague Geologic Surveys of 1883 to 1889 have numerous positive results. Arnold Hague, appointed in 1883 as geologist in charge of the survey of Yellowstone National Park and its vicinity, strongly and successfully advocates the preservation of the major features in their natural state. He and his team also survey more than 3,000 square miles of the Yellowstone region.

1886–1918: Because of the incompetence of the civilian leadership, the U.S. Army takes charge of Yellowstone from 1886 to 1918.

1887: In January 1887, the experienced Arctic explorer Frederick Schwatka and his team set off from Mammoth Hot Springs on an ambitious winter tour of the park. Schwatka himself had to drop out early because he was not used to high altitude. His team continued on and survived, but nearly lost their lives when they were stranded for 72 hours in a freezing, blinding snowstorm with little food or shelter.

1891: Congress passes the Forest Reserve Act, which allows President Benjamin Harrison to set aside—i.e., to "reserve"—parts of the public domain in order to protect natural resources. The President than establishes the nation's first Forest Reserve—the Yellowstone Park Timberland Reserve. It will become the first of many National Forests.

1894: The Lacey Act (named after its sponsor, Congressman John Lacey of Iowa) establishes the legal basis for protecting the park.

1915: The first Yellowstone park rangers are hired.

1917: Stagecoaches continue to carry passengers from railheads into the park until 1917.

1926: After touring the region with the Superintendent of Yellowstone, John D. Rockefeller, Jr., becomes charmed with the stunning mountain scenery. Beginning in 1926, over the next two years he therefore secretly begins buying 35,000 acres of land, with the intent of donating it to become part of Grand Teton National Park.

1929: The original Grand Teton National Park is established.

1950: Congress combines the original park with the Rockefeller lands and with adjacent areas to establish today's Grand Teton National Park.

1963: The Leopold Report, written by the environmentalist A. Starker Leopold, fundamentally changes National Park Service strategy to a new wildlife management policy of "letting nature take its own course."

1970: A new bear-management plan closes the Yellowstone open garbage pits in 1970.

1972: Congress establishes the John D. Rockefeller, Jr., Memorial Parkway to link Yellowstone and Grand Teton National Park.

1976: The United Nations designates Yellowstone as an International Biosphere Reserve.

1978: Yellowstone is named as a UNESCO World Heritage Site.

1978: The "Summer of Fire" in 1988 has a short-term impact on the park but no major long-term effects.

1994: The Greater Yellowstone Coalition enlarges its estimate of the best size for the Greater Yellowstone Ecosystem as being 20 million acres.

Appendix 1:
George Catlin Discusses the Prairie Native Americans

A self-taught American artist, George Catlin is famous today for his extensive travels across the American West to record, both in paintings and in words, the soon-to-vanish lifestyles of 50 tribes of Native Americans living west of the Mississippi, from present-day North Dakota to Oklahoma. He was such a determined man that he wrote: "If my life be spared, nothing shall stop me from visiting every nation of Indians on the Continent of North America."[1]

Catlin did precisely this from 1830 to 1836, and thereby created a collection of his paintings, which he called his "Indian Gallery." When on tour, it was very well-received, not only in the United States but also in London, Paris and Brussels. This Indian Gallery was donated to the Smithsonian Institution in 1879 by the widow of an American art collector, Joseph Harrison, Jr. Several hundred of Catlin's Native American portraits now hang in the Smithsonian American Art Museum.

Catlin recounted many of his experiences with the Native Americans in a magisterial two-volume study of these tribes. Lightly edited here, the excerpts given below come from Volume 1, "Letter—No. 5: Mouth of the Yellowstone," pp. 36–38. Later excerpts come from the Peter Matthiessen edition of Catlin's *North American Indians*, pp. 139–142 (see the Bibliography). Catlin writes:

These northwestern tribes are all armed with the bow and lance, and protected with the shield or arrow-fender, which is carried outside of the left arm, exactly as the Roman and Greek shield was carried, and for the same purpose....

There is one prevailing custom ... among all the tribes who inhabit the great plains or prairies of these western regions. The plains afford them abundance of wild and fleet horses, which are easily procured; and on their backs, at full speed, they can come alongside of any animal, which they can easily destroy.

The bow with which they are armed is small, and apparently an insignificant weapon, though one of great and almost incredible power in the hands of its owner, whose sinews have from childhood been habituated to its use and service. The length of these bows is generally about three feet, and sometimes not more than two and a half….

One of these little bows in the hands of an Indian, on a fleet and well-trained horse, with a quiver of arrows slung on his back, is a most effective and powerful weapon in the open plain. No one can easily credit the force with which these missiles are thrown, and the sanguinary effects produced by their wounds, until he has rode by the side of a party of Indians in chase of a herd of buffaloes; and witnessed the apparent ease and grace with which their supple arms have drawn the bow, and seen these huge animals tumbling down and gushing out their hearts' blood from their mouths and nostrils….

An Indian, therefore, mounted on a fleet and well-trained horse, with his bow in his hand and his quiver slung on his back, containing a hundred arrows, of which he can throw fifteen or twenty in a minute, is a formidable and dangerous enemy. Many of them also ride with a lance of twelve or fourteen feet in length … with a blade of polished steel.

[All of them also carry a shield] made from the skin of a buffalo's neck, which has been smoked and hardened with glue extracted from the hoofs. These shields are arrow-proof and will glance off [deflect] a rifle-shot by being turned obliquely, which they do with great skill….

In this wise then, are all these red knights of the prairies, armed and equipped … nothing can be more thrilling than a troop or war party of these fellows galloping over these green and endless prairies….

Catlin also tells us about the amazed reaction of the Mandan Indians to *Yellowstone*, the first steamship they had ever seen:

It happened that on this memorable day about noon [the Mandans were at that moment resorting to religious ceremonies to persuade their gods to send rain and thus break the severe drought that was destroying their corn crop], that the steamer *Yellow Stone*, on her first trip up the Missouri River, approached and landed at the Mandan Village, as I have described in a former epistle.

I was lucky enough to be a passenger on this boat, and helped fire a salute of twenty guns of twelve calibre [small cannons that fired a ball weighing 12 pounds], when we first came into sight of the village, some three or four miles below [downstream].

These guns introduced a *new sound* into this strange country, which the Mandans at first supposed to be *thunder*; and the young man upon the lodge [this Mandan was standing on top of an earthen lodge as part of the rain-making ceremonies], who turned it to good account, was gathering fame in rounds of applause, which were repeated and echoed through the whole village; all eyes were centered on him—chiefs envied him—mothers' hearts were beating high whilst they were decorating and leading up their fair daughters to off him in marriage, on his signal success [in generating the "thunder"]....

During all this excitement, [the young man, whose Mandan name translated as "The White Buffalo's Hair"] kept his position [on top of the lodge], assuming the most commanding and threatening attitudes; brandishing his shield in the direction of the thunder, although there was not a cloud to be seen, until he (poor fellow), being elevated above the rest of the village, espied, to his inexpressible amazement, the steam-boat ploughing its way up the windings of the river below; puffing steam from her pipes, and sending forth the thunder from a twelve-pounder on her deck!

The White Buffalo's Hair stood motionless and turned pale, he looked awhile, and turned to the chief and the multitude, and addressed them with a trembling lip—"My friends, we will get no rain! there are, you see, no clouds; but my medicine [spiritual power] is great—I have brought a *thunder boat!* look and see it! the thunder you hear is out of her mouth, and the lightning which you see [the flash of the cannons being fired]! is on the waters!"

At this intelligence, the whole village flew to the tops of their wigwams [their earthen lodges], or to the bank of the river, from which the steamer was in full view, and ploughing along to their utter dismay and confusion.

In this promiscuous throng of chiefs, doctors [distinguished Mandan men], women, children and dogs was mingled, The White Buffalo's Hair, having descended from his high place to mingle with the frightened throng....

A few moments later brought the boat in front of the village, and all was still and quiet as death; not a Mandan was to be seen upon the banks. The steamer moored, and three or four of the chiefs walked boldly down the bank on to her deck, with a spear in one hand and the calumet or pipe of peace in the other.

The moment they stepped on board they met (to their great surprise and joy) their old friend, Major Sanford, their [Native American] agent, which circumstance put an instant end to all their fears.

[The Native American agent was an official contact-point between the Native Americans and the American government.] The villagers were soon apprised of the fact, and the whole race of beautiful and friendly Mandans was paraded on the bank of the river in front of the steamer.

Appendix 2:
The "Putrified" [Petrified] Forest of Black Harris

The fur trapper Moses Harris (d. 1849) was known to his fellow trappers as "Black Harris" because of his dark facial complexion, not because he was a black trapper.

Not much is known about his life except that he was a member of the Ashley fur-trading expedition that headed up the Missouri River in 1823. He was a gifted storyteller, as the following account will show. Lightly annotated, edited, shortened here, it comes from George Frederick Ruxton's accounts of his own travels in the Rocky Mountains and elsewhere in the Far West in 1848.[1]

As Ruxton describes the scene, Black Harris is having a chat with a lady in a local tavern. Here is part of their conversation:

"Well, Mister Harris, I hear that you are a great traveler."

"Travler, marm," says Black Harris, "this n*****'s no travler; I are a trapper, marm, a mountain man, wagh!" [wagh means "really, truly"].

"Well, Mister Harris, trappers are great travelers, and you goes over a sight of ground in your perishiniations [travels], I'll be bound to say."

"A sight, marm, this coon's gone over, if that's the way your stick floats" [if that's what you mean"].

"I've trapped beaver on [and here he names many rivers] Platte and Arkansas, and away up on Missoura and Yaller Stone…. I've 'raised hair' [i.e., scalped] *more than one* Apache…. I've trapped in heav'n, in airth, and h— [Hell]; and scalp my old head, marm, but I've [even] seen a putrified forest."

"La [short for 'Lord'—'My goodness'], Mister Harris, *a what?*"

[He replies] "A putrified forest, marm, as sure as my rifle's got hindsights, and *she* shoots center [swearing by his accurate rifle]. I was out on the Black Hills [South Dakota, in winter]…. If there wasn't cold doin's about that time, this child [himself] wouldn't say so. The snow was about fifty feet deep, and the bufler [buffalo] lay dead on the ground like bees after a beein.' [In winter cold, bees will die if they run out of honey, e.g., if it is taken by

168

humans.] Not whar we was, though, for *thar* was no bufler, and no meat [nothing to eat]."

[He continues] "One day ... we got into a peraira [prairie], whar was green grass, and green trees, and green leaves on the trees, and birds singing in the green leaves, and this in February, wagh! Our animals was like to die when they see the green grass, and we all sung out, 'hurraw for summer doin's!'"

"'Hyar goes for meat,' says I, and I jest ups old Ginger at one of them singing birds, and down come the critter elegant; its darned head spinning away from the body, but never stops singing. When I takes up the meat, I find it stone, wagh!" [This means: "Now I need to kill an animal for food. So I aimed my rifle, and shot the head cleanly off a bird—but it never stopped singing, and when I picked it up I found that it was actually made of stone!"]

[Harris goes on] "'Hyar's damp powder and no fire to dry it,' I says, quite skeared." [He likens his situation to one in which his gunpowder has become wet and will not ignite in his rifle, which therefore cannot be fired. Harris had no immediate way to dry out his gunpowder.]

[Another trapper, named Rube, says to Harris] "Fire be dogged.... Hyar's a horse as'll make fire come." ["Forget about the lack of a fire: I'll make fire come all by myself!"]

[Rube then swings his axe at a cottonwood tree, but the tree is so hard—*it was made of stone*—that the axe just bounces off, with a big chip taken out of its blade. Another trapper, young Sublette, comes over, scrapes the tree with his hunting knife; breaks the grass around it like pipe stems; and snaps some of the leaves off a tree.]

When Harris asks him, "What's all this, boy?" Sublette replies "Putrefactions ... or I'm a n*****" [in this context, he means "or I'm a fool"].

[The lady asks] "La, Mister Harris, putrefactions! Why, [did you think] the leaves and the trees, and the grass smell badly?"

Harris replied: "Smell badly, marm! Would a skunk stink if he was froze to stone?" [Harris goes on to tell the lady that when he visited Laramie, Wyoming, he showed two well-educated men a piece chipped out of the tree. He said that both men called it a "putrefaction."]

To make his point, he then asked her: "So, marm, if that wasn't a putrified peraira, what was it? For this hos doesn't know, and *he* knows 'fat cow' from 'poor bull,' anyhow."

["Fat cow" was a female buffalo that was tasty and good to eat; "poor bull" was a male with flesh so tough that it should not be eaten. Harris is in effect saying: "I don't know the answer myself, but I *do know what makes good sense and what does not.*"]

Appendix 3:
Grizzly Bear Hazing Guidelines for Livestock Owners, Homeowners and the General Public

This information is drawn from the online March 2020 U.S. Fish & Wildlife report on the above subject. It has been considerably shortened and edited. Grizzly bears are officially listed as "threatened" under the provisions of the Endangered Species Act. This means that harassing, harming, pursuing, hunting, shooting, wounding, trapping, or collecting grizzly bears is illegal, except in cases of self-defense, e.g., using bear spray, or the need to protect other people.

Grizzlies can pose a threat to human safety and should be discouraged from using areas near homes or other human-occupied areas. Hazing discourages undesirable behavior in wildlife, and when properly conducted, does not create a likelihood of injury to grizzly bears to such an extent as to disrupt their normal behavior.

People may use the methods listed below to deter grizzly bears from the immediate vicinity (200 yards) of any human-occupied residence or potential conflict area, such as a barn, livestock corral, chicken coop, grain bin or schoolyard. If there is an immediate danger of attack, people may legally kill a grizzly bear in self-defense or in defense of others. Any such action must be reported to the U.S Fish & Wildlife Service within five days.

Acceptable hazing techniques include the following:

- Non-projectile noise-making, such as yelling, clapping, banging pots or other objects, vehicle and air horns, sirens, and public address systems.

- Lights, such as spotlights or flashing lights: These should be used in combination with yelling so the bear will associate these bright lights with a human presence.
- Car or truck pressure, namely, driving vehicles slowly toward bears—but *not* actually hitting them—can get bears to leave the immediate vicinity. Horns or sirens should be used at the same time.
- Dogs: Finnish Karelian bear dogs or trained guard dogs, used on a leash, can be an effective deterrent.
- Water: Hoses with a nozzle that creates an intense high pressure long-range stream, such as a fire hose, can be a good deterrent, too.
- Non-lethal projectiles: Stones, marbles, or wooden balls can be thrown or shot from a slingshot. Paintballs or noise-making projectiles (bangers and 12-gauge crackers) can be used. The loud explosive noise of a banger or cracker must occur *between* the shooter and the bear: any loud noise *behind* the bear will drive him toward you or toward any bystanders.

Unacceptable deterrence methods include screamers and whistlers (erratic flight patterns; higher fire risk in dry conditions); rubber bullets and rubber batons (higher risk of injury to the bear); and bean bag and aero sock rounds (at short range these can injure people). Livestock owners and homeowners can prevent or minimize losses from bear predation through good husbandry and deterrence by means of electric fences, guard animals, and human presence.

Appendix 4:
Litigation and Planning
History of Winter Use

This annotated chronology is drawn chiefly from the National Park Service's report on "Winter Use and Planning in Litigation," which is listed in the Bibliography.

1932: First request to park managers to plow roads year-round.

1949: First visitors using motorized oversnow vehicles, then known as snowplanes. (These consisted of passenger cabs set on skis and powered—without becoming airborne!—by a rear-mounted airplane propeller and engine.)

1955: Snowcoaches enter the park.

1963: First snowmobiles (a total of six) enter the park.

1967: Congressional hearing on plowing park roads year-round.

1968: Yellowstone managers formalize oversnow use instead of plowing.

1971: The park begins grooming roads; Yellowstone Park Co. opens the Old Faithful Snow Lodge.

1990: National Park Service issues first winter-use environmental assessment (EA) for Yellowstone and Grand Teton National Parks.

1992: Winter visitation exceeds threshold of 140,000 people per year, eight years earlier than expected.

1993: National Park Service begins to evaluate winter recreation in the greater Yellowstone Area.

1996–1997: This winter is one of the harshest winters of the 1990s, with abundant snow, very cold temperatures, and a thick layer of ice in the snowpack. Unable to get at the grass underneath the ice, more than 1,000 bison leave the park and as a result are then shot or shipped to slaughter—due to fears they could transmit brucellosis to the cattle in Montana. Concerned that the "groomed" (i.e., plowed) roads are increasing the number of bison leaving the park and then being killed by hunters, environmental groups file suit against the National Park Service in 1997. These groups allege that the National Park Service has failed to study the adverse environmental impacts of winter use. In 1997 the National Park Service develops a new winter use plan and EIS in response to these charges.

1999: A draft EIS (Environmental Impact Statement) is released; 46,000 public comments are received. Environmental organizations petition for the prohibition of trail grooming and snowmobile use in all National Parks.

2000: The final EIS is released and a Record of Decision is signed, banning snowmobiles and approving only snowcoach transportation. Snowmobile enthusiasts sue to overturn the ban.

2001: The National Park Service settles with snowmobilers' group and agrees to prepare a Supplemental EIS, i.e., a SEIS.

2001: The draft SEIS is released; it generates 357,000 comments.

2003: A final rule is published in the Federal Register; it will allow only 950 Best Available Technology (BAT) guided snowmobiles daily. BAT snowmobiles make less noise and are less polluting than earlier models. A Federal judge, however, directs the park to begin phasing out snowmobiles.

2004: Another judge halts the phase-out and requires temporary rules for the rest of the winter. The National Park Service releases a new EA, allowing 720 BAT snowmobiles driven only by approved drivers; 95,000 comments are received. This plan is approved, and winter use proceeds.

2007: A draft Final EIS is released. It allows 540 BAT guided snowmobiles in the park daily: 122,000 comments are received. A final rule is published in the Federal register.

2008: Federal court decisions cancel the new winter plan. The winter season opens with a modified version of the winter plan that was followed in 2004–2007, allowing 720 BAT guided snowmobiles daily.

2009: The winter season opens under an interim plan during the EIS process, allowing 318 BAT guided snowmobiles and 78 snowcoaches daily for the next two winters.

2010: The National Park Service begins preparing the next long-term plan.

2013: A final Winter Use Plan/SEIS is released, proposing to manage oversnow vehicles based on what are technically called "transportation events," e.g., smaller groups of vehicles, rather than on the total number of snowmobiles and snowcoaches allowed in the park each day. A Final Rule for winter use is released, authorizing oversnow vehicle use based on Transportation Events.

Appendix 5:
Waters of Yellowstone

Water plays a vital role in the ecosystems of Yellowstone National Park and its surrounding areas. This appendix considers them in their entirety. An excellent introduction to this subject is a 14-page National Park Service study of July 1, 2020 (listed in the Bibliography), which is the source of much of the information presented here.

The water that flows through the park and the Greater Yellowstone Ecosystem is truly a national treasure: the headwaters of seven great rivers are all located in this same region. These rivers flow from the Continental Divide through far-flung communities across the United States en route to the Pacific Ocean, the Gulf of California, and the Gulf of Mexico. Precipitation (rain and snow) falling on the mountains and plateaus of the Northern Rockies flows through the stream and river networks that provide essential moisture for much of the American West. Moreover, the rivers offer recreational opportunities, essential plant and wildlife habitats, and no end of scenic vistas. The water also drives the complicated geothermal activity of the region, and fuels the largest group of geysers on this planet. Both precipitation and groundwater gradually seep down into the geothermal "plumbing" over days or over many thousands of years. They are then superheated there by the Yellowstone volcano, and ascend to the surface as hot springs, geysers, mudpots, and fumaroles.

Yellowstone has some of the most significant near-pristine aquatic ecosystems found anywhere in the United States. The park has more than 600 lakes and ponds with a total of about 107,000 surface acres, 94 percent of which are associated with the Yellowstone, Lewis, Shoshone, and Hart lakes. There are also about 2,500 miles of running water in the 1,000 or so rivers and streams of Yellowstone. Thousands of small wetland habitats that are intermittently wet or dry make up about 3 percent of the Yellowstone landscape.

Yellowstone's inland lakes are an essential aquatic habitat for many resident species. Because in the park they are largely protected from many of the ecological stresses that may affect the waters outside the park, they can maintain their freshwater biodiversity, can support elaborate food chains, and can underpin many different plant and animal communities. Understanding the complexities of Yellowstone's lake resources thus helps park managers conserve the park's lake resources in the face of non-native invasive species, climate change, and pollution.

Yellowstone Lake itself is the biggest high-elevation lake in North America. It is 7,731 feet in elevation; covers up to 139 square miles with an average depth of 138 feet; contains more than 12,000,000 acre-feet of water; is a maximum of 430 feet deep, with a shoreline 141 miles long; and is covered by ice from mid–December to May or June. Many of the region's 1,000 to 3,000 annual earthquakes occur under Yellowstone Lake, causing uplift and subsidence events which continually reshape the shoreline of the lake. Finally, Yellowstone Lake is also the site of one of the most extensive conservation efforts by the National Park Service. As discussed in earlier pages of this book, lake trout were illegally introduced into Yellowstone Lake and have since then jeopardized the survival of the native population of cutthroat trout by eating them. Regarding some of the other lakes:

Lewis Lake is fed by the Lewis River and its tributaries. Shoshone Lake is the park's second-largest lake and is located at the head of the Lewis River southwest of West Thumb. It is a valuable wilderness resource and assessable only on foot or by boat through the Lewis River Channel. Originally barren of fish because of the waterfalls on the Lewis River, it now contains lake trout and brown trout (both inserted by park managers in 1890) and the Utah chub (introduced by bait fishermen). This large lake is the source of the Lewis River, which flows into the Pacific Ocean via the Snake River system. The U.S. Fish and Wildlife Service believes that Shoshone Lake may be the biggest lake in the lower 48 states that cannot be reached by car.

Heart Lake is located at the south end of the park near the base of Mt. Sheridan. It sits in prime bear country, and has several thermal areas along the northwest shore.

The Yellowstone River is 671 miles long and is the longest undammed river in the lower 48 states. The headwaters of the Yellowstone lie outside the southeast park boundary on Younts Peak in Wyoming. The river flows into Yellowstone Lake, leaves the lake at Fishing Bridge, and continues north-northwest until it leaves the park near Gardiner, Montana. The Yellowstone then continues north and east through Montana and joins the Missouri River just across the North Dakota state line. Its watershed drains one-third of the state of Montana. The river carves out the Grand Canyon of the Yellowstone in the middle of the park and runs over the Upper and Lower Falls. It is home to Yellowstone cutthroat trout. The Yellowstone River is one of the best recreational rivers in the United States and provides many opportunities for boating, fishing, bird-watching, and other forms of recreation. In addition, this river serves many downstream communities such as Billings, Montana, and is important to agriculture, industries and municipalities alike.

The Lamar River rises on the east side of the park. Its famous wildlife-filled valley is the site of pronghorn; rutting bison; bears; the most consistent viewing of wild wolves in the world; and first-rate fly fishing.

The Gardner River originates in the northwest corner of the park and ends up in the Missouri River. It flows into the Yellowstone, joining it near Rattlesnake Butte at the north entrance to the park.

The Snake River is a major tributary of the Columbia River. It begins in Yellowstone National Park and then turns south into Grand Teton National Park. The Snake River flows through Idaho and eventually joins the Columbia River in the state of Washington. The Snake is 1,040 miles long, of which 42 miles are in the park, and flows into Jackson Lake—a natural lake augmented by a dam, which has regulated downstream flows since 1907. Visitors can enjoy rafting, fishing, and photography on the river, which is home to a wide range of riparian and aquatic species, including the native Yellowstone cutthroat trout, and an endemic variety, the Snake River fine-spotted cutthroat trout. The 2009 Snake River Headquarters Legacy Act designated the river above Jackson Lake as a Wild and Scenic River.

The Firehole River, home to several species of trout, is a favored fly-fishing spot. Since most of the outflow from the park's geyser basins empties into the Firehole River, it is warmer and chemically-richer (due to its dissolved minerals) than the other watersheds.

The Gibbon River (a popular place to view rapids) and the Firehole River unite to form the Madison River, which eventually joins the Jefferson River and then the Missouri River on its way to the Gulf of Mexico.

Chapter Notes

QUOTE

1. Quoted in part in "Yellowstone National Park.com," p. 1, and in part in L.A. Haines (ed.), *Osborne Russell's Journey of a Trapper, or, Nine Years in the Rocky Mountains*, p. 13.

PREFACE

1. An ecosystem is in fact much more complicated than can easily be summarized. The U.S. Park Service, for example, lists these 11 component parts of the Greater Yellowstone Ecosystem: the Influence of Geology; Air Quality; Soundscapes; Water; Cycles and Processes; Winter Ecology; Beyond [man-made] Boundaries; Land Use; Wilderness; Winter Use; and Nature. (See, in the Bibliography, National Park Service, "Greater Yellowstone Ecosystem," pp. 1–6.)

2. After U.S. Geological Survey, "What is the difference between global warming and climate change?," p. 1.

3. After 2019 *Yellowstone Resources and Issues Handbook*, p. 72.

SETTING THE STAGE

1. A good source used here is the National Park Service paper on "Cycles and Processes" in the Bibliography.

2. After 2019 NPS Handbook on Resources and Issues, p. 61.

3. A partial list of these ranges would include the Tetons, the Wyoming Range, the Salt River Range, Wind Rivers, Absarokas, Beartooths, Gallatins, Madison, Tobacco Roots, Gravellys, and Centennials.

4. After Chang and Hansen, *Historic &*
Projected Climate Change in the Greater Yellowstone Ecosystem, p. 14.

5. Some of these comments are drawn from Marston and Anderson, "Watersheds and Vegetation of the Greater Yellowstone Ecosystem," p. 1 of the Abstract.

6. Quoted in *National Geographic* map, "Greater Yellowstone Region," back cover.

7. After Holdsworth, *Yellowstone and Grand Teton*, p. 3.

8. After Steingisser and Marcus, "Human Impacts on Geyser Basins," p. 7.

9. In North America, the words "bison" and "buffalo" both refer to the same animal. Purists insist that the use of the term "buffalo" is incorrect in the U.S. because "true buffalo" exist on other continents and are only distant relatives of the bison. This book uses the term "bison."

10. After Fraser, "The Crucial Role of Predators," p. 1.

11. Quoted in *Yellowstone Resources and Issues Handbook 2018*, p. 3.

12. Quoted in *Yellowstone Resources and Issues Handbook 2018*, p. 4.

13. After U.S. Forest Service, "Bridger-Teton National Forest—History and Culture," p. 1.

14. After Clayton, *Wonderscape*, p. 128.

15. After Huidekoper, *The Early Days in Jackson Hole*, p. 109.

16. See Williams, Darville, and Vering on "Improving Visitor Preparedness and Safety in the Bear Country of Yellowstone National Park."

CHAPTER 1

1. Some of the following comments are sourced to the National Park Service's

article on "Historic Tribes" in the Bibliography.

2. After Whittlesey, "Native Americans, the Earliest Interpreters," p. 278.

3. There are various lists of the tribes that once inhabited what is now Yellowstone National Park. The list used here is from the U.S. Park Service's official list of "Associated Tribes," which explains that "There are 26 current tribes that have historic connections to the land and resources now found within Yellowstone National Park." Similar but shorter lists can be found in Whittlesey, "Native American Indians, the Earliest Interpreters," p. 274, and National Park Service, *Yellowstone Resources and Issues Handbook 2019*, p. 16.

4. This and some of the following points are drawn from Yellowstone National Park, "Succession: Biological Progression," p. 1.

5. After *2019 Yellowstone Resources and Issues Handbook*, pp. 14–15.

6. Surrender speech of Chief Joseph, p. 1.

7. After *2018 Yellowstone Resources and Issues Handbook*, p. 31.

Chapter 2

1. In addition to the other sources cited in later endnotes, a brief National Park Service handout, "Expeditions Explore Yellowstone," pp. 1–3, has also been used here. The two most thorough sources on this subject are probably two volumes by Aubrey L. Haines of his *The Yellowstone Story*, both published in 1977, but these are too detailed for our purposes and have not been used in any depth here.

2. Quoted by Allen, *Lewis and Clark and the Image of the American West*, p. 1. Italics added.

3. Some of these comments on David Thompson are drawn from Hunt Janin's 2020 book on the explorers and writers of the American frontiers from 1528 to 1879 (see the Bibliography).

4. Quoted by Janin and Carlson in *Overland Explorations of the Trans-Mississippi West*.

5. Quoted by Golay and Bowman, *North American Exploration*, p. 387.

6. So much has been written about the Lewis and Clark expedition that no single source can be said to be predominant, but Carolyn Gilman's 2003 study, *Lewis and Clark: Across the Divide*, is one of the very best.

7. In the Bibliography, see Bergon (ed.), *The Journals of Lewis and Clark*.

8. After Bergon (ed.), *The Journals of Lewis and Clark*, p. 108.

9. Quoted by Whittlesey, "Native Americans, the Earliest Interpreters," p. 274.

10. Quoted in Golay and Bowman, *North American Exploration*, p. 356.

11. After Allen, *Lewis and Clark and the Image of the American Northwest*, p. 243; and Allen, *A Continent Comprehended*, p. 59.

12. The larger Western rivers could, under good conditions, i.e., with deep enough water, be navigated by at least several different kinds of boats. In terms of increasing size, these were: the dugout canoe; the pirogue; the flatboat; the Mackinaw; the keelboat; and, finally, the side-wheel and stern-wheel steamers. (Source: After O'Neil, *The Rivermen*, pp. 20–21.)

13. Quoted by Wheeler in *The Chroniclers*, pp. 117–118.

14. After Gilbert, *Westering Man*, p. 108.

15. After O'Neil, *The Rivermen*, pp. 28, 120–121.

16. Some of these comments on John Colter are drawn from Janin and Carlson, *Overland Explorations of the Trans-Mississippi West*, and from Lavender's Introduction to the Harris book on John Colter, pp. xi–xvii (see the Bibliography). See also the Janin and Faircloth article, "A Sense of Wonder," which is listed in the Bibliography.

17. After Golay and Bowman, *North American Exploration*, p. 326.

18. Quoted in Gilbert, *The Trailblazers*, p. 60.

19. Some of these comments are sourced to Golay and Bowman, *North American Exploration*, p. 344.

20. Quoted by Gilbert, *The Trailblazers*, p. 64.

21. After Golay and Bowman, *North American Exploration*, pp. 359–360.

22. After Sánchez *et al.*, *New Mexico: A History*, pp. 71–72.

23. Most of the information in this

section comes from the Janin and Faircloth article "A Sense of Wonder" and from *Bodmer's America*; see the Bibliography.

24. Quoted in Janin and Faircloth, "A Sense of Wonder," p. 41.

25. Some of these comments on Osborne Russell are from "Mountain Men in the American West," pp. 1–3.

26. Quoted in Utley, *A Life Wild and Perilous*, p. 89.

27. Quoted by Wheler, *The Scouts*, p. 16.

28. The quote is from Russell's *Journal of a Trapper*.

29. There was no love lost between the American trappers and the Blackfoot Indians. The mountain man and explorer "Old Bill" Williams (1787–1849), for example, was trapping alone near the source of the Yellowstone River when he was attacked by three Blackfoot Indians. Native American arrows hit him in the shoulder and thigh, but he managed to escape, armed only with his butcher knife. The Native Americans took his rifle, his mule, and his beaver pelts. After recuperating in his camp for two days, he began to track the thieves, and caught up with them four days later when they were asleep at night. He killed and scalped two of them without waking the third. Then, stirring up the campfire to give some light, he roused the remaining Blackfoot and waved the bloody scalps in his face. He did not harm the man, who ran off like an antelope. Later, asked by his relatives why he had not killed that Blackfoot, too, he replied: "Ef I'd a kilt that Injun, thyar would't a been nobody left to tell them Blackfeet how them bucks had gone under nor who'd a rubbed 'em out." (Source: Wheeler, *The Scouts,* pp. 16–17.)

30. Quoted by Miller in "The first written description of Yellowstone geysers in 1827," p. 2.

31. After Victor, "Introduction to *The River of the West*: Joe Meek's Years in the Rocky Mountains," pp. 5–6.

32. Quoted in Research Division, Yellowstone National Park, Interim Report on Northern Range Research, p. 4.

33. Quoted by Morgan, *Jedediah Smith and the Opening of the West*, p. 304.

34. Most of the information used here is from the 1919 edition of Wilson's 1910 autobiography, *White Indian Boy.*

35. Wilson, *White Indian Boy*, pp. 23–24.

36. This account is drawn from "Expeditions Explore Yellowstone," p. 2.

37. Quoted by Yellowstonenationalpark.com, p. 1, but no source given.

38. Quoted in Janin and Carlson, *Overland Explorations of the Trans-Mississippi West*, p. 164.

39. After National Park Survey, "Grand Canyon of the Yellowstone," p. 1.

40. After *National Geographic Magazine*, "When Yellowstone Explodes."

41. Some of these comments on the 1871 Hayden Expedition are drawn from the *Yellowstone Resources and Issues Handbook*, p. 19.

42. There was also a small U.S. Army expedition led by Captain J.W. Barlow in 1871. He discovered Heart Lake (lying south of the much larger Yellowstone Lake) and produced the first accurate map of the region, but these achievements were much less noteworthy than the results of the 1871 Hayden expedition and are not well-known to non-specialists today.

43. Moran joined the Hayden Expedition at his own expense and, with the backing of Jay Cooke and Company, owners of the Northern Pacific Railroad, he was welcomed as a member of the survey team. The railroad had a vested interest in Moran because it was trying to popularize the region in order to expand into the Mountain West. (Source: National Park Service article on "Thomas Moran's Diary.")

44. This account is drawn from Gilbert, *The Trailblazers*, p. 196.

45. A small copy of this map can be seen in Allen, *A Continent Comprehended*, p. 478.

46. The following information comes from the Yellowstone Historic Center, "Stagecoach Tourism," and "Early Rail Travel to Yellowstone."

47. Quoted by Wheeler, *The Chroniclers*, p. 147. Much of the information on Earl Dunraven that is used in this section is from this same source.

48. Quoted by Wheeler, *The Chroniclers*, pp. 147–148.

49. Quoted by Wheeler, *The Chroniclers*, p. 148.

CHAPTER 3

1. Much of the information used below comes from the PBS (Public Broadcasting System) article in the Bibliography on "The National Parks: America's Best Idea—Yellowstone National Park," pp. 1–2.

2. From Baillie-Grohman, *Camps in the Rockies*. Quoted in John Daugherty, *A Place Called Jackson Hole*, chapter 14, footnote 4.

CHAPTER 5

1. Important sources used in this chapter include the research of retired National Park Service expert Paul Schullery (see Bibliography).

2. Many of the following points are drawn from Yellowstone National Park, "Eat or Be Eaten!," listed in the Bibliography.

3. After Huidekoper, *The Early Days in Jackson Hole*, p. 23.

4. Donald Hough, a good-humored author and outdoorsman in Jackson Hole, offered this definition: "A dude is one who comes in for weeks or months, stays at a dude ranch or something like it, dresses more like a cowhand than a cowhand does, and in a kind of simple minded way tries to fit into the country. The dude is in the minority (compared to the tourist)—he, and especially she, takes up little space except when sitting down." (Source: Huidekoper, The Early Days in Jackson Hole, p. 101.)

5. In its heyday in the 1920s, the Bar BC Ranch was known as one of the best dude ranches in the West. Located on the west bank of the Snake River a few miles upstream from the hamlet of Moose, Wyoming, this ranch was in business from 1911 until 1986, when it became part of Yellowstone Park. (Source: Holdsworth, Jackson Hole and the Tetons, p. 104.)

6. After Harris, John Colter, pp 2–9.

7. After Preston, "Nature's Boundaries," p. 16.

8. This account is drawn from Forest Service, "Custer Gallatin National Forest," pp. 1–2.

9. Because the Colt was so slow to reload, some Western gunfighters carried two of them. In a gunfight, as soon as one

was empty, it could be dropped and the other revolver brought into play.

10. Some of these comments on the Beaverhead-Deerlodge National Forest are drawn from Forest Service information on its "Historic Period"—see website https:www.fs.usda.gov/bdnf.

11. Sources used here include Forest Service, "Caribou-Targhee National Forest," p. 1.

12. Some of the information used here comes Forest Service, "Welcome to the Bridger-Teton National Forest."

13. This information comes from Forest Service, "Shoshone National Forest."

14. After the two pieces on "Camp Monaco" listed in the Bibliography.

15. After Forest Service, "Shoshone National Forest," p. 1.

16. This account is drawn chiefly from the U.S. Fish and Wildlife Service, "National Elk Refuge," https://www.fws.gov/nwrs/threecolumn.aspx?id=21475110350. Accessed 21 September 2019.

17. Formerly known as Pierre's Hole and now the location of the Teton Geotourism Center in Driggs, Idaho, the Teton Valley commemorates the Hudson's Bay Company trader and Native American leader Pierre Tivanitagon, nicknamed "Big Pierre" or "Old Pierre," who was killed in a battle with the Blackfoot Indians in 1827.

18. The information presented here is drawn from the U.S. Fish and Wildlife Service, "Red Rock Lakes," pp. 1–7.

19. This section draws on the U.S. Fish and Wildlife Service, "Camas Refuge," pp. 1–4.

20. Some of this discussion follows Schullery, "The Greater Yellowstone Ecosystem," pp. 1–5.

21. After USGS, "Return of the Grizzly Bear," p. 1.

22. Quoted by O'Connor et al., Spectacular Yellowstone and Grand Teton National Parks, p. 18, citing Peacock and Peacock, The Essential Grizzly: The Mingled Fate of Men and Bears, pp. xiii, 43.

23. Grizzly bears are a top predator but, despite their fearsome reputation, meat makes up only about one-tenth of their diet: the rest consists of berries, seeds, and other foraged foods. They were labeled as "threatened" under the Endangered Species Act in 1975, and as their population recovered, efforts to remove

them from the list continued. The U.S. Fish and Wildlife Service removed the Yellowstone population of bears from the list in 2017. By 2018, the surrounding states began to organize trophy hunts for bears, but just hours before the first hunt was scheduled to begin in August 2018, a Federal judge halted the plan and restored the grizzlies' protection. The judge's ruling was appealed, and the new ruling upholds these protections. (Source: Smithsonian Magazine grizzly bear article listed in the Bibliography.)

24. After National Park Service, "Yellowstone Cutthroat Trout," pp. 1–9.

25. Much of this account is drawn from National Park Service, "Pronghorn," pp. 1–7.

26. After Yellowstone National Park Trips, "Important Food Source for Yellowstone Bears In Trouble," pp. 1–3.

27. Adapted from National Park Service, "The Greater Yellowstone Ecosystem," pp. 1–5.

28. Preston, "Saving the Charmed Goose: Reconciling Human Demands with Inherent Limitations in the Greater Yellowstone Ecosystem," pp. 5–6, 13.

Chapter 6

1. Many of the points made in this chapter are drawn from the 2018 edition of the Yellowstone Resources and Issues Handbook, pp. 54–55 and 107–130, and especially from the excellent 2019 National Park Service article on "Volcano," pp. 1–11. The text following, based on the latter account, has been lightly edited and shortened from the NPS article.

2. Some of the points used here come from the 2018 Yellowstone Resources and Issues Handbook, pp. 122–123.

3. For maps of glaciation in the Yellowstone area, see the 2018 Yellowstone Resources and Issues Handbook, pp. 124–125.

Chapter 7

1. This chapter is largely drawn from the 2019 National Park Service's Yellowstone Resources and Issues Handbook, pp. 131–142.

2. Quoted by the NPS in the Yellowstone Resources and Issues Handbook, p. 132.

3. After the NPS 2019 Yellowstone Resources and Issues Handbook, p. 139.

Chapter 8

1. See the 2019 Yellowstone Resources and Issues Handbook, pp. iii–iv, and 175–294, for excellent information on Yellowstone's wildlife. This is the source of much of the information used in this chapter.

2. This photo appears on p. 175 of the 2019 Yellowstone Resources and Issues Handbook.

3. Almost all the American muzzle-loading rifles of this era were single-shot weapons. The British did make "double rifles" that had two barrels, thus giving a hunter two shots, but these rifles were generally used to hunt big game in India or Africa, and were much too expensive for the typical American outdoorsman to afford.

4. After Catlin, North American Indians," pp. 66–67.

5. Some of the following comments are drawn from a National Park Service publication on the habitat of the bison, p. 1.

6. See National Park Service, "Study shows Yellowstone bison have positive effects on the landscape," in the Bibliography.

7. Some of the following comments are drawn from the National Park Service's report on "Elk," pp. 2–10, which is listed in the Bibliography.

8. After National Park Service, "Understanding the Limits to Wolf Hunting Ability," p. 3.

9. Many of the points made here are drawn from Yellowstone's 2019 Resources and Issues Handbook, pp. 265–285.

10. Quoted by Clifford, The Backbone of the World, p. 22.

Chapter 9

1. Quoted in Yellowstone Science, March 2015, p. 5.

2. After 2016 Yellowstone Resources and Issues Handbook, p. 78.

3. After 2019 Yellowstone Resources and Issues Handbook, p. 71.

4. After 2019 Yellowstone Resources and Issues Handbook, pp. 71–72.

5. This comment is from a private communication from Dr. Ann Rodman of 3 February 2020.

6. After National Park Service, "Climate Change," p. 2.

7. After National Park Service, "Climate Change, p. 3.

8. After Chang and Hansen, "Historic and Projected Change in the Greater Yellowstone Ecosystem," p. 18.

9. After Tercek, Rodman, and Thoma, "Trends in Yellowstone's Snowpack," p. 26.

10. After Tercek, Rodman, and Thoma, "Trends in Yellowstone's Snowpack," pp. 20, 26.

11. After Hansen, Piekielek, Chang, and Phillips, "Changing Climate Suitability for Forests in Yellowstone & the Rocky Mountains," p. 39.

12. After Gonzalez, "Climate Change and Ecological Impacts at Yellowstone National Park, USA," pp. 1–5.

13. Rome and Turner, "Implications of Global Climate Change for Biogeographic Patterns in the Greater Yellowstone Ecosystem," p. 382.

Chapter 10

1. The best sources on the Northern Range are probably the 2002 National Academy Press report on "Ecological Dynamics on Yellowstone's Northern Range; the 1997 National Park Service analysis of "Yellowstone's northern range: complexity & change in a wildland ecosystem"; and the 1992 study by the Research Division of Yellowstone National Park on "Interim Report Yellowstone National Park Northern Range Research." The first was also summarized in a 15-page document by the National Academies Press. All three of these papers are listed in the Bibliography.

2. Some the following descriptions are drawn from O'Connor, Spectacular Yellowstone and Grand Teton National Parks, pp. 65–73.

3. Some of the following discussion is drawn from the 2019 NPS Handbook on Resources and Issues, pp. 64–65.

4. It must be noted here that many factors, e.g., wolves and other predators, drought, winterkill, and hunting, can all contribute to low survival rates and thus to decreased elk numbers. In addition, elk numbers are only rough estimates, not exact counts, and do not necessarily "add up" to a sure total.

5. After the National Academies Press, Summary of "Ecological Dynamics on Yellowstone's Northern Range," 2002, p. 1.

6. After National Academy of Science, "Ecological Dynamics on Yellowstone's Northern Range," p. 1.

Chapter 11

1. One of the best studies of Yellowstone wolves is the 97-page Yellowstone Science report of June 2016 entitled "Celebrating 20 years of wolves," which is listed in the Bibliography and which has been used extensively in this chapter.

2. After Doug Smith, personal interview with Nicole Janin Sheehan, 27 January 2020.

3. After Doug Smith, personal interview with Sheehan, 27 January 2020.

Chapter 12

1. The source of this quote was probably Vol. ll of Grace Raymond Hebard's 1922 book on the Bozeman Trail, but the page number is not readily available.

2. This account is drawn from a private communication of 24 April 2019 from Rachel Phillips, the Research Coordinator for the Gallatin Historical Society/Gallatin History Museum.

3. Some of the following comments are drawn from the 2019 Yellowstone Forever article on "Safeguarding Yellowstone: The U.S. Army Years 1886–1918," pp. 1–7.

4. The following account is sourced to the Yellowstone National Park Trips article on "Deaths and Injuries at Yellowstone's Geysers and Hot Springs," pp. 1–3.

5. Quoted in "Protection of Game in Yellowstone National Park," p. 1.

6. The Lacey Act of 1894, Chap. 72, Sec. 4.

7. This account follows Lamplugh, "The Poaching and Saving of Yellowstone's Wildlife," pp. 1–3.

8. Quoted in Muir, The Wilderness Years, p. vii.

9. This quote is from Muir's April 1898 article in The Atlantic magazine.

10. Quoted by O'Connor, Spectacular Yellowstone and Grand Teton National Parks, p. 92, citing Muir but with no source or page number given.

11. Some of the points made in this section are sourced to Revisiting Leopold; Resource Stewardship in the National Parks," pp. 1–23.

12. The National Academy of Sciences is a private nonprofit society of scholars engaged in scientific and engineering research for the general welfare. It was chartered by Congress in 1863.

13. After Leopold Report, "The Goal of Park Management in the United States."

14. After the Summary of National Academies Press, Ecological Dynamics on Yellowstone's Northern Range.

15. After "Revisiting Leopold: Resource Stewardship in the National Parks," p. 11.

16. Some of the facts used here come from Reichard, "Old Yellowstone: Bear Feeding," pp. 1–7.

17. Quoted by Reichard, "Old Yellowstone: Bear Feeding," p. 5.

18. After National Park Service, "Bear-Inflicted Human Injuries and Fatalities in Yellowstone," p. 2.

19. Much of the following section is sourced to the 2019 Yellowstone Resources and Issues Handbook, pp. 161–174.

20. After the National Park Service handout on "Our Staff Offices," pp. 1–5.

21. Much of the following information comes from a National Park Service handout on "Yellowstone Center for Resources," pp. 1–3.

22. After the National Park Service handout on "Heritage and Research Center," pp. 1–5; and the Yellowstone Quarterly of May 16, 2019, pp. 1–3.

Chapter 13

1. The chief sources used here are the six articles on winter use of Yellowstone (see Bibliography, where they are listed under National Park Service, Winter use in Yellowstone).

2. After National Park Service, "Ski and Snowshoe," p. 2. Italics added.

3. Many of the comments of Yellowstone's animals during the winter are drawn from the National Park Service, "Winter Ecology," pp. 1–8.

4. This list is adapted from the National Park Service's article on "Winter Ecology," pp. 3–4.

5. Many of the points that follow here are drawn from the National Park Service's articles on "Winter Use Management," pp. 1–9, and "Winter Use Planning and Litigation," pp. 1–4.

6. After National Park Service, "Winter Use Management," p. 3. Italics added.

7. After National Park Service, "Winter Use Management," p. 2.

8. Some of the information used here is drawn from O'Connor, Spectacular Yellowstone and Grand Teton National Parks, p. 49.

Chapter 14

1. After the 2020 Yellowstone Resources and Issue Handbook, p. 93.

2. After Churchman, "Wicked Problems," pp. B-141-B-146.

3. After Levin et al., "Overcoming the tragedy of super wicked problems," pp. 123–152.

4. After Lybecker, "The Old West, the New West and the Next West." pp. 2–3.

5. Most of the points made here are sourced to Wilkinson's 4 June 2019 article on "The New West," (see the Bibliography), p. 5.

6. These points also come from the Wilkinson article cited above, pp. 5–6.

7. After the Wilkinson article cited in the Bibliography (p. 5).

8. After the NPR (National Public Radio) entry on this subject in the Bibliography.

9. After the NPR entry cited above.

10. This and the following comments are after McBeth et al., "The Science of Storytelling: Measuring Policy Beliefs in Greater Yellowstone," pp. 416–418.

11. Some of the following points are adapted from McBeth and Shanahan, "Public opinion for sale: The role of policy marketers in Greater Yellowstone policy conflict," pp. 321–324.

12. For an excellent summary of the history of wolf restoration in the Yellowstone region, see the 19 September 2019 National Park Service report listed in the Bibliography.

13. After Preston, "Saving the Charmed Goose," p. 13.

Chapter 15

1. After Ray, "A Healthy Look at Monitoring," in Yellowstone Science, p. 2.

2. After Debinski, "Insects as a Vital Sign in the Greater Yellowstone Ecosystem," p. 58. By adding the italics to this quote, we are calling attention to its most important point.

3. From the 2019 National Park Service publication "Vital Signs." p. 63.

4. The source of this section is Shanahan, "An Uncertain Future: the Persistence of Whitebark Pine in the Greater Yellowstone Ecosystem," pp. 67–71.

5. After Logan et al., "Whitebark pine vulnerability to climate-drive mountain pine beetle disturbance in the Greater Yellowstone Ecosystem," p. 895.

6. Some of these points are drawn from Ray et al., "Assessing the Ecological Health of the Greater Yellowstone Ecosystem," pp. 3–9.

7. Most of the following comments are drawn, with very little editing, from Thoma et al., "Patterns of Primary Production & Ecological Drought in Yellowstone," pp. 34–39.

Chapter 16

1. Some of these comments are drawn from pp. 1–5 of the NPS introduction to Visitor Use Management.

2. Most of these examples are taken from pp. 3–5 of the NPS commentary on Visitor Use Management.

3. Most of the following comments are drawn from the National Park Service piece on "Strategic Priorities," pp. 1–5.

4. This section draws chiefly on Noss et al., "A Multicriteria Assessment of the Irreplaceability and Vulnerability of Sites in the Greater Yellowstone Ecosystem," pp. 895–908.

5. After Noss et al., "A Multicriteria Assessment of the Irreplaceability and Vulnerability of Sites in the Greater Yellowstone Ecosystem," p. 895.

Chapter 17

1. Sources used in this chapter include "Beyond Boundaries," pp. 82–83, of the NPS 2019 Yellowstone Resources and Issues Handbook.

2. See the NPS 2019 Yellowstone Resources and Issues Handbook, p. 83.

3. See, in the Bibliography, the IUCN's 2017 Conservation Outlook on Yellowstone National Park.

4. Quoted by Schullery, "Greater Yellowstone Science: Past, Present, and Future," p. 11.

Conclusions

1. See Kieter's article on "The Greater Yellowstone Ecosystem Revisited" in the Bibliography.

1. Catlin, The North American Indians, Vol. 1, p. 15.

A Chronology

Appendix 1

1. Some of the points made in this section are drawn from the Smithsonian American Art Museum's piece on "George Catlin," pp. 1–2.

Appendix 2

1. See "Mountain Men" by Glen Rounds in the Bibliography, pp. 50–53.

Bibliography

AccessScience Editors. "Trophic Cascade in Yellowstone National Park." https: www. accessscience.com:443/. Accessed 19 November 2019.

Allen, John Logan (ed.). *Lewis and Clark and the Image of the American Northwest.* Mineola: Dover Publications, 1991.

______. *North American Exploration: A Continent Comprehended.* Vol. 3. Lincoln: University of Nebraska Press, 1997.

Ambrose, Stephen E. *Undaunted Courage: Meriwether Lewis, Thomas Jefferson, and the Opening of the American West.* New York: Touchstone, 1997.

Athearn, Robert G. *The Mythic West in Twentieth-Century America.* Lawrence: University Press of Kansas, 1986.

Bergon, Frank (ed.). *The Journals of Lewis and Clark.* New York: Penguin, 2003.

Bodmer's America: Karl Bodmer's Illustrations to Prince Maximilian of Wied-Neuweid's Travels in the Interior of North America 1832–1834. London: Joselyn Art Museum and Alecto Editions, 1991.

Brunson, Mark, and Lynn Huntsinger. "Synthesis Paper—"Ranching as a Conservation Strategy: Can Old Ranchers Save the New West?," in *Rangeland Ecology & Management* 61(2), March 2008, pp. 137–147.

Capps, Benjamin. *The Old West: The Great Chiefs.* New York: Time-Life Books, 1975.

Catlin, George. *North American Indians.* (Peter Matthiessen, ed.) New York: Penguin, 2004.

______. *The North American Indians, Being Letters and Notes on Their Manners, Customs, and Conditions, Written During Eight Years' Travel Amongst the Wildest Tribes of Indians. In two volumes—Vol. 1.* Edinburgh: John Grant, 1903.

Churchman, C. West. "Wicked Problems," in *Management Science,* 14(4): B-141–B-146.

Clayton, John. *Wonderscape: Yellowstone National Park and the Evolution of an American Cultural Icon.* New York: Pegasus Books, 2017.

Clifford, Frank. *The Backbone of the World: A Portrait of the Vanishing West Along the Continental Divide.* New York: Broadway Books, 2002.

Daugherty, John. *A Place Called Jackson Hole: A Historic Resource Study of Grand Teton National Park.* Moose: Grand Teton Natural History Association, 1999.

Debinski, Diane M. "Insects as a Vital Sign in the Greater Yellowstone Ecosystem," in *Yellowstone Science,* 17 September 2019, pp. 58–60.

Deweese, Chelsea. "A Guide to Yellowstone's Gorgeous & Underrated Northern Region." Gardiner: Chamber of Commerce, April 07, 2018.

Farquhar, Brodie. "Wolf Reintroduction Changes Ecosystem in Yellowstone." http://www. yellowstonepark.com/things-to-do/wolf-reintroduction-changes-ecosytem. Accessed 16 December 2019.

Farrell, Justin. "The Battle of Yellowstone: Morality and the Sacred Roots of Environmental Conflict." https://environment.yale.edu/news/article/justin-farrell-book-the-battle-for-Yellowtone/. Accessed 09 December 2019.

Fraser, Caroline. "The Crucial Role of Predators: A New Perspective on Ecology." Yale Environment 360. https://e360.yale.edu/features/the_critical_role_of_predators _a_new_perspective_on_ecology. Accessed 7 February 2020.

Gilbert, Bil [*sic*]. *The Trailblazers.* New York: Time-Life Books, 1973.

_____. *Westering Man: The Life of Joseph Walker.* Norman: University of Oklahoma Press, 1985.

Gilman, Carolyn. *Lewis and Clark: Across the Divide.* Washington: Smithsonian Books in association with the Missouri Historical Society of St. Louis, 2003.

Golay, Michael, and John S. Bowman. *North American Exploration.* Hoboken: Wiley, 2003.

Golding, Jenny. "The Northern Range—Yellowstone's Wildlife Hub." http://www.yellow stonenationalparklodges.com/connect/yellowstone-hot-spot/the-northern-range-yellowstones-wildlife-hub/. Accessed 20 April 2019.

Gonzalez, Patrick. "Climate Change and Ecological Impacts at Yellowstone National Park, USA." Washington, D.C.: Climate Change Response Program, U.S. National Park Service, December 4, 2012.

Greater Yellowstone Coordinating Committee. "About" (i.e., "About this Committee.") https://www.fedgycc.org. Accessed 14 May 2020.

Haines, Aubrey L. *Yellowstone National Park: Its Exploration and Establishment.* Washington, D.C.: U.S. Department of the Interior, National Park Service, 1974.

Haines, L.A. (ed.). *Osborne Russell's Journal of a Trapper, or, Nine Years in the Rocky Mountains.* Lincoln: University of Nebraska Press, 1965.

Hansen, Andrew, and Linda Phillips. "Trends in vital signs in Greater Yellowstone: application of a Wildland Health Index." *Ecosphere.* August 2018. 9(8). Article e02380. www.esajournal.org. Accessed 22 September 2019.

Hansen, Andrew; Nate Piekielek; Tony Chang; and Linda Phillips. "Changing Climate Suitability for Forests in Yellowstone & the Rocky Mountains." *Yellowstone Science,* 23(1), 2015.

Harris, Burton. *John Colter: His Years in the Rockies.* (David Lavender, ed.). Lincoln and London: University of Nebraska Press, 1993.

Hert, Tamsen Emerson. "Yellowstone, the Word's Wonderland." WyoHistory.org: A Project of the Wyoming State Historical Society. https:www.wyohistory.org/encyclopedia/Yellowstone-worlds-wonderland. Accessed 14 December 2019.

Hine, Robert V; John Mack Faragher; and Jon T. Coleman. *The American West: An Interpretive History.* 2nd ed. New Haven: Yale University Press, 2017.

Holdsworth, Henry H. *Yellowstone & Grand Teton: Wildlife Portfolio.* Helena: Far Country Press, 2001.

_____, and Charlie Craigshead. *A Portrait of Jackson Hole & the Tetons.* Helena: Far Country Press, 2007.

Huidekoper, Virginia. *The Early Days in Jackson Hole.* Moose: Grand Teton Natural History Association, 2006.

"Human Impact and the Future—Yellowstone National Park." https://visityellowstonen ationalparkyall.weebly.com/human-impact-and-the-future.html. Accessed 31 August 2019.

International Union for Conservation of Nature and Natural Resources. "Yellowstone National Park: Conservation Outlook: (1) Summary and (2) Full Assessment." https://worldheritageoutlook.icun.org/explore-sites/wdpaid/2013. Finalized on 09 November 2017.

Janin, Hunt. *Fort Bridger, Wyoming.* Jefferson, NC: McFarland, 2001.

_____, and Ursula Carlson. *Overland Explorations of the Trans-Mississippi West: Expeditions and Writers of the American Frontier.* Jefferson, NC: McFarland, 2020.

_____, and Nicki Faircloth. "A Sense of Wonder: The Engravings of Karl Bodmer," in *Persimmon Hill.* Oklahoma City, 21(4), Winter 1993, pp. 5–12.

Jewell, Judy and W.C. McRae. *Montana.* Berkeley: Avalon Travel, 2015.

Keiter, Robert B. "The Greater Yellowstone Ecosystem Revisited: Law, Science, and the Pursuit of Ecosystem Management in an Iconic Landscape" in *University of Colorado Law Review* 91(1), 2020.

_____, and Mark S. Boyce. *The Greater Yellowstone Ecosystem: Redefining America's Wilderness Heritage.* New Haven: Yale University Press, 1991.

Lamplugh, Rick. "The Poaching and Saving of Yellowstone's Wildlife." https://www.yellow stonereports.com/report.php?date=2019&cid=4034. Accessed 25 November 2019.

Larson, T.A. *History of Wyoming.* 2nd ed., revised. Lincoln: University of Nebraska Press, 1990.

"Legacy on the Landscape—30 Years After the 1988 Fires." *Yellowstone Resources and Issues Handbook 2018.* Yellowstone National Park.

Legends of America. "'Old Bill' Williams—Mountain Man and Explorer." https:www.legendsofamerica.com/old-bill-williams/. Accessed 21 May 2020.

Leopold, A. Starker, *et al.* [The Leopold Report.] "The Goal of Park Management in the United States," in *Wildlife Management in the National Parks.* National Park Service, 1963. http:/www.nps.gov/history/history/online_books/leopold/leopold4.htm. Accessed 21 July 2009.

Levin, Kelly; Benjamin Cashore; Steven Bernstein; and Graeme Auld. "Overcoming the Tragedy of Super Wicked Problems: Constraining Our Future Selves to Ameliorate Global Climate Change," in *Policy Sciences.* 45 (2, 123–152.) 23 May 2012.

Logan, Jesse; William W. Macfarlane, and Louisa Willcox. "Whitebark Pine Vulnerability to Climate-Driven Mountain Pine Beetle Disturbance in the Greater Yellowstone Ecosystem," in *Ecological Applications.* 20(4), 2010, pp. 895–902.

Lybecker, Donna. "The Environmental Politics and Policy of Western Public Lands: The Old West, the New West and the Next West." https://open.oregonstate.education/environmentalpoliticsandpolicsandpolicy/chapter1/chapter-1/. Accessed 22 January 2020.

MacDonald, John Gordon. "History of Navigation on the Yellowstone River" (1950). University of Montana, *Graduate Student Theses, Dissertations & Professional Papers.* 2565. https://scholarworks.usmt.edu/etd/2565. Accessed 7 October 2019.

MacNulty, Daniel R.; Daniel R. Stahler; C. Travis Wyman; Joel Ruprecht; and Douglas R. Smith. "The Challenge of Understanding Northern Yellowstone Elk Dynamics After Wolf Reintroduction." *Yellowstone Science,* Wolf Issue 24(1). 2016.

_____, Daniel R. Stahler, and Douglas W. Smith. "Ys 24–1. Understanding the Limits to Wolf Hunting Ability." htpps://www.nps.gov/yell/learn/ys-24–1-understandng-the-limits-to-wolf-hunting-abil... Accessed 9 January 2020.

Maguire, James H., Peter Wild and Donald A. Barclay. *A Rendezvous Reader: Tall, Tangled, and True Tales of the Mountain Men, 1805–1850.* Salt Lake City: University of Utah Press, 1997.

Manns, Timothy R. "History of the Park Ranger in Yellowstone National Park." Yellowstone National Park, April 18, 1980. Unpublished manuscript.

Marston, Richard A., and Jay E. Anderson. "Watersheds and Vegetation of the Greater Yellowstone Ecosystem." https://conbio.onlinelibrary.wiley.com/doi/labs/10.111/j.1523.1991.tb00147.x. Accessed 11 September 2019.

McBeth, Mark K.; Elizabeth A. Shanahan; Ruth J. Arnell; and Paul Hathaway. "The Intersection of Narrative Policy Analysis and Policy Change Theory," in *The Policy Studies Journal* 35(1), 2007, pp. 87–108.

_____, and Elizabeth A. Shanahan. "Public Opinion for Sale: The Role of Policy Marketers in Greater Yellowstone Policy Conflict," in *Public Sciences* 2004, pp. 319–338.

_____, Elizabeth A. Shanahan; and Michael D. Jones. "The Science of Storytelling: Measuring Policy Beliefs in Greater Yellowstone," in *Society and Natural Resources,* 18 2005, pp. 413–429.

Miller, M. Mark. "The First Written Description of Yellowstone Geysers in 1827." www/yellowstonegate.com/2013/04/ia-tale-i-first-written-description-of-yellowstone-geysers-daniel-t-potts-1827/. Accessed 6 June 2019.

Montana State University. "Health of the Greater Yellowstone Ecosystem." ScienceDaily, 11 September 2018. www.sciencedaily.com/release/2018/09/1809lll32107.htm. Accessed 22 September 2019.

Moran, Thomas. "Thomas Moran's Diary." https://www.nps.gov/yell/historyculture/thomasmorans.diary. Accessed 14 December 2019.

Morgan, Dale L. *Jedediah Smith and the Opening of the West.* Lincoln: University of Nebraska Press, 1967.

Morris, Joseph M., and Mark K. McBeth. "The New West in the Context of Extractive Commodity Theory: The Case of Bison-Brucellosis in Yellowstone National Park," in *The Social Science Journal,* 40:2 2003, pp. 233–247.

"Mountain Men and Life in the Rocky Mountain West." www.mman.us/russellosborne biohtml. Accessed 6 June 2015.

Muir, John. *The Wilderness Journeys.* Edinburgh: Canongate Classics, 1996.

National Academy of Sciences. *Ecological Dynamics on Yellowstone's Northern Range.* Washington, D.C.: National Academy Press, 2002.

National Academy Press. Summary of the NAP's 2002 report on *Ecological Dynamics on Yellowstone's Northern Range.* https://www.nap.edu/read/10328/chapter2#6. Accessed 31 August 2019.

National Forest Foundation. "What Are the Differences Between National Parks and National Forests?" https://www.nationalforests.org/blog/category/national-forest-system. Accessed 12 March 2013.

National Geographic Magazine. "When Yellowstone Explodes." https:www/national geographic.com/magazine/2009/08/Yellowstone/. Accessed 19 June 2020.

National Geographic Society. "Geotourism Mapguide: Greater Yellowstone Region—Idaho, Montana, and Wyoming, including Yellowstone and Grand Teton National Parks." www.yellowstonegeotourism.org. Washington, D.C.: National Geographic Society, revised 2015.

_____. "Greater Yellowstone Region: Idaho, Montana, and Wyoming." Washington, D.C.: National Geographic Society, 2015.

National Park Service. "Elk." https://www.nps/gov/yell/learn/nature/elk.htm. Accessed 14 May 2020.

_____. "Explore in Winter," "Winter Safety," "Winter Use Management," "Ski and Snowshoe," "Ride a snowmobile or snowcoach," "Play in the Snow" and "Winter Use and Litigation." Accessed 13 February 2020.

_____. "Grand Canyon of the Yellowstone." https://www.nps.gov/thingstodo/yell-grand-canyon-of-the-yellowstone.htm. Accessed 25 April 2020.

_____. https://www.nps.gov/yell/learn/nature/bison.htm. "Habitat" (i.e., habitat of bison). Accessed 14 May 2010.

_____. "Museum of the National Park Ranger." https://www.nps.gov/yell/planyourvisit/museum-of-the-national-park-ranger.htm. Accessed 9 July 2020.

_____. "Strategic Priorities." https://www.gov/yell/learn/management/strategic-priorities.htm. Accessed 7 February 2020.

_____. "Study Shows Yellowstone Bison Have Positive Effects on the Landscape." https://www.nps.gov/yell/learn/news/19052.htm. Accessed 17 April 2020.

_____. "Sustainability." https://www.nps.gov/yell/getinvolved/sustaiability.htm. Accessed 7 February 2020.

_____. "Visitor Use Management." https://www.nps/gov/yell/learn/management/visitor-use-management.htm. Accessed 25 March 2020.

_____. "Volcano." https://www.nps.gov/yell/learn/nature/volcano.htm. Accessed 6 January 2020.

_____. "Water." (Updated July 1, 2020.) https://www.nps.gov/yell/learn/nature/water.htm. Accessed 14 July 2020.

_____. "Winter Use Management." https://www.nps/gov/yell/learn/winter-use-management.htm. Accessed 9 February 2010.

_____. "Winter Use Planning and Litigation." https://nps.gov/yell/learn/management/winter-use-planning-and-litigation.htm. Accessed 13 February 2020.

_____. "Yellowstone Lake." https:www.nps.gov/yell/learn/nature/Yellowstone-lake.html. Accessed 23 June 2020.

_____. "Yellowstone National Park: Climate Change." https://www.nps.gov/yell/learn/nature/climate-change.htm. Accessed 6 July 2020.

National Park System Advisory Board Science Committee. "Revisiting Leopold: Resource Stewardship in the National Parks." Washington, D.C. August 25, 2012.

Noss, Reed F.; Carlos Carroll; Ken Vance-Borland; and George Wuerthner. "A

Multicriteria Assessment of the Irreplaceability and Vulnerability of Sites in the Greater Yellowstone Ecosystem," in *Conservation Biology*, August 2002, Volume 16, No. 4, pp. 895–908.

NPR [National Public Radio]. David Quammen article, "Is Yellowstone National Park In Danger of Being 'Loved to Death'?" April 18, 2016. https://www.npr.org/2016/04/18/47468556/is-yellowstone-national-park-in-danger-of-being-loved-to-death. Accessed 30 June 2019.

Old Faithful Virtual Visitor Center. "Grand Prismatic Spring." https://www.nps.gov/features/yell/ofvec/exhibits/treasures/thermals/hotspring/grandprismatic.htm. Accessed 31 March 2020.

O'Neil, Paul. *The Rivermen.* Life-Time Books, 1975.

PBS (Public Broadcast System). "Ecotourism in Yellowstone: A One Act Play." https://rampages.us/tutene/ecosystem-in-yellowstone-a-one-act-play/. Accessed 17 June 2020.

______. "The National Parks: America's Best Idea: Parks—Yellowstone National Park." www.pbs/nationalparks/parks/yellowtone/2/. Accessed 4 January 2020.

Polis, G.A. and D.R. Strong. "Food Web Complexity and Community Dynamics," in *American Naturalist,* 147(5), 1996, pp. 813–846.

Preston, Charles R. "Saving the Charmed Goose: Reconciling Human Demands with Inherent Limitations in the Greater Yellowstone Ecosystem," in *Yellowstone Science,* 13(4), Fall 2005, pp. 5–14.

"Protection of Game in Yellowstone National Park: An 1894 Report from Congressman Lacey to the House Committee on Public Lands, p. 1." www.yellowstone-online.com/history/lacey3/lacey2.html. Accessed 26 November 2019.

Ray, Andrew M. (ed.); David P. Thoma; Kristin L. Legg; David M. Diamond; and Andrew J. Hansen. "Assessing the Ecological Health of the Greater Yellowstone Ecosystem." https://www.nps.gov/articles/assessing-the-ecological-health-of-the-greater-yellowstone-ecosystem.htm. Accessed 16 December 2019.

______ (ed.). "Vital Signs: Monitoring Yellowstone's Ecosystem Health." https://www.nps.gov/subjects/yellowstonescience/index.htm. Accessed 1 October 2019.

______, David Thoma; Kristin Legg; Robert Diehl; Adam Sepulveda; Mike Tercek; and Robert Al-Chokhachy. "Vital Sign Monitoring is Good Medicine for Parks," in *Yellowstone Science,* "Vital Signs: Monitoring Yellowstone's Ecosystem Health." pp. 4–13. https://www.nps.gov/subjects/yellowstonescience/index.htm. Accessed 1 October 2019.

Research Division, Yellowstone National Park. "Interim Report: Yellowstone National Park Northern Range Research, April 1992."

Ripple, William J., and Robert L. Beschta. "Trophic Cascades in Yellowstone: The First 15 Years After Wolf Reintroduction." Biological Conservation (2011), doi:10.1016/j.biocon.2011.11.005. Accessed 18 November 2019.

Roberts, Steve. "Beaver Dick Leigh, Mountain Man of the Tetons." https://www/wyohistory.org/encyclopedia/beaver-dick-leigh-mountain-man-tetons. Accessed 15 February 2020.

Rodman, Ann (ed.). *Yellowstone Science.* Special Issue: "Ecological Implications of Climate Change on the Greater Yellowstone Ecosystem." 23(1), March 2015.

Romme, William H., and Monica G. Turner. "Ecological Implications of Climate Change in Yellowstone: Moving into Unchartered Territory?," in *Yellowstone Science,* 23(1), 2015, pp. 6–14.

______, and ______. "Implications of Global Climate Change for Biogeographic Patterns in the Greater Yellowstone Ecosystem," in *Conservation Biology,* 5(3), September 1991, pp. 373–386. Accessed 28 March 2020.

Rounds, Glen (ed.). *Mountain Men: George Frederick Ruxton's* [1848] *Accounts of Fur Trappers and Indians in the Rockies.* New York: Holiday House, 1966.

Sánchez, Joseph P.; Robert L. Spude; and Art Gómez. *New Mexico: A History.* Norman: University of Oklahoma Press, 2013.

Schullery, Paul. "The Greater Yellowstone Ecosystem." https://web.archive.org/web/

2006925064249/http://biology.usgs.gov/s+t/noframe/r/114.htm. Accessed 30 June 2019.

______. "Greater Yellowstone Science: Past, Present, and Future," in *Yellowstone Science,* 18(2), 2010, pp. 7–13. Accessed 13 April 2020.

______. "The Northern Range." Private Communications of 2019 regarding the Northern Range, and the reporting on this subject that was carried out by the National Research Council of the National Academy of Sciences.

Shanahan, Elizabeth A; Mark K. McBeth; Paul L. Hathaway; and Ruth J. Arnell. "Conduit or Contributor? The Role of Media in Policy Change Theory." Published online: *Policy Science* 14, 2008, pp. 115–138.

Shanahan, Erin K. "An Uncertain Future: The Persistence of Whitebark Pine in the Greater Yellowstone Ecosystem, in *Yellowstone Science,* 27(1), 2019, pp. 67–71.

S.J. & Jessie E. Quinney College of Natural Resources, Utah State University. "Yellowstone Elk Don't Budge for Wolves, Say Scientists." *Science Daily.* 26 March 2019. Accessed 9 January 2020.

Smith, Douglas W. (ed.) *Celebrating 20 Years of Wolves,* in *Yellowstone Science,* 24(1), June 2016. www.nps.gov/yellowstonescience. Accessed 18 December 2019.

Smithsonian American Art Museum. "George Catlin." https://americanart.si.edu/artist/george-catlin-782. Accessed 3 October 2019.

Smithsonian Magazine. "Protections for Grizzlies in the Greater Yellowstone Area Upheld in Court." https://www.smithsonianmag.com/smart-news/good-news-bears-protections-grizzlies-... Accessed 24 July 2020.

Steingisser, Alethea, and W. Andrew Marcus. "Human Impacts on Geyser Basins," in *Yellowstone Science,* 17(1), 2009. Accessed 7 June 2020.

"Surrender Speech of Chief Joseph." www2.gsu.edu/~eslmlm/chiefjoseph.html. Accessed May 29, 2019.

Tercek, Mike; Ann Rodman; and David Thoma. "Trends in Yellowstone's Snowpack." *Yellowstone Science,* 23(1), 2015.

Teton Geotourism Center. "Discover the Teton Scenic Byway." discovertetonvalley.com/geotourism-center. Accessed 17 May 2020.

Thoma, David P.; Seth M. Munson; Ann W. Rodman; Roy Renkin; Heidi M. Anderson; and Stefanie D. Wacker. "Patterns of Primary Production & Ecological Drought in Yellowstone," in *Yellowstone Science,* 27(1), 2019, pp. 34–39.

"Trophic Cascade," in the National Park Service report on "Cycles and Processes." http://www.nps.gov/yell/learn/nature/cycles-and-processes.htm. Accessed 26 March 2018.

Tyrrell, Kelly April. "Can Yellowstone Forests Recover from Frequent Fires?," in *Yellowstone Insider,* 28 May 2019, https://yellowstoneinsider.com/2019/05/27/can-yellowstone-forests-recover-from-freq... Accessed 28 May 2019.

Uhler, John William. "Yellowstone National Park Challenges." https://www.yellowstone.co/challenges.htm. Accessed 14 February 2020.

U.S. Fish and Wildlife Service. "Camas Lake." https://www.fws.gov/refuge/s_lake/. Accessed 21 September 2019.

______. "Camas National Wildlife Refuge." https://www.fws.gov/refuge/Camas/about.html. Accessed 21 September 2019.

______. "Red Rock Lakes." https://www.fsw.gov/refuge/Red_Rock_Lakes/about.html. Accessed 21 September 2019.

U.S. Forest Service. "Beaverhead-Deerlodge National Forest." https://www.fs.usda.gov/bdnf/ Accessed 19 September 2019.

______. "Bridger-Teton National Forest: History & Culture." https://www.fs.usda.gov/detail/btnf/history-culture/?cid=fsbdev3_0663669. Accessed 15 February 2020.

______. "Bridger-Teton National Forest." https://www.fs.usda/gob/btnf/. Accessed 19 September 2019.

______. "Caribou-Targhee National Forest." https://www.fs.usda/gov.main/ctnf/learning/history-culture. Accessed 19 September 2019.

______. "Custer Gallatin National Forest: Welcome to the Historic Main Boulder Ranger

Station." https:www.fs.usda.gov/detail/custergallatin/learning/history-cuture?cid=stelprd5127786. Accessed 18 September 2019.

______. "Shoshone National Forest." https://www.fs.usda.gov/main/shoshone/about-forest. Accessed 20 September 2019.

U.S. Geological Survey. Northern Prairie Wildlife Research Center. "Yellowstone Wolf Restoration." http://www.usgs.gov/centers/npwrc/science/yellowstone-wolf-restoration?qt-science_center_objects=0#qt-science_center_objects. Accessed 14 December 2019.

______. "Return of the Grizzly Bear." https://www.usgs/news/return-yellowstone-grizzly-bear?qt-news_science_products=1#qt-news_science_products. Accessed 7 July 2020.

______. "What Is the Difference Between Global Warming and Climate Change?" https://usgs.gov/faqs/what-difference-between-and-climate-change-1?qt-news_science_products+0#qt-news_science_pro... Accessed 31 October 2019.

U.S. National Park Service. "Associated Tribes." https://www.nps.gov/yell/learn/historyculture/associatedtribes.htm. Accessed 28 September 2019.

______. "Bear-Inflicted Human Injuries and Fatalities in Yellowstone." https://www.nps.gov/yell/learn/nature/injuries.htm. Accessed 30 November 2019.

______. "Climate Change." https://www.nps.gov/yell/learn/nature/climate-change.htm. Accessed 17 June 2019.

______. "Cultural History: Humans and the Teton Landscape." https://www.nps.gov/grte/learn/historyculture/cultural.htm. Accessed 18 September 2019.

______. "Cycles and Processes." https://www.nps.gov/yell/learn/nature/cycles-and-processes.htm. Accessed 14 September 2019.

______. "Enemy at the Gates: Aquatic Invasive Species." Yellowstone Resources and Issues Handbook 2019.

______. "Expeditions Explore Yellowstone." https://www.nps.gov/yell/learn/historyculture/expeditions.htm. Accessed 10 June 2019.

______. "Greater Yellowstone Ecosystem." https://www.nps.gov/yell/nature/greater-yellowstone-ecosystem. Accessed 1 August 2019.

______. "Heritage and Research Center." https://www.gov/yell/learn/historyculture/collections.htm. Accessed 2 December 2019.

______. "Historic Tribes." https:www.nps.gov/yell/learn/historyculture/historic-tribes.htm. Accessed 1 June 2019.

______. "Legacy on the Landscape—30 years after the 1988 fires." Yellowstone Resources and Issues Handbook 2018.

______. "Our Staff & Offices." https://www.nps.gov/yell/learn/management/staffandoffices.htm. Accessed 2 December 2019.

______. "Park History." https://www.nps.gov/yell/learn/historyculture/park-history.htm. Accessed 19 April 2019.

______. "Pronghorn." https://www.nps.gov//yell/learn/nature/pronghorn.htm. Accessed 14 October 2019.

______. "Timeline of Human History." https://www.nps.gov/yell/learn/historyculture/timeline.htm. Accessed 18 April 2019.

______. "Wolf Restoration." https://nps.gov/yell/learn/nature/wolf-restoration.htm. Accessed 20 September 2019.

______. "Yellowstone Announces Strategic Priorities." https://www.nps.gov/yell/learn/news/19017.htm. Accessed 24 May 2019.

______. "Yellowstone Center for Resources." https://www.nps.gov/yell/learn/management/ycr.htm. Accessed 2 December 2019.

______. "Yellowstone Cutthroat Trout." https://www.nps.gov/yell/learn/nature/yellowstone-cutthroat-trout.htm. Accessed 14 October 2019.

______. *Yellowstone Science* 24–1 Celebrating 20 Years of Wolves." https://www.nps.gov/yell/learn/yellowstone-science-24–1-celebrating-20years-of-wolves.htm. Accessed 12 June 2019.

______. "YS 24–1 Yellowstone Wolf Facts." https:www.nps.gov/yell/learn/us-24–1-yellowstone-wolf-facts.htm. Accessed 12 June 2019.

Utley, Robert M. *A Life Wild and Perilous: Mountain Men and the Paths to the Pacific.* New York: Henry Holt, 1997.

Victor, Mrs. Frances A. Fuller. *The River of the West.* Hartford and Toledo: R.W. Bliss, 1870. (The first 21 chapters of this book are available online at https://user.xmission.com/drudy/mtman/jmeekint.html. Accessed 6 June 2015, this is the source used here.)

Wacker, Stefanie D. "Invasive Plants as Indicators of Ecosystem Health," in *Yellowstone Science,* 27(1), 2019, pp. 64–66.

Wertz, Pamela Krewson. "'Geodesigning' Solutions for the Future of Yellowstone National Park." https://news.psu/edu/story/5799450/20/19/o2/academics/geodesingning-solutions-future-yellowstone-national-park. Accessed 29 April 2020.

Wheeler, Keith. *The Chroniclers.* Alexandria: Time-Life Books, 1976.

______. *The Scouts.* Alexandria: Time-Life Books, 1978.

Whittlesey, Lee H. "Native Americans, the Earliest Interpreters: What Is Known About Their Legends and Stories of Yellowstone National Park and the Complexities of Interpreting Them." Yellowstone Center for Resources, Yellowstone National Park, 6th Biennial Scientific Conference; no date given for the Conference but believed to have been held in about 2001.

Wilkinson, Todd. "The New West: For Some New West towns, it's Gut-check Time Amid Huge Change." Buckrail.com, Jackson Hole news. Accessed 5 June 2019.

Williams, Pat Stephens; Ray Darville; and Sally Vering. "Improving Visitor Preparedness and Safety in the Bear Country of Yellowstone National Park," in *Yellowstone Science,* "Vital Signs: Monitoring Yellowstone's Ecosystem Health," pp. 79–80.

Wilson, Elijah Nicholas. (Howard R. Driggs, ed.). *White Indian Boy: My Life Among the Shoshones.* Colorado Springs: Piccadilly Books, 2009.

Wislizenus, F.A. *A Journey to the Rocky Mountains in the Year 1839.* New York: Cosimo Classics, 2005.

Wyoming Historical Markers. "Camp Monaco." https://www.waymarking.com/waymarks/WMDEWG_Camp_Monaco. Accessed 1 June 2020.

Wyoming State Historical Society. "Camp Monaco." https://www.wyohistory.org/field-trips/camp-monaco. Accessed 1 June 2020.

Yellowstone Forever. "Explore Yellowstone's Northern Range This Winter." https://www.yellowstone.org/come-play-in-yellowstones-northern-range/. November 5, 2018.

______. "Safeguarding Yellowstone: The U.S. Army Years 1886–1918." https://www.yellowstone.org/safeguarding-yellowstone-the-us-army-1886–1919. Accessed 25 November 2019.

Yellowstone Historic Center. "Stagecoach Tourism" and "Early Rail Travel to Yellowstone." No publication data given. Accessed 30 June 2019.

Yellowstone National Park. "Eat or Be Eaten!" https://visityellowstonenationalparkyall.weebly.com/yellowstones-wildlife.html. Accessed 2 June 2020.

______. https://www.yellowstonenationalpark.com/history.htm. Accessed 30 May 2019.

______. "Climate Change Explorer V1.0." https://www.nps/gov/features/yell/climate explorers/index.html. Accessed 18 June 2009.

______. "Enemy at the Gates… Aquatic Invasive Species." Yellowstone Resources and Issues Handbook 2019.

______. "Greater Yellowstone Ecosystem." Yellowstone Resources and Issues Handbook 2020.

Yellowstone National Park Lodges. "Yellowstone's Northern Range Features Best Wildlife Viewing in the Lower 48 States; Options Abound for These Who Want to Observe Wolves, Elk, Bison, Bears and More." https://www.yellowstonenationalparklodges.com/press-releases. Accessed 7 January 2010.

Yellowstone National Park Trips. "Deaths and Injuries at Yellowstone's Geysers and Hot Springs." https://wwww.yellowstonepark.com/things-to-do/cautionary-tale. Accessed 23 November 2019.

_____. "Important Food Source for Yellowstone Bears in Trouble." https://www.yellow stonepark.com/park/grizzly-food-source. Accessed 14 October 2019.

Yellowstone Science. "Special Issue: Ecological Implications of Climate Change on the Greater Yellowstone Ecosystem." 23(1), March 2015.

_____. "Vital Signs: Monitoring Yellowstone's Ecosystem Health." April 2019 27(1).

Yellowstone Wolf Project, 2011 Annual Report. National Park Service, Yellowstone Center for Resources. YCR-2012–01. Accessed 16 December 2019.

_____. *Yellowstone's Northern Range: Complexity and Change in a Wildland Ecosystem.* Mammoth Hot Springs: National Park Service, 1997.

Yellowstone Wolf Project 2018: Wyoming, Montana, Idaho. "Succession: Biological Progression." https://visityellowstonenationalparkyall.weebly.com/succession.html. Accessed 13 June 2020.

"Yellowstone Wolf Project Annual Report 2018." Yellowstone Center for Resources. National Park Service, 2018.

Yonk, R.M., and J.K. Lofthouse. "A Review on the Manufacturing of a National Icon: Institutions and Incentives in the Management of Yellowstone National Park," in *International Journal of Geoheritage and Parks* (2020), https://doi.org/10.1016/j.ijeop.2020.05.004. Accessed 5 June 2020.

Index

9 781476 681078